TANNHÄUSER: POET AND LEGEND

UNIVERSITY OF NORTH CAROLINA
STUDIES IN THE GERMANIC LANGUAGES
AND LITERATURES

Initiated by RICHARD JENTE (1949–1952), established by F. E. COENEN (1952–1968)

Publication Committee

SIEGFRIED MEWS, EDITOR

JOHN G. KUNSTMANN GEORGE S. LANE HERBERT W. REICHERT

CHRISTOPH E. SCHWEITZER SIDNEY R. SMITH RIA STAMBAUGH PETRUS W. TAX

For other volues in the "Studies" see pages 200 ff.

Send orders to: (U.S. and Canada)
The University of North Carolina Press, P.O. Box 2288
Chapel Hill, N.C. 27514
(All other countries) Feffer and Simons, Inc., 31 Union Square, New York, N.Y. 10003

NUMBER SEVENTY-SEVEN

UNIVERSITY
OF NORTH CAROLINA
STUDIES IN
THE GERMANIC LANGUAGES
AND LITERATURES

Composed by
EKENÄS TRYCKERI AKTIEBOLAG
Ekenäs - Finland

Tannhäuser: Poet and Legend

With Texts and Translations of his Works

by

J. W. THOMAS, 1916 —

CHAPEL HILL

THE UNIVERSITY OF NORTH CAROLINA PRESS

1974

Library of Congress Cataloging in Publication Data

Thomas, John Wesley, 1916—
    Tannhäuser: poet and legend.

    (University of North Carolina studies in the Germanic languages
and literatures, no. 77)
    English and Middle High German.
    Bibliography: pp. 193—99.
    1. Tannhäuser. I. Tannhäuser. II. Title. III. Series: North
Carolina. University. Studies in the Germanic languages and literatures,
no. 77.
PT1658.T3Z9   831'.2   73-15986
ISBN 0-8078-8077-9

Manufactured in the U.S.A.

PREFACE

The name Tannhäuser is well-known, but the figure which it brings to mind varies greatly from person to person. The medievalist recalls a thirteenth-century poet who distinguished himself primarily by his ironical songs, the folklorist remembers the subject of one of Germany's oldest and most popular ballads, the musicologist thinks of Wagner's hero and the legendary singers' contest at Wartburg. One objective of the present work is to present a composite picture of the figure so that one scholar may become better acquainted with the Tannhäuser of the other, in keeping with present trends away from narrow specialization. A second aim is to provide the student of medieval German literature with a diplomatic edition of a significant poet who composed in all three of the chief lyric forms of his day — *Leich*, minnesong, and *Spruch*. It is hoped that the student may also gain something from a critical treatment which differs somewhat from the usual textual and historical approaches. A third, and most important goal of the volume is to make Tannhäuser's songs and the ballad about him available to those with a limited command of Middle High and Early New High German. For these readers an English translation is supplied which attempts to reproduce as accurately as possible both form and content. The greatest works of the German Middle Ages, once the exclusive property of the medievalist, are now widely read in English in paperback editions, and it is felt that the nonspecialist with literary interests may also enjoy Tannhäuser's lesser, but highly original compositions. Although the work was prepared for a diverse audience, it assumes that the reader has some knowledge of the medieval period and dispenses with all but the most pertinent background material.

The author wishes to thank Professors Siegfried Mews and Petrus Tax for many valuable suggestions and the staffs of the University of Vienna Library and the Austrian National Library for their kind assistance in locating and making available the extensive literature on Tannhäuser.

CONTENTS

INTRODUCTION

Nothing is known of the life of the thirteenth-century poet and composer Tannhäuser except for what can be learned from the relatively few lines of verse which have been ascribed to him by medieval anthologists. As far as can be determined, he appears in no official document of his time and is mentioned by no contemporary. However, since he frequently refers to himself and others in his songs, literary historians have accumulated a considerable amount of biographical material, much of which is of dubious validity. For the biographers have seldom fully weighed the fact that Tannhäuser was a humorist — with a marked tendency toward irony — and that he composed to amuse, rather than to enlighten his audience. It is certain that nothing he says about himself is to be fully trusted, and it is well to be cautious in assessing his remarks about other people and about current events.

The mystery of Tannhäuser begins with the name itself, the source of which is four songs in the Manesse Manuscript — in them the poet refers to himself as "tanhusere." Since this designation was placed at the head of the section in which Tannhäuser's verse appears, without a given name, *von, her, meister,* or any other title, it is clear that the scribe could not identify the poet more closely. There were many places called Tannhausen with which the poet might have been associated, but it is also true that "der tanhusere" (the backwoodsman) would have been a good pseudonym for a professional humorist in a sophisticated, courtly society. Such pen names were certainly not uncommon among the poets of the day; one thinks of "Der elende Knabe," "Gast," "Meister Irregang," "Suchenwirt," "Rumsland," "Der Unverzagte," among others. If the name is fictitious, one is inclined to assume that the poet was a *Spielmann* or goliard, associated with no particular family, castle, or town. His occasional displays of learning, his bits of French, Italian, and Latin, and his *pastourelle*-like songs could also point to the goliard.[1] However, most scholars who have dealt with Tannhäuser believe

---

[1] E. Kück, rev. of *Zu Tannhäusers Leben und Dichten,* by Alfred Oehlke, *AfdA,* 17 (1891), 208, says that the poet was a goliard: "Nun hat aber die höchst eigentümliche zerfahrene gelehrsamkeit, die zuweilen heidnisch naive, keineswegs rohe sinnlichkeit Tannhäusers nirgends im deutschen minnesang, wol aber in der lat. vagantendichtung ihres gleichen; es ist sicher viel eher erweisbar, dass er vagant, fahrender kleriker, als dass er adliger war, was durch jenes ja freilich nicht ausgeschlossen wird." Wilhelm Brauns, "Zur Heimatfrage der Carmina Burana," *ZfdA,* 73 (1936), 195, insists that Tannhäuser was a *Spielmann* or goliard: "Wie schon gesagt, sind die Pastourellen nur einem Fahrenden angemessen; wenn nun Siebert ... ihren frivol-parodistischen Zug

that his knowledge is drawn from courtly verse, rather than from biblical, theological, or classical lore. And they maintain that the poet's subject matter, his general tone, and his attitude toward political events and the higher nobility indicate that he was a knight.[2]

If the poet did belong to the minor nobility, the question arises as to whether he can be identified with a specific family. His language points to a South German or Austrian origin, but does not indicate more. Most of the earlier Tannhäuser scholarship makes him a member of a prominent Austrian Thannhausen family which is first mentioned in a Salzburg document of 1275.[3] More recent scholarship usually connects him with one of the families of minor nobility which were located in the vicinity of Nürnberg. This is because of a reference by Tannhäuser to that city. As a result of an erroneous translation of a word in one of his songs, several scholars maintain that he belonged to a family which took its name from the village of Tannhausen, southeast of Nürnberg. One has attempted to identify the poet with a Liupolt Tanhusaer, presumably of that village, who appeared in a document of 1246.[4] A third family which has been claimed for Tannhäuser is that of the Lords of Tanne, whose ancestral home was apparently in Untersiegsdorf on the Traun River between Salzburg and Linz.[5] Several times during the nineteenth century the inhabitants of Untersiegsdorf

---

bestreitet und sie wörtlich verstehen will, so bekennt er sich zu einem Irrtum in der Grundauffassung, der in bezug auf die Gattung der Pastourelle von einer längst dahingegangenen Generation von Germanisten (und Romanisten) geteilt worden ist." Anton Wallner, rev. of *Der Dichter Tannhäuser: Leben, Gedicht, Sage*, by Johannes Siebert, *AfdA*, 53 (1934), 175-79, expresses the belief that the poet was a *Spielmann* or goliard. Paul Kluckhohn, "Ministerialität und Ritterdichtung," *ZfdA*, 52 (1910), 153, n. 1, inclines toward the same view.

[2] Ludwig Wolff gives a concise summary of the majority opinion in *Die deutsche Literatur des Mittelalters: Verfasserlexikon*, IV (Berlin: Walter de Gruyter, 1953), 355.

[3] However, Robert von Raab, "Die Tannhausen im Mittelalter," *Mittheilungen der Gesellschaft für Salzburger Landeskunde*, 12 (1872), 1-33, states that extant historical documents cannot establish whether or not the poet was a member of the Salzburg-Carinthian Thannhausen family.

[4] Karl Weller, "Zur Lebensgeschichte des Tanhäusers [sic]," *Festgabe für Karl Bohnberger*, ed. Hans Bihl (Tübingen: Mohr, 1938), pp. 154-63. Franz Martin, "Der Tannhäuser — kein Salzburger," *Mitteilungen der Gesellschaft für Salzburger Landeskunde*, 80 (1940), 85-86, also refers to the document and assumes that the poet is either Liupolt or Siboto Tanhusaer. Johannes Siebert, "Zum Tannhäuser," *ZfdA*, 77 (1940), 55-60, presents arguments against both possibilities. Wolff, p. 356, states that Siboto could not have been the poet since the former was a member of the Order of Teutonic Knights during the period when Tannhäuser was presumably wandering from court to court in search of a generous and permanent patron. Actually, all of the evidence which is supposed to link the poet with the Tanhusaers of the 1246 document or with the Bavarian village of Thannhausen is most tenuous.

[5] Otto Denk, "Der Minnesänger Tannhäuser und seine Heimat," *Das Bayerland*, 28 (1916-17), 225-28, claims that this is the most probable home of the minnesinger. He also tells of a sixteenth-century picture in a church in nearby Bergen which apparently depicts the hero of the Tannhäuser ballad.

considered erecting a monument to the poet, but the plan was never carried out. The most interesting, and least plausible, of the theories as to Tannhäuser's identity is that he was the Heinrich von Ofterdingen who appears as a character in the thirteenth-century poem, "Der Sängerkrieg auf der Wartburg."[6] Several scholars have maintained that Heinrich, like others in the poem, was an actual minnesinger,[7] and August Wilhelm Schlegel suggested that he was the author of the *Nibelungenlied*.[8] Other works, including the "Sängerkrieg" itself, have also been attributed to him.[9] The attempts to determine Tannhäuser's family by means of the armorial bearings pictured in the illumination in the Manesse Manuscript have been unsuccessful, for the escutcheon shown there is that of none of the Tannhäuser, Thannhausen, Tanne, or Ofterdingen families.[10] It is clear that the artist, like the scribe, knew nothing of the poet and was drawing from one of Tannhäuser's songs for inspiration. The painting shows a front view of a handsome young man who is dressed in a greenish blue tam and robe and a white mantel on which a large cross is sewn. Red and green vines wind on both sides of the standing figure. It is an artist's representation of a pilgrim and is based on Tannhäuser's so-called crusade song. The vines perhaps refer to the predominance of spring songs among his works.

Although there are wide differences of opinion as to Tannhäuser's origins, relatively little disagreement exists as to the authorship of the works which medieval scribes have attributed to him. Everyone accepts all the verse which appears after his name in the Manesse Manuscript as being his. Opinion is about evenly divided with regard to the authenticity of the *Sprüche* which are ascribed to Tannhäuser in the Jena Manuscript. The majority of scholars who have commented on the poem about table manners which follows his name in a late fourteenth-century manuscript have refused to accept it as his. And no one considers genuine the verse which the fifteenth-century Kolmar and Wiltener Manuscripts attribute to Tannhäuser, except that which is a corruption of verse in the Manesse Manuscript. Nevertheless, some scholars believe that Tannhäuser

---

6 C. T. L. Lucas, *Ueber den Krieg von Wartburg*, Historische und literarische Abhandlungen der königlichen Deutschen Gesellschaft zu Königsberg, No. 4, Part 2, 1838. But F. Zander, *Die Tanhäuser-Sage und der Minnesinger Tanhäuser* [sic]: *Zur öffentlichen Prüfung der Schüler des Königl. Friedrichs-Collegiums* (Königsberg, 1858), p. 20, objects that Tannhäuser was considerably younger than any actual Heinrich von Ofterdingen would have been.

7 Erich Schmidt, *Charakteristiken* (Berlin: Weidmann, 1901), p. 42, cites a Henricus dictus de Oftindinch who appears in a document of 1257.

8 Josef Körner, *Nibelungenforschungen der deutschen Romantik* (Leipzig: Haessel, 1911), p. 153. According to Karl Reuschel, "Die Tannhäusersage," *Neue Jahrbücher für das klassische Altertum, Geschichte und deutsche Literatur*, 13 (1904), 666, the well-known German scholar, Franz Pfeiffer, shared Schlegel's view.

9 Wolfgang Golther, "Tannhäuser in Sage und Dichtung des Mittelalters und der neuen Zeit, *Walhalla*, 3 (1907), 46.

10 Alfred Oehlke, *Zu Tannhäusers Leben und Dichten*, Diss. Königsberg 1890, p. 6.

composed a great deal more than is extant and has been identified as his.[11] The present study treats the Manesse and Jena poems: in all, seven *Leiche*, six minnesongs, and four *Spruch* cycles.

The discussion of the poet's compositions presents them according to subgenres, rather than as they appear in the manuscripts, and stresses particularly matters of form and style. The conclusion is reached that the most typical characteristic of his genius is irony, and it is largely around this element that the chapter on sources and reception turns. The consideration of the legend begins with an explanation of its probable origin and continues with a history of how it flourished during the Middle Ages, vanished in the seventeenth century, was revived by the Romantics, and again declined during the present century. Throughout the account an attempt is made to evaluate the impact of the legend on medieval and modern German literature.

[11] Among them, Helmut de Boor, *Die höfische Literatur: Vorbereitung, Blüte, Ausklang, 1170-1250*, 8th ed. (München: Beck, 1969), p. 370.

Five of Tannhäuser's *Leiche* are *Tanzleiche,* apparently the earliest of this sub-genre. They were sung to accompany dancing[12] — so much is clear — but whether sung only by a *Vorsänger* or by *Vorsänger* and dancers responsively, we do not know for certain. It is not unlikely that both methods of performance were used, the first part being sung by the *Vorsänger* and the second part by him and the dancers in turn. Consistent with their function, these *Tanzleiche* are lighthearted in mood with lively rhythms. There is an undercurrent of ironic humor which sometimes surfaces to a broad smile, but never becomes crude or coarse. They are carefully structured, with introduction, main theme, description of the dance, and conclusion — which usually admonishes the listeners to be happy. The audience for which Tannhäuser composed was courtly and sophisticated. It enjoyed clever eroticism, but not obscenity, and was sufficiently educated to appreciate the poet's humorous inventions in literature, history and geography. Some of his *Tanzleiche* were composed for the court at Vienna and might be considered the spiritual, perhaps even the historical ancestors of the modern Viennese operetta; a mixture of irony and wit, naive sentimentality, and joyful affirmation of the senses.

The first *Leich*, as it appears in the manuscript, is a panegyric on Duke Friedrich II of Austria, otherwise known as Friedrich the Warlike. The duke was Tannhäuser's patron, and, according to several of the *Sprüche*, a very generous one. A reference in the *Leich* to a crown for the monarch dates it as having been composed in the spring of 1245. The negotiations over the raising of Austria to a kingdom took place during the early months of that year; and in May Emperor Friedrich II gave the duke a ring as a pledge of the coming coronation. The *Leich* probably was composed for the specific purpose of announcing the momentous occasion and might have been sung and danced before the emperor, who was in Vienna when the commitment was made. It is the first instance of the *Leich* form being used for eulogy. History does not tell us why the duke was not crowned.

The work begins with a nature introduction which expresses the joy and delight of the spring season and has words of praise for an anthropomorphic May who has brought them. In the second versicle May is compared with the

---

12 Margarete Lang, *Tannhäuser*, Von deutscher Poeterey, 17 (Leipzig: Weber, 1936), p. 86, questions as to whether one really danced to *Tanzleiche*, but her argument is quite unconvincing.

duke, and in the following versicles Friedrich's accomplishments and princely attributes are lauded in fairly regular iambs and lines consisting primarily of four or more feet. Starting with versicle 15,[13] a more personal side of the ruler is portrayed and we see him as a sponsor of festivals and even as a singer of Tannhäuser's songs at dances. He is the gay prince who seeks entertainment and shares it with his subjects. This view of him is accompanied by a change in the rhythm, which becomes somewhat faster, as indicated by a marked increase in trimeter and dimeter lines.

Versicles 15 to 19 inclusive form a transition in content and metrics. The narrator turns from the princely singer to the dance which is being sung. Short lines of one or two feet predominate as the narrator gives the invitation to the dance (which, of course, is already going on), tells of his sweetheart, and refers to the dancers by name. In the last versicle he tells the young people that, since God has given them voice and feet, they should sing, dance, and be happy. This admonition brings us back to the joyous season of the introduction. It has been suggested that the early part of this and of the other *Tanzleiche*, where the rhythm is regular and measured, was an accompaniment to the stately *tanz*, while the second and livelier part was sung to a fast-moving *reie*.[14]

Technically, the incorporating of a eulogy into a dance song was successful, with transitions in content, mood, and metrics being carried out expertly, if somewhat abruptly. And yet there is a definite impression of incongruity; even more, the impression that a skillful artist is making fun of us by combining incompatible elements as if they belonged together. Another touch of irony is seen in the use of terms to describe Friedrich which are particularly associated with heroic and Arthurian literature: *degen, helt, vermezzen, waleis*. And when the singer maintains that no misfortune can befall anyone who sees the prince once a week, he is comparing Friedrich to the grail in *Parzival*. One scholar speaks of "die parodistischen Anspielungen auf das Epos."[15] As will be seen, deliberate incongruity, straight-faced deception of his audience, and parody are basic characteristics of Tannhäuser's style. The effect on the *Leich* is, of course, humorous, but the praise heaped on Friedrich does not seem to be the less sincere for that. The poet's haste to mention himself first among the poor whom his ruler is aiding and the use of diminutives in speaking of the dancers are also

---

[13] Since the manuscript does not indicate the limits of the separate versicles, there is some disagreement as to how the *Leiche* were divided. The references here are to the arrangement in the chapter, "Tannhäuser's Verse," of this volume.

[14] Johannes Siebert, *Tannhäuser: Inhalt und Form seiner Gedichte* (Berlin: Vogt, 1894), p. 76.

[15] Ernst Bernhardt, "Vom Tannhäuser und dem Sängerkrieg auf der Wartburg," *Jahrbücher der Königlichen Akademie gemeinnütziger Wissenschaft zu Erfurt* (Erfurt: Carl Villaret, 1900), p. 96.

amusing. Other medieval poets who eulogized Friedrich in their verse are Neidhart von Reuenthal, Ulrich von Liechtenstein, and Bruder Werner.[16]

The second work in the manuscript is just as unique in medieval German verse as the first, however in quite different ways. It, too, begins with a nature introduction, but here the description of the beauties of nature is much longer. Then comes the main body of the composition, and this time it contains a true narrative. While wandering over the heath the singer encountered a maiden whose charm was such that he immediately fell in love. He greeted her, begged for her favor, and told of his complete devotion. They walked together through the clover, embraced, kissed, and at last fully consummated their love. At this point appears a brief reference to the dance in progress, which, however, does not hold the singer's attention. Thrilled by the memory of his experience, he praises women's goodness and declares his eternal loyalty to his ladylove. With this, the singer announces the end of the dance, advises the maidens to reject false sorrowing, and (with propriety) to be joyful. He promises that the men will join them in so doing.

The poem is very symmetrical in structure and its separate parts are carefully balanced. The number of verses in the nature introduction is exactly one-half the number in the love story, is equal to that in the dance section, and is three times that in the conclusion. The poet has been just as careful and meticulous in joining the separate parts and giving a unity of mood and theme to the whole. The nature description of the introduction carries over to the main narrative and even to the dance section. The latter looks back to the love story and comments on it. A springtime mood prevails from beginning to end with no discordant or extraneous notes.

The metrical pattern of the composition is the most uniform of all the Leiche. Indeed, the work may not be a Leich at all.[17] If one were to omit two couplets, the work would fall naturally into 25 four-line stanzas with iambic tetrameter lines and alternating rhyme. The only metrical variations between these stanzas would be those which are found in most minnesongs: masculine versus feminine rhyme and presence or absence of an Auftakt, neither of which has any significant effect on the melody. Without the two couplets there would be no reason to suspect that the composition was not a minnesong except for its position between two Leiche. And since the scribe who put it there may never have heard the work sung, this is not an adequate basis for classifying it, particularly because the similarity of the content to that of Leich III would explain their being placed together.

The location of the two couplets strengthens the evidence against the work being a Leich. One of them comes at the very beginning. Manuscripts with notation show that some songs are introduced by musical embellishments, which

---

[16] Neidhart in the song, "Owe lieber sumer diner süeze bernden wünne;" Ulrich in his *Frauendienst*; and Bruder Werner in the song, "Ich han geklaget unde klag ez an."

[17] De Boor, p. 372: "Es ist eher ein Erzähllied als ein Leich."

7

are sometimes assumed to be instrumental preludes and sometimes to be vocal flourishes that employ the vowel of the initial syllable of the text. Tannhäuser may have supplied such an initial embellishment with a full text of its own: the first of the two couplets. The second couplet appears in the love story after the narrator has declared his devotion and just before the love-making begins. And immediately in front of the couplet in the manuscript stands the only paragraph in the composition. The singer paused here, presumably repeated the initial flourish with a new text, and then went on with the regular melody. If one does not count the verses of the nature introduction or of the conclusion, the second couplet stands exactly in the middle of the composition. With regard to content, it leads directly to the climax of the work and marks the point at which it takes another direction, one which has no precedent in German courtly verse. What lies between the first and second couplets is a traditional minnesong; what follows the second couplet is a new type of courtly love song, which is set off from the first by the musical embellishment. Another and perhaps more plausible explanation for the two couplets is that Tannhäuser used a melody — maybe not his own — which had a refrain and that he used the music of this refrain as a prelude to the two parts of his composition. He could have gotten the idea from the *rondeau*, which occasionally begins with a two-line refrain. In any case, the work probably should be considered a *Lied*, rather than a *Leich*. However, the traditional designation will be preserved here for convenience.

Since the conventional minnesong or *Minneleich* tells of the longing and frustration rather than the fulfillment of love, it is customary for scholars to call *Leich* II an imitation of a French *pastourelle*[18] or of a goliard song, such as the seduction songs in the *Carmina Burana*.[19] One supporter of the latter thesis presents this work and *Leich* III as evidence that the poet was not a knight, but a *Spielmann* or goliard.[20] The comparison of Tannhäuser's composition to a *pastourelle* or goliard song is not particularly apt. The poet may well have been familiar with such works, but his verse was not significantly influenced by them. The *pastourelle* is specifically *Standesdichtung*: it tells of the attempt of a knight to seduce a shepherdess. It is a humorous contest in which one of the participants is discomfitted. The erotic goliard song does not necessarily have a knight as its hero, but in other respects it resembles the *pastourelle*. It emphasizes wit and humor, which is often coarse and sometimes obscene. Tannhäuser's work differs from both in that it is a story of courtly lovers, even though class itself is not

---

18 Wolfgang Golther, "Die Quellen der Dichtung des 'Tannhäuser'," *Bayreuther Blätter*, 12 (1889), 132; Ernst Elster, *Tannhäuser in Geschichte, Sage und Dichtung*, Veröffentlichungen der Abteilung für Literatur der deutschen Gesellschaft für Kunst und Wissenschaft zu Bromberg, 3 (Bromberg, 1908), p. 4; Karl F. Kummer, ed., *Die poetischen Erzählungen des Herrand von Wildonie und die kleinen innerösterreichischen Minnesinger* (Wien: Hölder, 1880), p. 68.

19 *Carmina Burana: Faksimile-Ausgabe der Benediktbeuerer Liederhandschrift*, ed. Bernhard Bischoff (München: Prestet, 1967), fols. 73v, 91v, 96v-97r, and others.

20 Brauns, pp. 194-95.

stressed. Moreover, in spite of some timidity on the part of the lady, the love scene is by no means a casual seduction. A deep and lasting attachment is formed which evokes in the narrator a feeling of great joy rather than of triumph. The consummation of love is only touched upon, and then with tact and restraint. One is reminded particularly of Walther's "Under der linden." Even the background is treated differently than in the typical *pastourelle* or goliard song. Tannhäuser does not describe merely a rural scene, but rather an ideal landscape of springtime beauty which serves as a leitmotif. The blooms of the heath, just as the wreath of red flowers on the maiden's head are symbols of youth, high spirits, and joyous dancing.

When one considers the popularity of *Mädchenlieder* and courtly *Dorfpoesie* in thirteenth-century Germany, it is strange that the Romance *pastourelle* was not adopted by Tannhäuser or one of his contemporaries. But no shepherdess appears in any minnesong or *Leich*. However, if *Leich* II is not a German *pastourelle*, it is also not a conventional minnesong. Its frank, though discreet treatment of love's fulfillment is considered by some to be a sign of the decadence of chivalric ideals, an indication of a decline in good manners at the court of the undisciplined Duke Friedrich II.[21] One scholar considers the work to be auto-biographical, a product of the poet's own relationship to "die flotten Wiener Mädchen."[22] Actually, it tells a fresh and natural story which must have been a delight to a society that was surfeited with fifty years of plaints from frustrated and languishing lovers. It is this tradition which supplies the song with its subtle humor, for when the author unexpectedly exceeds the limits of the courtly lyric and allows a fine lady to respond to love, the effect is a sympathetic, but amused surprise. Tannhäuser's penchant for irony is expressed in the implied ridicule of the artificial conventions of the minnesong. With respect to the dancing which the composition accompanied, one should assume it to be of a single type, the *tanz*, because of its unvaried and moderate rhythm. In general, however, works with a spring setting were sung to *reien*.[23]

Leich III also presents a love story against an Arcadian background of flowering spring. It begins with a nature description which gradually becomes a tale about the narrator and his sweetheart. He relates how he had crossed the blooming heath and entered a forest which rang with bird song and was traversed by a brook. He had followed it and found by a pool his lady, whose physical charms are described in intimate detail. He had declared his love and she had gladly submitted to him. In thinking back over his adventure he is filled with joy and praises her as the best of women. He then speaks to the dancers and refers to the instruments which accompany their singing, but he cannot stop thinking

---

[21] De Boor, p. 371.
[22] Bernhardt, p. 96.
[23] Wolff, p. 359, calls *Leich* II "einen ausgelassenen Wintertanz." However, Bernhardt, p. 96, maintains that all *Tanzleiche* were intended for *reien*.

of his loved one. Suddenly the breaking of the fiddle's string brings song and dance to an end.

Like *Leich* II, this work can be taken as simply an idyllic love story. However, the irony is a little more pronounced here and there is some parody. The narrator dwells on the love scene a bit longer and mixes some light wit in with his expressions of affection, as in the passage: "si iach si litte es gerne. dc ich ir tete als man den frowen tut dort in palerne." This, together with the slightly daring description of the lady's person, contrasts sharply with the treatment of ladies and love in the traditional minnesong and thereby produces a humorous effect. The suspicion of parody is awakened when the conventional prayer of the knight that God may watch over the lady is extended to include the hope that no one else is watching over her, also by the lady's suggestion that he sing her a song about the beauties of May when it is obvious that he has something quite different in mind. However, not until one notices the unusual vocabulary of the *Leich* does the intent to parody become clear.[24] The object of Tannhäuser's irony now is not the minnesong, but courtly epic verse. The first part of the *Leich* is adorned with a baroque display of French borrowings. There are over twenty of them — words such as *tschoie, dulz, schantieren, parlieren* — some of which are used several times. Since all of this preciosity is restricted to introduction and love story, leaving the dance section in the author's usual simple and unaffected speech, the contrast is such as to place both the language and the eroticism of Arthurian romance in an amusing light. A reference to *tavel runde* and *massenie* leaves no doubt as to the comparison which Tannhäuser seeks to evoke.[25] Once more he has produced humor, not by ridiculing his characters, but by tricking his audience: by treating a literary convention with which it was familiar in a manner that it did not expect. It has been suggested that the author intended his irony to cover not only euphuistic art, but also the pretentious language and superficial manners which — it is assumed — characterized the courts of the mid-thirteenth century.[26] The objections to this thesis are simply that the medieval poets were considerably less inclined to associate literature and life than the Romantic scholarship of modern times has supposed, and that there

---

[24] Wolff, p. 361, writes, "Der 3. Leich parodiert die höfische Neigung, sich mit romanischen Fremdworten einen prunkenden Mantel umzuwerfen." De Boor, p. 373, agrees, "Solche ohrenfällige Häufung kann nur bewußte Absicht sein, und eine andere als eine parodistische ist bei diesem Dichter nicht denkbar." However, Siebert, *Tannhäuser: Inhalt und Form*, p. 82, disagrees, as does Lang, p. 49.

[25] It is quite possible that Tannhäuser was thinking in particular of the flowery description of the idyllic scene at the Cave of Love in *Tristan*, for Gottfried also refers to "Artuses tavelrunden und alle ir massenie." The lines are 16900-01 in Friedrich Ranke, ed., *Gottfried von Strassburg, Tristan und Isold*, 14th ed. (Dublin and Zürich: Weidmann, 1969).

[26] Helmut de Boor, *Das späte Mittelalter: Zerfall und Neubeginn. 1250-1350.* 3rd ed. (München: Beck, 1967), p. 265: "Die Veräußerlichung des höfischen Lebens zu oberflächlichem Preziösentum wird in der kauderwelschen Sprache des jungen Helmbrechts hörbar, wie sie auch der Tannhäuser in seinem dritten Leich verspottet hatte."

is little evidence to prove that Tannhäuser's society was more decadent than that of the preceding generation.

The more obvious eroticism of *Leich* III as well as the stronger overtone of humor has caused it to be associated not only with the *pastourelle* but also with the *mal mariée* songs. With regard to the former, one may object once again that there is no shepherdess; with respect to the latter, that there is no husband. Nevertheless, the composition does reveal similarities to the *mal mariée* songs in the emphasis on the consummation of love as well as in the use of a background of field and forest beauty. The unswerving and sincere devotion of the narrator to his sweetheart, however, establishes a tone which is quite dissimilar to any previous songs of seduction in either French or German. The division of this *Leich* into definite units on the basis of content is not as clear as in either of the preceding works. The nature introduction mentions not only the lady of part two, but also the dance of part three, while the last versicle — except for the final three lines — is devoted to the narrator's love instead of to the dance or its conclusion. A separation into parts on the basis of rhythm is also not obvious, for short and long lines, iambs and dactyls are scattered fairly evenly throughout the work. References to *springen* and *reien* indicate the type of dance to which the last three versicles were sung, and it is quite likely that the entire composition accompanied a *reie*. There is nothing in either *Leich* II or *Leich* III to indicate when or where they were composed.[27]

As do a host of minnesongs, the following *Leich* begins with the praise of a lady and a declaration that none has been so highly acclaimed as she. With this introduction, a long and impressive catalogue of famous women of literature unfolds which is liberally padded with names invented for the occasion. Characters and events of courtly literature are paraded at length, but many of them are deliberately scrambled. However, everything is related in such a factual manner that even today there is little agreement as to the extent of Tannhäuser's fabrication.[28] Parzival enters the story of Troy by breaking down the city's wall; Wigamur takes Gahmuret's place as the hero of the tournament at Kanvoleis; and Tristan fills in for him as the husband of Belakane. *Eneide, Der Trojanerkrieg, Lanzelet, Tristan, Wigalois, Die Krone,* and other medieval works contribute characters and incidents, sometimes accurately, sometimes in deliberate confusion.

---

27 Kummer, p. 67, states that the *Leiche* are arranged chronologically in the manuscript, but presents no evidence of this. Oehlke, p. 41, presents the theory that *Leiche* III, V, and IV were composed in that order, because it reflects the increasing complexity of the motif of the broken string or bow at the end.

28 Siebert, *Tannhäuser: Inhalt und Form,* p. 86, is reluctant to believe that Tannhäuser invented characters: "Es entzieht sich denn auch noch manches der Erklärung, ohne daß daraus der Schluß gezogen werden darf, der Dichter habe einzelnes einfach erfunden." Lang, p. 66, also assumes that the poet is referring to works which have been lost. However, de Boor, *Die höfische Literatur,* p. 373, thinks it improbable that Tannhäuser is naming characters from literature which has disappeared and speaks of "bewußte Verdrehungen von barocker Lustigkeit."

The *Leich* not only reveals Tannhäuser's familiarity with the epic verse of his day, but also tells something of the literary background of his audience. For a humorist profits little from private jokes.

At last the narrator turns from the heroines of the past to his sweetheart, who is as lovely as any. Her beauty is portrayed with enthusiasm and, once more, in somewhat intimate detail. She is not only physically very attractive, but has also the other virtues poets laud: good manners, constancy, and kindliness. Above all she possesses that which Tannhäuser values most, a joyous spirit: "ir zimt wol dc lache*n*." However, although the narrator is extravagant in his praise, the appearance of his loved one is not at all what the listener was led to expect. After the procession of goddesses and queens — Juno, Pallas, Venus, Medea, Helen, Dido, and others — the audience is presented with a young dancer with a flower in her yellow hair, who is described affectionately, but in quite irreverent terms. After telling of his sweetheart and declaring his love, the narrator turns from the one dancer to the dance itself and to others who are or should be there. The final stanza announces the conclusion of the festivities, opposes whoever would spoil the happiness of the dancers, and ends abruptly with the breaking of the fiddler's bow.

Leich IV has more sharply defined segments than do the two preceding works and the parts are meticulously balanced. Counting dimeter lines as half-lines, there are 4 lines in the introduction, 58 in the parade of celebrities, 58 devoted to the narrator's sweetheart, 22 to the dance, and 8 to the conclusion. This means that the two main sections are exactly equal in length and the conclusion is twice as long as the introduction. If the *Leich* is divided into two parts instead of five, there are 120 lines devoted to the main theme and 30 to the dance, a ratio of precisely four to one. Such figures are to some extent a result of chance and could be slightly altered by a different partition of the work. However, they do indicate that Tannhäuser was a careful craftsman who, though he may not have counted verses, was interested in creating a symmetrical work of art.

Unlike the first three *Leiche*, this work does not have a nature introduction. Yet, references to crocuses, roses, and bird song in the conclusion identify it as a spring song — which is reflected in the rhythm. Metrically, the composition is divided into two distinct parts, the second beginning with the discussion of the narrator's sweetheart. What goes before is told for the most part in iambic tetrameter lines which show little variation in tempo; what comes after is largely in dimeter and trimeter lines, with only enough longer lines to provide contrast. The frequent omission of the *Auftakt* in the second part also serves to vary the rhythm. Once more one might assume that the *Leich* accompanied first a *tanz* and then a *reie*.

The transitions between the five segments of the work are made more quickly than in the two preceding *Leiche*, but are done smoothly. The last line of the introduction — "Ich gehorte nie wib so wol gelobe*n*, als ma*n* si tût" — is enough to shift the attention from the narrator's lady to those of literature. The final line of this segment and the first of the following one bring us back to the heroine. The narrator's joy in his love leads to his joy in the dance and thus ties in with the following section. Allusions to the beauties of spring connect the dance with the conclusion.

Except for the dance section, the content of *Leich* IV differs considerably from that of the first three, even though the ironical treatment of the content is quite similar in all. Here it takes the form of parody. Where other poets have compared their ladies to Dido or Isolde, Tannhäuser lists twenty-two such famous beauties, including new inventions. Where others have demonstrated their learning by references to episodes in fiction, he runs the full gamut of the courtly epic of the day, purposely confusing characters and events as he goes. There is throughout a carefully calculated mixture of the familiar and the bizarre, designed to achieve an effect which has been called grotesque.[29] Ironical humor appears again in the poet's exceeding the limits of courtly propriety in his descriptions of the female form.

Most important with regard to *Leich* IV is the fact that its melody is extant, although perhaps in a form slightly different from the original. A late thirteenth-century musician's handbook in the Munich library contains among other compositions a Latin *conductus* which begins with "Syon egredere nunc de cubilibus" and ends with "eia et eia, quia nunc dictaturi: Der sait der ist enzwai." A comparison of the music with the text of *Leich* IV shows that the *conductus* melody fits Tannhäuser's verses somewhat better than the Latin ones, indicating the priority of the secular setting. The melody consists largely of similar variations on a single theme, but it is pleasant, and has been praised as the most beautiful of all extant *Leich* melodies.[30] It is the only extant music for a dance *Leich*.

The fifth *Leich* resembles the preceding one, but instead of a parade of great ladies and lovers, there is a travelogue of exotic lands. In rapid succession we hear of Morocco's mountains of gold, of the mightly rulers of Persia and India, of colorful Bagdad and Jerusalem. After more geography of the Middle East, the narrator turns to Southeast Europe: to Constantinople with its famous sea nymph, to Bulgaria, Hungary, and Russia. He then jumps to Western Europe: France, England, the five kingdoms of Spain, and Ireland — each with its special characteristic or interesting bit of history. Then, by way of cold Norway and Denmark, the narrator moves to the familiar territory of Austria and Bavaria. After a brief tribute to the dead Friedrich II of the former and the living Otto II of the latter, the travelogue is finished and the love story and dance begin.

---

29 Ferdinand Mohr, *Das unhöfische Element in der mittelhochdeutschen Lyrik von Walther an* (Diss. Tübingen, 1913), p. 67; Wolff, p. 360.

30 Hans Spanke, "Eine mittelalterliche Musikhandschrift," *ZfdA*, 69 (1932), 63. Siebert, *Der Dichter Tannhäuser: Leben, Gedichte, Sage* (Halle: Niemeyer, 1934), pp. 58-68, reconstructs the melody as he thinks it was before it was adapted to the Latin text. Hugo Kuhn, *Minnesangs Wende* (Tübingen: Niemeyer, 1952), pp. 110-19, gives an extensive discussion of the musical structure.

This latter section, unlike those of the previous *Leiche*, is not restricted to a purely local scene, but starts by telling of great men — Saladin, Ermerich, Roland, and others — whose prowess, however, was no greater than that of the narrator when he discovered his sweetheart alone. Shifting rapidly back and forth in time from the girl of his adventure to the same one who is now dancing with him, he tells of her beauty and charm. He calls for the musicians: flutist, tambourinists, trumpeter — but the fiddler's string breaks again and thus signals the end of the song. Thereupon the narrator encourages himself to be happy and to dance merrily wherever there is singing.

The *Leich* shows fewer and less distinct divisions than the preceding ones. The travelogue starts without introduction and proceeds in general from the remote to the familiar until it ends with the praise of Otto. The narrator's joy in having found, as he hopes, a generous sponsor leads to his joy in his lady, and so the second segment begins. This is not really a love story, but rather a listing of heroes which is introduced and concluded by references to his sweetheart. The transition to the dance section is made when the narrator invites others to take a partner as he has done. However, he had referred to the dance several times before and he continues to speak of his lady, so no clear separation is apparent. This is also true of the dance section and the conclusion, for he has already mentioned ending his song before the string breaks.

Rhythmically the *Leich* falls into four parts, the first two of which coincide with the travelogue, the last two with lady's section and dance section respectively. The first eleven versicles have essentially the same *Ton,* which consists of four hexameter lines — occasionally with interior rhyme. The following six versicles have a somewhat livelier *Ton* that is made up of two heptameter lines — usually broken by interior rhyme — and a trimeter line. One of the versicles of this group has a variant of the second *Ton* which repeats each long line once. The third part includes the next five versicles, which are composed in four different variants of the second *Ton*. The last part has eight versicles, each with a different *Ton* that is made up almost entirely of short lines. The concluding verses are distinguished by the prominence of dactyls. The development from part to part is consistently in the direction of increased complexity and diversity. The tempo — as indicated by short lines — also gradually increases. The first two parts taken together are twice as long as the last two.

Leich V has received particular attention from those scholars who have attempted to put together a biography of Tannhäuser. One suggests that it was composed as a greeting to Otto II when, in 1247, he was appointed governor of Austria after the death of Friedrich.[31] Others assume that the verses,

> ich gesach nie fursten me so milten noch so richen
> so rehte lobelichen.
> heia tanhusere nv la dich iemer bi im vinden.

---

[31] Wolff, p. 362.

indicate that the poet was for a time a protégé of the Bavarian duke.[32] It has also been assumed by some that Tannhäuser is telling facts about himself when his narrator says he has been in a few of the lands he lists, and they connect these travels with participation in a crusade or pilgrimage to Jerusalem. It has even been suggested that the *Leich* indicates his route there (through Bulgaria and Constantinople)[33] and back (by way of the Western Mediterranean, Spain, France, England, and Denmark).[34] One scholar cites the *Leich* as proof that Tannhäuser took part in the Cyprian War of 1231—1233.[35]

Actually, the work tells little about either the poet or its composition. A comparison of the brief mention of Otto here with the long eulogy of Friedrich in *Leich* I makes it seem unlikely that *Leich* V was composed as occasional verse. And though the lines quoted certainly indicate that the poet was looking for a patron, there is no evidence that he found one. As far as travel in the Middle East is concerned, the *Leich* offers less support for than against the assumption of such a journey. For the confused geography which it presents, together with the inclusion of fictional lands from courtly novels and the poet's own imagination, weighs against any personal knowledge of the region. To be sure, Tannhäuser's editors have labored valiantly to put his geography in order and to identify all of the places he mentions with actual cities and countries, but the results have been largely unconvincing. The one indisputable biographical fact which comes from the *Leich* is that it was composed between 1247 and the year of Otto's death, 1253.

The humor of *Leich* V stems largely from parody of the literary vogue of exotic lands. The crusades had stimulated interest in far-away countries and strange customs, and the poet who could tell of them from first-hand knowledge would not lack an audience. The so-called *Spielmannsepen* were set in distant kingdoms, and even works the action of which took place primarily in Western Europe often exploited the charm of exotic lands and people. Tannhäuser's narrator is determined to surpass all others as he displays his gazeteer of regions that he has seen or of which he has heard, mixing the actual and the fictional in a truly surrealistic manner. References to characters in Wolfram's *Willehalm* suggest that this work may have been the special object of the mockery. The parody carries over to the story of the narrator's sweetheart. In *Leich* IV he had paraded the famous ladies of literature. Now he tells of great heroes (including one of his own invention) and indicates that he could have told of many more had

---

32 Joseph Haupt, "Die Sage vom Venusberg und dem Tannhäuser," *Berichte und Mittheilungen des Altertums-Vereins zu Wien*, 10 (1869), 315; Gustav Heinrich, "Die Tannhäuser-Sage," *Ungarische Revue*, 6 (1886), 828; Lang, p. 152; Oehlke, p. 9; Zander, p. 25; and others.

33 Gustav Ehrismann, *Geschichte der deutschen Literatur bis zum Ausgang des Mittelalters: Schlussband* (1935; rpt. München: Beck, 1966), p. 266.

34 G. Rosenhagen, "Die Leiche des Tannhäuser und des Ulrich von Winterstetten," *ZfdPh*, 61 (1936), 272.

35 Wolff, p. 357.

he wished. Additional humor is provided in the love story by the pretentious use of French, such as: *bel amye, bel amur, foret,* and *Schampenie* (MS spellings).

To the comic effect of parody is added that resulting from the narrator's inconsistency in the use of time, place, and person. When he first speaks of his sweetheart, she is dancing before him. Then he tells of finding her alone in the forest. Once more she is at the dance, again back in the forest, and again at the dance. Sometimes he speaks of her in the third person, sometimes he addresses her directly. The result is an amusing confusion, similar to that produced by the mixing of real and invented places and historical and fictional heroes.

The matter of a patron, which appears briefly in *Leich* V, is central to the sixth *Leich*. In an introduction the singer bewails the deterioration of a society which has lost its joy, shows no appreciation for his songs, and has seen the death of princely generosity. This munificence becomes the theme of the following verses as the poet first presents a list of open-handed rulers of the immediate past and then a catalogue of living nobles, whose virtues seldom include a readiness to share their wealth. The gallery of portraits begins with those of Emperor Friedrich II and his sons, King Heinrich and King Konrad, all three of whom are lauded as models of royalty, whose passing the singer laments. Then other German princes who have died during Tannhäuser's lifetime are brought forward and praised, one by one, especially for their *milte*.

The second group, the living princes, are treated with appropriate tact. They too have their virtues, but generosity is mentioned in connection with only two. At last the register of nobility comes to an end and the singer asks where he should look to find a lord who values fame and honor. For he will gladly spread the praises of one who is worthy and knows how to show appreciation properly. The singer then announces that such a prince exists and that he will name him. But what follows is a statement — in four unrhymed and irregular lines — that the kindness of charming ladies can help those who are held fast by the bonds of love. After this a blank space of almost nine unfilled lines appears in the manuscript.

Various opinions have been expressed with regard to the end of the *Leich*. One scholar believes that it is complete as far as content is concerned and that only the meter and rhyme of the final lines have been corrupted.[36] Others maintain that Tannhäuser's ending was lost and that the last three or four verses were supplied by someone else.[37] It is generally assumed that the *Leich* as we have it is almost complete and that the catalogue of princes is not followed by a love episode and a dance section. What may have happened is this: The Manesse scribe noted that the *Leich*, as it appeared in the manuscript he was copying, had no obvious conclusion like those of the preceding *Leiche*. He, therefore, left a space so that the final stanza or stanzas could be filled in later and went on. A search failed to turn up the missing ending and the scribe added one of his

---

[36] Kück, p. 212.
[37] Siebert, *Tannhäuser: Inhalt und Form,* p. 97; Oehlke, p. 12; Wolff, p. 363.

own.[38] The main reason for believing that the *Leich* is essentially complete is its length. The previous five *Leiche* take up from one and one-half to a little more than two columns of manuscript each. *Leich* VI fills exactly two columns, so if the extant portion had been followed by a love story and a dance, the *Leich* would have been much longer than the others. Another reason to assume that little, if anything, is missing is that the *Leich* as it is shows the same general structural pattern that is seen in the other *Leiche*. The introduction is made up of three short versicles in a *Ton* which consists of dimeter, trimeter, and tetrameter lines, rhyming a a a. Following the introduction come thirty-two versicles in a second *Ton*, that has alternate tetrameter and trimeter lines which rhyme a b a b. Then a third *Ton* appears, of indeterminate length, which is made up of trimeter couplets. There are nine lines in the introduction, ten lines in what appears to be the conclusion, and the main body is divided by its content into two fairly distinct parts. As with *Leich* II, one might well question as to whether this is actually a *Leich*. For it may have had a basic melody (repeated thirty-two times), which was preceded and followed by another melody which served as prelude and, in a variant form, as finale. The absence of any reference to dancing indicates that the work is not a *Tanzleich*.

Leich VI has been discussed primarily as an expression of Tannhäuser's political sympathies in the struggle between the Hohenstaufens and the papacy. It has been noted that the work not only begins with praise of Friedrich II and his sons, but mentions primarily their supporters and includes only a single ecclesiastical prince — an ally of the Hohenstaufens. It has even been maintained that the presumably lost ending would have proclaimed Konradin, the last of the family, as the model of living monarchs.[39] However, although there are indications in several of his other works that Tannhäuser favored the Empire over the papacy, it is a mistake to class the *Leich* as primarily a political document. For some of the princes listed and praised were opponents of the Hohenstaufens and others seem to have remained relatively neutral in the conflict between Empire and Church. It is much more probable that Tannhäuser, if he had a purpose beyond pure entertainment, was interested in his own well-being rather than that of the Hohenstaufens.

The preponderance of Hohenstaufen supporters among the higher nobility listed in the *Leich* can be explained as easily by geographical as by political considerations. For all the living princes mentioned were from the eastern half of the Empire, where the papal influence was less strong. The singer's references to the courts of Saxony, Braunschweig, Brandenburg, and Silesia has led some to assume that Tannhäuser spent his later years wandering through Central and Eastern Germany.[40] This may be so. However, the prominence of the area in the

---

[38] The manuscript indicates that the last four lines are in the same hand as the rest of the *Leich*.

[39] Oehlke, p. 30.

[40] De Boor, *Die höfische Literatur*, p. 370; Siebert, *Der Dichter Tannhäuser*, p. 26.

Leich may be due to the increasing importance of its princes in the political and economic affairs of Germany as well as by its relative proximity to Vienna — the only lasting residence of the poet, as far as we know. His nearness to Austria might also explain why the king of neighboring Bohemia is singled out for praise.

By checking the dates of the deceased princes against those of the living, the time of composition of the *Leich* has been established as being between the spring of 1264 and that of 1266.[41] Tannhäuser was certainly no longer young then and, since no later date has been established for any of his works, may have been at the end of his professional career. The opening lines, which remind one of Walther's "Owe war sint verswunden alliu miniu jar," certainly give the impression of one who is nostalgically looking back on a period which was not only quite different, but is now rather remote. Nevertheless, neither Tannhäuser's poetic techniques nor his propensity for irony have significantly changed. The accumulation of names of people and places, which characterizes the fourth and fifth *Leiche* is also a distinguishing feature of this one. He apparently did not invent celebrities in *Leich* VI as in the others — although this possibility cannot be entirely discarded, since not all those mentioned have been positively identified. The poet does make several errors with regard to relationship and to whether a prince was alive or deceased, but this could well have been accidental. Still, the irony of two passages is clear, and the ending may have been a joke on his audience. Certainly Tannhäuser had not become overly serious with age. His prayer that God may have mercy on the souls of those who are dead to generosity and honor is only another way of saying, "They're practically deceased, why not bury them?" And the remark that the margraves of Brandenburg were very wise, especially at hanging on to their wealth, was surely good for a laugh at those courts which resented the rising power of Brandenburg.

It may be that the most amusing part of the *Leich* is the conclusion. For it is not necessary to believe either that the unrhymed final lines are a corruption of the real ending or that the real ending was lost. It may be that Tannhäuser intended to stop with the last lines which are indisputably his:

> ich wil de*n* furste*n* nenne*n*.
> ob ir in welt erkenne*n*.
> Sin grus vn*d* och sin lache*n*.
> dc ka*n* mir froide machen.

Such an ending is humorous in that it leads the audience on and then fails to satisfy its curiosity. The ending is also practical, for an additional couplet could immortalize any prince who cared to pay the singer's price for fame. And the latter has already indicated that the space at the end was for sale. Apparently there were no satisfactory offers.

---

[41] Wolff, p. 358, dates the composition between 27 April 1264 and 4 April 1266.

The last of the *Leiche* (XVI)[42] is very short, consisting of five brief versicles each of which presents a riddle. Riddle verse was popular during the medieval period, and it appeared in various types of literature: sometimes as incidental inclusions in longer works, such as *Parzival* and *Der Wartburgkrieg*, occasionally in polystrophic songs, like "Das Traugemundslied," but usually in individual *Spruch* stanzas. Such *Rätselsprüche* were composed primarily by middle-class poets and were largely the product of a folk, rather than a courtly tradition. As a result the language used and the scenes described often lacked the refinement of courtly verse. The riddles were sometimes didactic and frequently drew from Biblical stories. This *Leich* is the only one of Tannhäuser's works which is not told in the first person. The first versicle relates that a woman killed her husband and all her children, which so enraged the former that he killed her in turn and all her servants; later other children were born to them. In the second we learn of a man, not born of woman, who took a wife who never had a father or mother. The third tells of a dog which barked so loudly that everyone living heard it. The fourth states that the earth is higher than the heavens, as wise masters have often learned in years past. The last versicle tells of a child which, while in its mother's womb, killed its father as he was singing of God and reading the truth to the other children.

As the work consists of only fourteen lines in all and the manuscript does not separate the versicles in any way, early nineteenth-century scholars assumed that it was a *Spruch* stanza which presented a single puzzle. Since no solution could possibly satisfy all of the conditions posed, it was classed as nonsense verse or as a teasing mixture of riddle and tall tale. Toward the end of the century, however, the poem was divided into versicles, and the individual riddles were soon solved by comparing them with other Latin and Middle High German versions to which answers are appended.[43]

The first riddle is the only one which does not appear elsewhere, but there is fairly general agreement as to its solution: Eve caused the death of Adam and all her descendants by her sin; when Adam also sinned, this judgment on them was confirmed. One scholar objects that, since the second riddle treats Adam and Eve, the first must have another subject. He suggests night and day, which continually destroy and renew themselves and their offspring, the hours.[44] Solutions to the next three riddles are: Adam was not born of woman, and he took a wife who never had parents; the dog in Noah's ark barked so loudly that

---

42 Where the arrangement in this study is different from the order in the manuscript, the latter will be indicated by the proper Roman numeral.

43 The riddles are treated primarily by the following: Gustav Roethe, "Tannhäuser's Rätselspruch," *ZfdA*, 30 (1886), 419-20; Richard Maria Werner, "Zu Tannhäuser," *ZfdA*, 31 (1887), 363-64; E. Kück, "Zu Tannhäusers Rätselspruch," *AfdA*, 17 (1891), 79-80; Fritz Loewenthal, *Studien zum germanischen Rätsel* (Heidelberg: Winter, 1914), pp. 64-67; Anton Wallner, "Eine Hampfel Grübelnüsse," *ZfdA*, 64 (1927), 81-83.

44 Loewenthal, p. 65.

everyone alive heard him; Christ's presence on earth in the Sacraments makes it higher than the heavens. The answer to the final puzzle is a little more involved. In 1170 Archbishop Thomas Becket was murdered in Canterbury Cathedral on the order of King Henry II. We see, therefore, that the child (Henry), while in its mother's womb (the Church), killed its spiritual father (the archbishop), while the latter was singing of God to the other children (ministering to the spiritual needs of his congregation).

One can imagine that the medieval performance paralleled the modern history of the *Leich*. Tannhäuser would probably have sung it straight through without a pause, with the result that no one would have been able to decipher it. When the perplexed audience protested that it had no meaning, he would have sung it again, hesitating after each versicle to allow opportunity to guess its meaning. Each of the five versicles has a separate *Ton*.

Tannhäuser is known primarily for his *Leiche*. Five of them are dance *Leiche* — probably the first in German literature — and have a lighthearted, joking mood which is appropriate to their function. This mood is evident also in the other two *Leiche*, although the sixth makes a more serious impression because of the narrator's nostalgia and his search for a patron. The versicles of the *Leiche* fall into groups which divide the works into more or less distinct segments according to content and sometimes according to rhythm. Relatively few different *Töne* are used, which gives several *Leiche* the appearance of *Lieder* and suggests that the poet was not very inventive with regard to music composition.

The six minnesongs fall into three groups of two songs each: summer songs, winter songs, and *minne* parodies. All of the summer and winter songs were probably sung for dancing, and the parodies may have been. Unlike the dance songs of Neidhart, they have no narrative. Since none contain references to historical events or persons, they cannot be dated,[45] but there is some indication that not all were composed at the same period in the poet's career. With regard to form, the songs are quite representative of their period. The rhyme schemes are complex, although not unusually so for a time which stressed technical virtuosity. Five of the songs have three stanzas (the favorite number among thirteenth-century composers), the remaining one has five stanzas (the second most popular number). All stanzas have *Stollen* form and most are somewhat longer than average for the period, especially among those which do not tell a story.[46] The mood varies from carefree gaiety to light melancholy. Tannhäuser's characteristic irony extends from a tactful, but detailed description of his sweetheart's figure to slapstick parody of the standard conventions of *minne*.

The poet's two summer songs (VII and XV) are closest to the stereotype of the classical minnesong. Indeed, one scholar calls them "höfische Lieder, ganz im alten Stile" and suggests that they may have been composed before the poet developed a style of his own.[47] But the very fact that they are obviously dance songs distinguishes them from the formal courtly lyric of the late twelfth and early thirteenth century, which does not mention dancing. The first of the summer songs begins with a brief dance invitation that is followed by a description of scenes and sounds of spring — leafy forests, singing birds, and blooming fields — among which all life becomes young again. The stanza concludes with the narrator's saying that he too could be happy if the object of his affection so wished. The second stanza continues with the portrayal of the beauties of May which have brought joy to all the world. The singer alone is sad, and only the lady's kindness can change that. The final stanza is devoted entirely to her and his feelings toward her. She was cordial to him when she saw him at the

---

45 Kummer, p. 67, believes that the songs are in chronological order in the manuscript.
46 A detailed analysis of the structure and metrics of Tannhäuser's songs appears in Günther Müller, "Strophenbindung bei Ulrich von Lichtenstein," *ZfdA*, 60 (1923), 47.
47 Oehlke, p. 33; Wolff, p. 359, likewise thinks that they belong to the tradition of "hohe Minne."

21

dance, but society is so watchful that he cannot find a way to be alone with her. The song is divided about equally between nature and the lady, and, in spite of the singer's pangs of love, the prevailing mood is that of happy springtime. Besides, the lady — in contrast to the conventional heroine of the minnesong — has not tried to discourage him. There is certainly nothing new in this composition. It is a variant of a pattern — beauties of nature, beauty of a lady, love for the lady — which was often used in the mid-thirteenth century. However, the language is not at all hackneyed nor is the impression one of obvious imitation.[48] Despite the familiar content and structure, the expression is fresh and the emotion genuine.

The other summer song is composed in the longest and most intricate *Ton* of those by Tannhäuser in the Manesse Manuscript. It consists of sixteen lines which rhyme: a a b c d e e b c d f d f f b b. The *Stollen* and the first half of the *Abgesang* are made up of dimeter and trimeter lines, usually without an *Auftakt,* but the end of the *Ton* has a pentameter and a hexameter line which break the staccato effect of the short lines and perhaps indicate a change in the tempo of the melody. The first stanza is taken up by an account of the flowering heath and of forest birds competing in song. Then in the long final line the singer injects a personal note — as in the introduction to the previous song — by saying that much of his sorrow is leaving him. In the following stanza we discover the reason for his sadness when he tells of how he sang to happy young people under the linden in years past, and adds that merriment has now disappeared from society and no one cares for his singing. In the last stanza the narrator says that his sorrow nevertheless would end if his lady would console him. He then would praise her above the beauty of May and show that no one else pleased him so much. He concludes by asking her to observe how nicely he acts when thinking of her.

The progression of the stanzas — joys of May, deterioration of society, hopes for consolation from the lady — follows no established pattern and is the invention of the poet. His use of the final three lines in each stanza is especially noteworthy. The first, a pentameter, sums up or emphasizes what has been said in the thirteen preceding short lines; the second and third lines, dimeter and hexameter respectively, show how the singer is affected by the situation. The first stanza contains the traditional nature introduction and is exceptional only in that the description of nature here, as in the preceding work, takes up a much greater than average percentage of the total composition. The theme of the second stanza — the changing times and the corruption of society — appears frequently in the lyric verse of the thirteenth century, but it is most unusual to find it in the customarily lighthearted and frivolous summer dance song. The treatment of the singer's feelings toward the lady in the third stanza is traditional

---

[48] Lang, p. 111, believes the song was strongly influenced by Neidhart and cites a number of parallels which, however, do not establish the dependence of Tannhäuser's work on those of the older poet.

until one comes to the last two lines. Here there is certainly a humorously ironic implication that the lady would ordinarily not expect such proper behavior from the singer when he was thinking of love. Despite some melancholy notes, the song ends in a light vein which is quite in keeping with a celebration of the rites of spring.

Because of the middle stanza, the song has been attributed to the poet's later years. Of course, one cannot positively identify the narrator with his creator. However, the implication that the former has fallen on hard times sufficiently agrees with similar statements in the *Leiche* and *Sprüche* to warrant the assumption that a certain amount of autobiography appears in the stanza. If so, it was composed after the death of Tannhäuser's generous patron, Duke Friedrich.

The first of Tannhäuser's winter songs to be discussed here (XI) is the most charming of his minnesongs. Composed for Christmastide festivities, it dispenses with the nature introduction, which establishes a bleak and melancholy mood for the typical winter song. Instead, the narrator starts with a summons to merriment, a promise of joy, and an offer to sing for a dance. With this, he calls attention to the *vortenzerinne*, who soon commences a solo dance to show the others what steps are to be used. The rise and fall of the sash at her hips as she glides forward gives him a warm feeling of pleasure. With the second stanza an enthusiastic and frankly sensuous description of her beauty begins. This description pours out through the rest of the song as if the narrator could not say enough to do justice to his subject. At first he addresses her directly, praising hair, eyes, lips, cheek, throat, breasts, and interrupts his compliments at times to encourage her to dance on — and to whirl so as to expose more of her figure. In the third stanza, with a sudden change of direction, the narrator describes her tiny feet, her legs, and — quite unexpectedly — her thighs, hips, and mons. The last stanza tells us that the girl is not only beautiful, but that she talks entertainingly and leads a virtuous life. The narrator pledges his heart that he has seen nothing so fine in the entire country.

Although the song gives an initial impression of simplicity and lack of sophistication, there is nothing naive or accidental in its composition. The basis is the cataloguing technique which is so characteristic of Tannhäuser's verse. To avoid monotony, the narrator continually changes his audience. First he addresses the group as a whole, then the beautiful dancer, again the group, and finally — in the ecstatic last stanza — himself. The description is also broken up by references to the dance. The narrator volunteers to sing for the dance, starts the *vortenzerinne* off, tells the others when they should begin, and later even gives instructions as to specific dance movements. He reminds one of the caller at a modern square dance, and he may actually have been performing just such a function.

Tannhäuser's chief means for maintaining interest and creating suspense throughout his lengthy enumeration of feminine charms lies, of course, in his arrangement of them. It soon becomes apparent to the listener (and the reader) that the narrator, having started at the top of the lady's head, is proceeding steadily downward. At the moment of greatest tension, he breaks off and, beginning at her feet, moves upward. Then, when it appears that he has been just teasing and can go no further, he does. The audience was no doubt thinking of the song in which Walther too describes the head and feet of his lady, and breaks off, saying:

> ob ich da enzwischen loben muoz,
> sô wæne ich mê beschowet hân.[49]

The surprise comes when Tannhäuser allows his narrator's fancy to take over once the limits of his vision have been reached.

The *Ton* of the song has a structure in which short and long lines alternate throughout. The effect is that of a dance tune, but one with a deliberate tempo. It is no doubt a *tanz*, rather than a *reie* melody. The rhyme scheme is simpler than that of either of the summer songs.

The second winter song (VIII) begins in the traditional way with a description of a winter scene — a faded heath and a forest barren of leaves — and a cry of regret that nature should look so dismal. The atmosphere of gloom carries over to the singer's own affairs when, at the end of the first stanza, he says he will be greatly pained if his lady should forget him. In the following stanza the singer asks his audience to help him thank his lady for her kindness, since he can expect a reward from the white one, should he make her red grey be brown. If he brings her the apple Paris gave Venus, she will even permit him to be called her *amis*. In the last stanza we learn that she opposes his every wish and that he would leave her if he could. She wants the sun, the moon, and the North Star from him. A comparison of this song to the preceding ones is revealing with regard to the character of the poet: he can be relatively serious about joy, but sorrow evokes his laughter. He ridicules the idea of service to a lady and, in doing so, pokes fun at the lady, the singer, and even the audience. For the song is half finished before they can guess that the lament is a fake and that they have been tricked.

Although there is no mention of dancing, there can be little doubt but that it is a dance song; probably all thirteenth-century songs of the seasons are. The *Ton*, with its constantly changing line-lengths and its predominance of dimeter and trimeter verses, points to a *reie*, rather than a *tanz*, although winter songs were usually sung to the latter. It has been suggested that this song and the following two were influenced by Ulrich von Liechtenstein's *Frauendienst*.[50] If so, they were composed after 1256, the year in which Ulrich's novel was completed. However, neither here nor elsewhere does Tannhäuser refer to

---

[49] Karl Lachmann, ed., *Die Gedichte Walthers von der Vogelweide*, 13th ed., rev. by Hugo Kuhn (Berlin: Walter de Gruyter, 1965), 54, 19-20.
[50] Oehlke, p. 41; F. Mohr, p. 66.

Frauendienst, and there are many earlier works from which he could have got the idea for *minne* parody.

The above composition exaggerates the lover's plaint in an established lyrical form, the winter song, to produce comedy instead of pathos. The impression given is that this occurred almost as an afterthought and with no intent to create a particular type of verse. To be sure, in the true *minne* parodies (IX and X) the design to exploit the humorous potential in the concept of service is obvious from the start. The first begins by saying, "steter dienest der ist gv̊t" and then for three stanzas presents a list of the lady's demands. She wants him to exchange the Danube for the Rhône, build her an ivory house on the surface of a lake, and bring her, among other things: a Galilean mountain on which Adam sat, a tree from India, Parzival's grail, the apple of Paris, and Noah's ark. If he accomplishes these tasks, she will give him whatever he asks — when Mouse Mountain melts like snow. The singer thanks her, calls her the very soul of kindness, and is happy in anticipation of his reward, although he is a little troubled about finding the ark. The plaint appears in the refrain, in which regret is voiced that the lovely, beautiful, and kind one does not turn his pain to joy. Thus the stanzas and the refrain present contrasting points of view — cautious optimism and helpless despair — and so accentuate the humor of the situation. In the thirteenth-century performance, the refrain would have been sung by the audience.

The *Ton* of the song is quite long, the verses are relatively uniform in length, and the rhyme scheme is simpler than those of the summer and winter songs. The stanzas are made up almost entirely of tetrameter and pentameter lines, which would indicate a moderate rhythm. The refrain, however, consists of tetrameter and trimeter lines, which favor a more rapid tempo. If the song was used for dancing, one might assume that the dancers alternated between *tanz* and *reie*. Tannhäuser was apparently the first poet to compose songs with *minne* parody as the central theme. But traces of it appear in both epic and lyric works from the beginnings of courtly verse and it is sometimes quite pronounced in *Parzival* and the works of Neidhart. The connection of impossible deeds to *minne* was not new and the moving of a river is mentioned in several earlier songs. Friedrich von Hausen's lady insists that those who try to keep her from her lover will sooner change the Rhine into the Po than succeed.[51] Ulrich von Gutenburg's knight says in one song that it would be easier to separate the Moselle from the Rhine than his loved one from his heart, and in another that it would be harder to get him to renounce her than to turn the Rhine into the Po.[52] Heinrich von Morungen applies the simile of the impossibile task directly

---

51 Karl Lachmann, Moriz Haupt, and Friedrich Vogt, eds., *Des Minnesangs Frühling*, 34th ed., rev. by Carl von Kraus (Stuttgart: S. Hirzel, 1967), 49, 8-9.
52 Lachmann, *Des Minnesangs Frühling*, 71, 39-40; 75, 6-7.

to the lady when his knight claims that it would be easier to bend down a tree with a word than to get her to grant his request.[53]

The song is the only one by Tannhäuser to be included in a second manuscript, appearing in one of the early fifteenth century[54] as well as in the Manesse Manuscript. In addition, there is a ten-stanza revision and expansion of the work in the Kolmar Manuscript. One might, therefore, assume that this was the most popular of Tannhäuser's songs.

The following *minne* parody also gives the theme of the song — service and reward — at the very beginning. Then the singer asks the audience to thank the lady for her kindness to him which, as it turns out, consists only of promises. Once more there are requests for fantastic exploits and presents. The former include interfering with the normal flow of Rhine, Elbe, and Danube, controlling both weather and seasons, digging a moat around the earth, and flying like an eagle. As gifts, she would like, among other things: a star, the light of the moon, and the fabled salamander who lives in fire. A humorous leitmotif is supplied by the lady's repeated assurance — nine times in three stanzas — that the singer will certainly get what he wants if he satisfies what she appears to consider quite reasonable desires. His reaction is to proclaim, "ir he*r*ze ist ganzer tvge*n*de vol," but only the actual performance could show whether this is intended to be mock naivité or open sarcasm. The refrain throws further light on the situation by hinting that the lady is not serious and is only putting the singer off. The refrain also makes fun of the minnesong convention which insists that the lady's name be kept secret.

The *Ton* provides an interesting contrast between stanza and refrain. The structure of the former is very simple, consisting of twelve tetrameter lines with alternating rhyme. The refrain, on the other hand, is quite complex in form, having verses of one, two, three, four, and five feet. The predominance of dimeter and trimeter lines also indicates a more rapid tempo than that of the stanza. The simplicity of the alternating rhyme of the stanza likewise contrasts with the virtuosity of the refrain, which has a a a a b b b.

It has been pointed out that Tannhäuser is reluctant to take misfortune seriously. Perhaps for the same reasons, he does not take a scornful woman seriously enough to give her substance as a character. The lady in the first three songs is quite well-defined for a heroine of minnesong. She is a graceful and beautiful dancer who laughs readily and talks in a charming manner. She has curly hair, pink cheeks, tiny feet — to name only a few of the physical characteristics given. But the lady of the last three songs is not described at all. We know what she says, but no more. And her words appear in indirect discourse. She is, therefore, a complete abstraction, merely a symbol of the exaggerated *Minnedienst* which is the source of Tannhäuser's ironic laughter. Laughter is central to all of the

---

53 Lachmann, *Des Minnesangs Frühling*, 127, 32-33.
54 Berliner Hs. Ms. germ. 2°922.

songs. In the summer songs it is a laughter of pure enjoyment of the spring, the dancing, and the sight of the beautiful girl who has herself such a talent for laughter. (The touch of melancholy in the second summer song comes from the awareness that there is not as much laughter as in former years.) In the first winter song the appearance of the girl causes the singer to laugh with pleasure; the chief source of his laughter here, no doubt, is the surprise of his audience when he describes her form so completely. The laughter of the last three songs is evoked in part by the hapless figure of the lovelorn knight and in part by the awareness that an established literary convention is being parodied.

One sees in Tannhäuser's minnesongs a skillful use of form to emphasize content and avoid monotony. The stanzas of the first five end in a line which is significantly longer than the others and is used to sum up the impressions of the stanza. The *Stollen* of three of the songs also end with a line which is longer than average and serves a similar purpose. The uniform structure of the stanzas of the *minne* parodies is balanced by the more complex form of their refrains. Rhyme is used to give unity to individual stanzas, but never to link them with each other. In five songs the *Stollen* are connected by rhyme; in two of them *Aufgesang* and *Abgesang* are joined in this way. The poet likes to rhyme in series; the sequence a b c appears in four of the songs.

The nineteen *Sprüche* are composed to four different *Töne* and, with a few exceptions, develop four specific themes. The *Sprüche* are more realistic than the minnesongs, but some have allegorical implications. The scale of mood is greater, ranging from the genuine sorrow at the loss of Duke Friedrich to the broad humor of complaints about hard biscuits and salty meat. Structurally, however, they are less varied than the minnesongs, the rhyme schemes are in general simpler and the rhythms more regular. Frequent touches of irony and occasional parody characterize the *Sprüche*, except the last four, which are openly didactic.

The first of the *Spruch* cycles to be discussed (XII) does not have a theme which carries through all of its five poems. However, the first three are linked by a common symbol, that of the home. Since many lyric poets of the Middle High German period were penniless wanderers, it is not surprising that the theme of home ownership should appear with some frequency. One thinks immediately of Walther's sad complaint in his song which begins, " 'Sît willekomen her wirt:' dem gruoze muoz ich swîgen," several verses of which are echoed in the first two *Sprüche* of this cycle. Herger, Spervogel, and Ulrich von Singenberg also treated the subject before Tannhäuser, and Friedrich von Sunnenberg, Der Meissner, Helleviur, and Der Unverzagte after him.[55] The series begins by comparing the narrator's present situation with that of former times. Then he had fond relatives, and the most distinguished members of society enjoyed his company — then he was a property owner. But those who were once glad to see him now either greet him in a cursory manner or turn their backs on him. He has to give way to those who formerly had to yield to him. They who were once dependent on the generosity of others now have homes of their own, while he is no better off than he was twenty years before. His life is insecure, he has to find food and shelter with others. And anyone who thinks this is pleasant should try it.

The second *Spruch* continues in a similar vein. When things go badly for the narrator as he wanders from place to place, he thinks of Nürnberg and how nice it would be for him there. He would rather have enough there where he was known than have nothing among strangers — his audience may well

---

55 Lachmann, *Des Minnesangs Frühling*, 27, 6-10; 22, 16-21; Karl Bartsch, ed., *Die Schweizer Minnesänger* (1886; rpt. Darmstadt: Wissenschaftliche Buchgesellschaft, 1964), p. 37; Georg Holz, Franz Saran, and Eduard Bernoulli, eds., *Die Jenaer Liederhandschrift* (1901; rpt. Hildesheim: Georg Olm, 1966), I, 114, 56-57, 71.

believe that. But the singer admits that he has done some things which he now regrets, and he thinks he would be better off financially if he had been as wise before as he is at present. He wasn't sufficiently aware of his own weaknesses, and now has to suffer for it. This is why he almost never invites people to his home, and why he hears everyone say, "Be on your way, stranger!" He doesn't know whether or not they get pleasure out of treating him in this manner. Although the situation described here and in the preceding *Spruch* might seem to be a sad one, it does not ring true as a serious attempt to win sympathy. The ironical comments about having many relatives when one is rich and few guests when one has no house point to mock-pathos, as do the asides to the audience and the hints of prodigality and dissipation. Whether one considers it as wry humor, pathetic humor, or gallows humor, the intended effect was certainly comic. The reference to Nürnberg is used by some scholars as support for the theory that the poet originally came from there or from the surrounding area.

The home-symbolism and the ironic humor which appear in the background of the first two *Sprüche* dominate the third. Some naive persons have advised the singer to build himself a house, and he speculates as to who might be expected to assist with its construction. Imprudence and Sir Do-Nothing will show up at once, as well as a long-time acquaintance by the name of Never-Rich. Indigence and Indecision are loyal servants who will stand by him, as always. And he can assume that Sir Trouble and Sir Unready will be there, for they are his frequent companions. If his house is completed by this retinue, there surely will be snow falling down his neck from the rafters in winter. Tannhäuser uses his characteristic cataloguing technique together with allegory. All of the prospective helpers are closely associated with the narrator, and one should regard them not as exterior phenomena, but as traits of the narrator himself. These are the personal weaknesses to which he refers in the second *Spruch* of the cycle, the irresistible inner forces which fix his character. The humor is that of the ironic self-depreciation which Neidhart had made popular.[56] Here, as elsewhere in Tannhäuser's verse, one can assume that accounts of the narrator's misfortunes are intended to be comical.

The personification of abstract concepts appeared early in the history of courtly song but at first they were limited in number and scope and went little beyond such figures as *minne, saelde, meie, sumer, winter,* and *vrouwe werlt.* After Tannhäuser, however, this tendency became much stronger, perhaps as a result of his influence. At any rate, one can see the effect of this *Spruch* on

---

[56] Tannhäuser may have been familiar with Neidhart's stanza which tells of his troubles with the run-down fief of Reuenthal: Edmund Wiessner, ed., *Die Lieder Neidharts,* Altdeutsche Textbibliothek, 44 (Tübingen: Niemeyer, 1955), p. 58.

several later poems.[57] As it appears in the manuscript, the *Spruch* is shorter by two lines than the others in the cycle. It seems likely that the lines dropped out in the process of transmission, probably from the middle of the poem. They may have listed additional helpers.

Tannhäuser's encyclopedic style is most pronounced in the fourth *Spruch*, which consists entirely of a list of rivers and their locations. The series begins with the Tiber and, with a few side excursions, describes a rough arc as it moves to the north and west past the Arno, Tronto, Po, and Isère to the Seine, then eastward to the Moselle, Rhine, and Neckar, northeast to the Elbe, back to the Meuse, east to the Neisse, south to the Váh, Tisza, and Moldau, and finally ends with the Danube at Vienna. The narrator thereupon invites anyone who might doubt his placement of the rivers to go and look for himself. One of them, the Tronto, is incorrectly located — it is said to flow by Pescara[58] — and another, the *tuzer*, has not been positively identified.[59] But, in general, the geography is sufficiently accurate for some scholars to assume that the *Spruch* gives the actual itinerary of a journey by the poet. It has been suggested that he took this circuitous route home to Vienna after returning to Italy from the crusade of 1228.[60]

When one reads the *Spruch,* the question as to its purpose immediately comes to mind. There are two answers, which are not mutually exclusive. The first is that the song is simply a geography lesson in verse, comparable to the modern poem by means of which we recall the lengths of the months, "Thirty days hath September..." At a time when most people were illiterate, a great deal of information was rhymed, purely as an aid to the memory: charms, incantations, proverbs, riddles, even rules of table etiquette. In this instance, a rough map of Western and Central Europe could be constructed by humming through a tune. The earliest example of such a verse atlas is the Merigarto-fragment of the late eleventh century, which lists springs, streams, and lakes whose waters have great medicinal, even miraculous effects. The second possibility is that the *Spruch*

---

57 Reinmar von Zweter maintains that Indecision never builds a solid house; both walls and roof will be as undependable as he: Gustav Roethe, ed., *Die Gedichte Reinmars von Zweter* (1887; rpt. Amsterdam: Rodopi, 1967), p. 496. Bruder Werner finds that the house he has built has been taken over by Indigence and Indecision: Anton E. Schönbach, "Die Sprüche des Bruder Wernher, II," *Sitzungsberichte der philosophisch-historischen Klasse der Akademie der Wissenschaften,* 150 (1905), I, 95. Süßkind von Trimberg's home is invaded by equally troublesome guests: Where-To-Seek, Nothing-Found, Distress of Do-Without, and Meager-Wealth: Carl von Kraus, ed., *Deutsche Liederdichter des 13. Jahrhunderts* (Tübingen: Niemeyer, 1952), I, 424.
58 If one assumes with Oehlke, p. 70, that the *pitschier* of the manuscript refers to Pescara, the geography is incorrect. It is possible, however, that the author was thinking of Piceno, which is on the Tronto.
59 The manuscript reads, "diu tuzer gat viur rezzen." If this is not the poet's own invention, the most plausible guess would be the Töss which flows past Rüti in Switzerland.
60 Siebert, *Der Dichter Tannhäuser,* p. 23.

parodies those authors who try to impress their audiences by stressing the extent of their travels or by more subtle geographic name-dropping. Tannhäuser may have been thinking of Walter's poem which refers to the latter's wanderings throughout the empire from the Seine to the Mur and from the Po to the Trave.[61] Or he may have had in mind the lines in which Walther praises his fellow Germans:

> Von der Elbe unz an den Rîn
> und her wider unz an Ungerlant
> mugen wol die besten sîn,
> die ich in der werlte hân erkant.[62]

It is interesting that the above verses — like Tannhäuser's *Spruch* — were composed in Vienna.

The last *Spruch* of the cycle is the most traditional in content. A wise man gives his son certain rules for behavior when he is at court. He is to avoid arrogant people and is to emulate and associate with those who are respected. Then he, too, will have praise and honor. He is not to remain where he sees evil being done, and is always to flee wanton debauchery. He is to drink in such moderation as to give no one offense. He is to speak well of women so that they may speak well of him. If he follows this advice, he will get along excellently with them. The didactic spirit which permeated the Middle Ages found expression in scores of similar codes of good conduct, and Tannhäuser's *Spruch* does not differ greatly from many others. However, once more there is a hint of his light irony, although one would need to have seen the original performance to be certain. The wise man does not set forth his precepts as a guide for life in general, but for behavior at court — which may lend them a somewhat calculating tone. And the advice to compliment ladies so that one may enjoy their good will could also have slyly mercenary implications.

The *Ton* for the *Spruch* cycle is simple and regular, consisting of ten iambic heptameter lines with feminine endings and the rhyme scheme: a b a b c c d d e e. Some, but not many of the *Auftakte* are lacking, and occasionally a dactyl replaces an iamb. Most of the lines are broken by a caesura after the first four feet. The rhyme scheme indicates that the stanza consists of *Aufgesang* and *Abgesang*, and the fact that two lines — probably either the c c or the d d couplet — could drop out implies that the first part of the *Abgesang* melody was repeated. A plausible reconstruction of the melodic pattern, therefore, would be: A A B B A. A late approximate date of composition, 1263—1268, has been assigned to the cycle because of the reference in the first *Spruch* to twenty years of homelessness.[63] The assumption is that Tannhäuser was prosperous until after the death of Duke Friedrich.

---

[61] Lachmann, *Die Gedichte Walthers von der Vogelweide*, 31, 13-14.
[62] Lachmann, *Die Gedichte Walthers von der Vogelweide*, 56, 38-57, 2.
[63] Oehlke, p. 41.

The second of the *Spruch cycles* (XIII) uses the allegory of the sea of life as its theme. The sea is rough and dangerous, but its worst feature is that it drives one where it wills with no regard for one's own desires. The cycle begins with an idyllic picture of courtly life in the sunny south, in Apulia. Some knights are hunting in the fields with falcons, others in the forest with hounds. One group is out walking for recreation, another is riding about to see the sights. But the narrator has no share in such pleasures. There is no falconry or deer hunting for him. He wears no wreath of roses over the meadows and no one may expect to find him with fair maidens in the garden. For he is out on the sea.

The second *Spruch* of the cycle pictures the narrator as the eternal wanderer. Though he sings happy songs, his life is difficult. It is an aimless drifting from place to place as if he were driven before a storm. While aware that his shabby appearance offends people, he has to be concerned primarily with bare survival on land and sea. However, he knows that some day he inevitably will have to pay the innkeeper of this world his due. The sketch is essentially a description of Everyman at the mercy of a capricious fate, struggling day by day to save himself, but aware that in the end death must triumph.

The following *Spruch* is more personal and specific. The narrator asks rhetorically if anyone has suffered as much as he has from unwarranted confidence, and then tells of being for five days in a terrifying storm at sea off Crete in which he would have died had not God intervened. The waves broke the oars, the winds tore away the sails and nearly drove the ship on the rocks. The crew had never experienced such winds before, and their cries greatly oppressed the narrator. There was no escaping, one simply had to wait and endure. Although the language in the *Spruch* is realistic, still the first and last statements invite comparison to the sea of life.

In the fourth *Spruch* the narrator turns from a storm of the past to one of the present, and from an equivocal to a definitely light and ironical tone. Winds from Barbary are buffeting him as are others, simultaneously, from the direction of Turkey. And the waves are making him seasick. If this is a punishment for his sins, may God preserve him! His drinking water is cloudy, his biscuits are hard, the meat is too salty, and the wine is mouldy. And the odor which comes up from the bowels of the ship is no good companion for the journey — if he had his choice, he would prefer the fragrance of roses. Besides all this, it is difficult for him to be happy on a diet of peas and beans. If God wants to give him a reward, he would like to have better food and drink. The analogy to life, with its hardships, sins, punishments, and rewards is obvious.

The last *Spruch* of the cycle begins with an exclamation that the man who can ride wherever he pleases is indeed fortunate, and can scarcely appreciate the situation of one who must always wait for favorable winds. With this, Tannhäuser's urge to catalogue takes over and his narrator lists all the names of winds that he knows and, characteristically, at least one which he himself invented. He concludes by saying that he wouldn't know these names if he were ashore. He wishes he had never learned them, for he went to sea to serve God, not to become so familiar with winds. Construed in the light of the central allegory, this means that, although he set forth on the sea of life in the service of God, he was not prepared to encounter so many adverse forces.

The traditional interpretation of this *Spruch* cycle is that its stanzas make up a crusade song which tells of Tannhäuser's personal experiences on a journey from Italy to Palestine in 1228.[64] One may, of course, raise the objections that there is no mention of a crusade or of the Holy Land, that the descriptions of land and sea are generalized and literary,[65] and that there is no more reason to assume a medieval *Ich-Dichtung* is autobiographical than that a modern song in the first person gives real incidents in the life of the author. On the other hand, it is probable that the cycle was influenced by crusade songs and that it parodied them to some extent. Heinrich von Rugge praises the crusading spirit in one of his songs and then tells of an evil man who believed it better to stay at home and pass the time pleasantly with the ladies[66] — which is just what the narrator in Tannhäuser's first *Spruch* wishes he had done. And when Walther says:

> möht ich die lieben reise gevaren über sê,
> sô wolte ich denne singen wol, und niemer mêr ouwê,[67]

he may have inspired the irrepressible younger poet to send his narrator on such a journey and then have him sing "owe!" It is also perhaps significant that

---

64 Siebert, *Der Dichter Tannhäuser*, p. 18; Richard M. Meyer, *Deutsche Charaktere* (Berlin: Hofmann, 1897), p. 62; Günther Currle, "Die Kreuzlyrik Neidharts, Tannhäusers und Freidanks und ihre Stellung in der mittelhochdeutschen Kreuzzugslyrik" (Diss. Tübingen, 1957), p. 72; Wolff, p. 363; Wolfgang Golther, *Die deutsche Dichtung im Mittelalter* (Stuttgart: Metzler, 1912), p. 385; de Boor, *Die höfische Literatur*, p. 370; and others. Siebert, *Der Dichter Tannhäuser*, p. 18, calls the crusade of 1228 the first definite fact that we know of Tannhäuser's life. Lang, p. 121, and Bernhardt, p. 91, suggest that the work was composed later, perhaps in the forties. Wolfgang Mohr, "Tanhusers Kreuzlied," *DVjs*, 34 (1960), 347-48, objects to all attempts to derive exact history from the *Spruch* cycle and maintains that it contains nothing which is necessarily an expression of personal experience. With regard to its essentially literary character, he says, "Topoi rücken das einmalig und zufällig Wirkliche in übergeordnete objektive Zusammenhänge, so daß man es nicht mehr als etwas Einmaliges, sondern als Zeichen für etwas Allgemeineres und Typisches nimmt. Und genau so will die Seesturmstrophe Tanhusers verstanden sein."

65 There are differing opinions concerning the nature of the descriptions in the cycle. Currle, pp. 72-73, believes that the verses were composed during the journey and not later, "denn der Eindruck des fürchterlichen Seesturms ist noch zu frisch." De Boor, *Die höfische Literatur*, p. 374, also stresses the new spirit of realism in the work. Conversely, W. Mohr, p. 347, speaks of *Scheinrealismus* which is borrowed from the courtly novels of the early thirteenth century.

66 Lachmann, *Des Minnesangs Frühling*, 98, 28-31.

67 Lachmann, *Die Gedichte Walthers von der Vogelweide*, 125, 9-10.

another song of Walther tells of a mighty wind which causes pilgrims to lament.[68] In contrast to the idealistic songs of Heinrich, Walther, and others, there was verse by several of Tannhäuser's contemporaries in which they were less than enthusiastic about journeys to the Holy Land. Freidank's *Sprüche* concerning Acres bitterly attack its citizens, Christian as well as heathen, for their exploitation of the crusaders. He describes Palestine as a place "dâ got noch man nie triuwe fand."[69] The crusader Neidhart also is unhappy with his treatment by fellow Christians (the French) and is most anxious to return to Germany. The first stanza of his song is similar to Tannhäuser's first *Spruch* in that both begin with a description of nature and end with a lament that the singer had to depart.[70] Neidhart concludes his song by proclaiming that only a fool would want to stay through the summer. One should wait no longer, but sail back over the sea, for a man is best off at home in his own parish. Tannhäuser's ironic nature and his tendency toward parody might have been challenged either by the idealism of Walther or the scepticism of Neidhart. In any case, his cycle about the sea of life seems to have drawn from the traditional crusade song, with humorous effects. However, there is nothing in these *Sprüche* which mark them as products of direct, rather than allegorical experience.

The *Ton* of the *Spruch* cycle is interesting because of its variations on a simple pattern. There are sixteen trimeter, tetrameter, and hexameter verses with regularly alternating rhyme: 4a 3b 4a 3b 3c 3d 3c 3d 6e 6f 6e 6f 3g 3h 3g 6h. Half of the verses make up the *Aufgesang*, half the *Abgesang*, with the last four being a repetition of the *Stollen*. The melodic structure, therefore, seems to have been: A A' B A". As can be seen, the three *Stollen* are not quite alike. The first alternates tetrameters and trimeters, the second has only trimeters, while the last has three trimeters and a hexameter. However, since the tetrameters lack the *Auftakt*, it would be easy for the same melody to fit them and the trimeters. For the hexameter in the third *Stollen,* one might guess either that the normal melodic line was repeated or that it was replaced by the fourth line of the *Abgesang*.

With one exception, the *Sprüche* in the following cycle (XIV) deal with the singer's poverty or his search for a patron. Songs as these *Gehrsprüche* were composed by most, perhaps all of the itinerant poets of the medieval period, and in general should be considered as advertisements for employment, rather than as mendicant verse. By Tannhäuser's day they had become recognized as belonging to a specific type of song, and thus, like the minnesong, were vulnerable to parody. The narrator begins by expressing the hope that God will take pity on him because he is not a lord,[71] for that is why he gets none of the gold

---

[68] Lachmann, *Die Gedichte Walthers von der Vogelweide*, 13, 12-15.
[69] H. E. Bezzenberger, ed., *Fridankes Bescheidenheit* (1872; rpt. Aalen: Otto Zeller, 1962), p. 212.
[70] Wiessner, pp. 24-26.
[71] Kluckhohn, p. 153n, cites this statement as an indication, though not proof, that Tannhäuser was not a nobleman.

which is sent up from Italy. The lords divide it while the poor stare in amazement, looking on woefully as the former have their pouches filled. From Thuringia, too, comes a good deal of wealth, that — on his word — he would never touch. As stupid as he is, he could find there one who would support him well, but he would rather stay poor than forsake the crown. He speaks highly of the king, although he does not know if he will be rewarded for it.

The political references in the *Spruch* are to one of the conflicts between the Hohenstaufens and the papacy. In 1245 Pope Innocent IV excommunicated Emperor Friedrich II and the following year supported the attempt of Landgrave Heinrich Raspe of Thuringia to supplant Friedrich's son, Konrad IV, as king of Germany. With the aid of large sums of papal money, Heinrich was elected. But since only ecclesiastical electors were present at the voting, many of the German princes continued to recognize Konrad. Heinrich died in 1247 and his position as anti-king (*Gegenkönig*) was assumed by Count William of Holland. If one may judge from the praise which is given in *Leich* VI to the then deceased King Konrad, the poet may well have been rewarded for his refusal to join the king's enemies. The *Spruch* was apparently composed in 1246.

Where politics dominates the first *Spruch*, art pervades the second. The narrator says that he should be at court, where his singing could be heard. However, he is troubled by the lack of good tunes. To the lady who gave him some, he would sing all sorts of courtly things. He would sing most sweetly of all beautiful ladies. He would sing of the heath, of leafy trees, and of May; of summertime and dancing; of the cold snow and rain and wind. He would sing of father, mother, and child. The narrator then asks who will help him, for he cannot find any melodies. Style and content combine very successfully to make the *Spruch* one of Tannhäuser's most lyrical compositions. As employed here, his cataloguing technique creates a truly poetic impression as he repeats "Ich sunge" six times and charms the imagination with familiar poetic themes. The last subject mentioned, however, is unusual, for no medieval secular song deals primarily with the relationship of father, mother, and child.

One cannot know, of course, whether or not the narrator's complaint that he has run out of melodies reflected the situation of the author. As has already been indicated, it seems that Tannhäuser was not very inventive as a composer. The music to *Leich* IV consists of variations on a single theme, whereas a *Leich* usually has a series of different melodies. In addition, the relatively small number of *Töne* in Tannhäuser's other *Leiche* suggest that few melodies were employed. The minnesingers were for the most part far less gifted as composers than as poets. A new tune was a prized acquisition and much of their music was borrowed from France and Provence. The hero of Ulrich's *Frauendienst* recounts at some length an episode in which he received an Italian melody from a lady admirer.[72] Moreover, he is careful to report the favorable reaction of the public to his own music.

---

[72] Lachmann, *Ulrich von Lichtenstein*, pp. 112-14.

In the following *Spruch* the narrator admits that beautiful women, fine wine, choice food, and two baths a week are consuming his property, but says that he can live without care as long as he still has something to mortgage. However, when he finally has to pay up, he will be in trouble and his pleasure will turn to distress. The women will become ugly when he has to leave them, and the good wine will sour as soon as he has nothing to pawn to get it. He then advises himself not to worry about the situation, for he doesn't know any rich lords who will avert the hardships which threaten him. The traditional *Gehrspruch* is a plea from one who needs the bare necessities of life, the minimum of food, shelter, and clothing. Tannhäuser opposes this figure with the portrait of a self-acknowledged wastrel who is deliberately squandering his property with high living. For the most part, Tannhäuser scholarship takes it for granted that the song is autobiographical. This assumption is not necessarily valid. The poet may or may not have been a profligate, but he certainly was a professional humorist whose chief stock in trade was the parody of established literary conventions. An additional comic effect is achieved by the seeming incongruity of listing two baths a week with wine and women and by the statement that there is no reason to be concerned because no one is going to help him. The comment that the women will become ugly and the wine sour is, of course, a reference to Aesop's philosophical fox.

The fourth *Spruch* of the cycle is more serious, and it is probably autobiographical. The narrator bewails the loss of the hero of Austria who had housed him so well. Now life is sad, for he is homeless and does not know where to turn. Who will take his patron's place and, like him, provide for fools as well as proud guests. The narrator seeks blindly, for he has no idea where such a generous person may be found. If his patron were still living, he would never have to ride with the chill wind in his face and hear those with houses call out, "Oh my, wanderer, how do you get cold so quickly?" Friedrich II of Austria died in 1246 in a battle against the Hungarians at the Thaya River. The *Spruch* apparently was composed soon afterwards. The mood is sombre, but not without Tannhäuser's characteristic irony: the narrator needs to find someone who will take care of a fool.[73] There is also ironical humor in the question of the householders.

The fifth *Spruch* is closely connected with the preceding one. The narrator tells of what he had possessed — a beautiful house in Vienna, the fief of Leupoldsdorf near Luchsee, fine estates at Himberg — and prays that God may reward his departed benefactor. He wonders if he ever will again receive the income from these properties. No one should reproach him if he mourns the duke, for all of his joy has died with him. The narrator then asks himself where he is going to live and if he knows anyone who will help improve his difficult

---

73 Wolff, p. 355, maintains that the narrator includes himself among the "proud guests." However, the phrase is significant only if one assumes that the narrator counts himself among the fools.

situation, which, alas, has continued for some time. The death of his patron, he says, was certainly a cause for grief. What is chiefly of interest in the *Spruch* is the detailed listing of the former property of the narrator, a bit of realism which is most unusual in Middle High German lyric verse. Medieval poets, especially lyric poets, composed largely in symbols, abstractions, and generalities, rather than in terms of specific phenomena. Walther, for all his ecstatic joy in at last receiving a fief, tells us neither of what it consists nor where it is, but only how he feel about it. Tannhäuser also lets us know what these possessions mean to his life, but for him they have an objective significance in themselves, quite aside from his sense of loss.[74] The amount of property which Friedrich reportedly gave the narrator has been advanced as proof that Tannhäuser was a nobleman.[75] The duke, it is said, would never have invested a nameless minstrel with such extensive holdings. One can, of course, not be at all sure of what the unpredictable Friedrich would have done, assuming that the account of the property was not fictional.

In the last *Spruch* of the cycle Tannhäuser returns to catalogues and comedy. The narrator's steed moves too heavily and his pack horse too lightly, his servants have to go on foot. His house has no roof, his chamber no door, his cellar has fallen in, his kitchen has burned down, the cross beams of his barn have collapsed, and his hay is used up. No flour is milled, no bread is baked, no beer is brewed for him. His clothing is too thin, and no one needs envy or belittle his furnishings and equipment. This is neither autobiography nor a description of a specific scene, but a mock-pathetic picture of the dilemma of an impoverished nobleman on his dilapidated estate. It must have been a familiar situation in thirteenth-century Austria and one well suited to evoke laughter.

In this cycle Tannhäuser takes a traditional lyric theme, the singer's need, and develops it in a variety of ways. In the first *Spruch* the singer is in want by his own choice, and thus demonstrates his loyalty to the king. In the second, the need is for melodies, and it serves as a pretext to list subjects for songs. The third parodies the *Gehrspruch*, while the fourth and fifth combine it with a dirge. The last *Spruch* exploits the comic potential of need. The *Ton* for these *Sprüche* is almost the same as for the preceding cycle. There are nine lines, instead of ten, and the final line rhymes with the last couplet: a b a b c c d d d. It seems likely that the same melody, slightly altered at the end, was used for both cycles.

The last *Spruch* cycle appears in the Jena Manuscript under the name "Der tanuser." As has been stated, there is a difference of opinion as to whether or

---

[74] De Boor, *Die höfische Literatur*, p. 375, describes this characteristic of the poet well when he says with regard to this passage: "Das ist die bare Wirklichkeit ohne Beschönigung. Aber sie ist erlebt mit der dichterischen Beeindruckbarkeit eines Mannes, für den alles Erlebnis Abenteuer und der reale Vorgang plastisches Bild wird."

[75] Wolff, p. 355.

not it is genuine.[76] The objections to assigning it to Tannhäuser are based primarily on the religious content and the consistently serious mood. The chief evidence for its authenticity are the witness of the fourteenth-century scribe — who should know more about it than we — and the fact that certain elements of form and style are typical of Tannhäuser. Three characteristics of its form point to him: the length of the stanza, the rhyme scheme of the *Aufgesang*, and the long final line. The twenty-line *Ton* of the poem is considerably longer than most *Töne* of the period, including those of Tannhäuser in the Manesse Manuscript. However, he has two of sixteen lines there, and his stanzas as a whole are longer than those of the great majority of his contemporaries.[77] The rhyme scheme of the *Aufgesang*, a b c d a b c d, is more important as a link to Tannhäuser. He liked to rhyme in series this way. One of his undisputed poems has the identical rhyme scheme in the *Aufgesang* and three others have similar ones: a b c a b c, a a b c d d b c, and a a b c d e e b c d. This means that the *Aufgesang* rhyme of nearly one-half the poet's unquestioned minnesongs and *Sprüche* resembles that of the Jena *Ton*. But the most distinctive structural element in this work is the long final line of the stanza, which is also the most characteristic element of Tannhäuser's *Töne*. In all of his minnesongs the final line is longer than the others and in the *Sprüche* it is as long or longer. The element of style in the Jena work which especially reminds one of the Tannhäuser verse in the Manesse Manuscript is the use of catalogues.

Even though the content and mood of the work may on first reading seem foreign to Tannhäuser, they appear less so on closer examination. The first stanza begins with a nature introduction, as do three of his *Leiche* and three of his minnesongs. To be sure, the employment of a nature introduction was widespread, but few poets used it as frequently as did he. As concerns the chief theme of the cycle, the penitence of a sinner, one remembers that three of Tannhäuser's other *Sprüche* allude rather pointedly to excesses in the narrator's past and imply regret for them. The mood, too, though lacking Tannhäuser's usual irony, has something of his cheerfulness and optimism: the soul is in no great danger, for God will certainly forgive. All in all, there is nothing which weighs strongly against Tannhäuser's authorship and much that supports it.

The Jena work is commonly referred to as a penitent song. The singer depicts himself as a penitent, to be sure, but there is a question as to whether the four

---

[76] Among those who accept the Jena *Sprüche* as genuine are Meyer, p. 65; Bernhardt, p. 102; and Alfred Rottauscher and Bernhard Paumgartner, *Das Taghorn: Dichtungen und Melodien des bayrisch-österreichischen Minnesangs* (Wien: Stephenson, 1922), I, p. 45. Those who doubt that Tannhäuser was the author include Siebert, *Der Dichter Tannhäuser*, p. 237; Karl Bartsch, *Deutsche Liederdichter des zwölften bis vierzehnten Jahrhunderts*, 4th ed. (Berlin: Behr, 1901), p. LXVIII; and Wolff, p. 366.

[77] The average stanza length of Tannhäuser's other *Lied* and *Spruch Töne* is 12.5 lines. A random check of 100 *Töne* by twelve of his contemporaries revealed an average stanza length of 8.94 lines. The average stanza length of the *Töne* of none of the twelve equalled that of Tannhäuser.

stanzas make up a single song or a cycle of separate *Sprüche* which have a common theme. The problem has to do with the original performances. When Tannhäuser sang these stanzas, did he sing all of them together and in a particular order, or might he have sung them individually at different times? One can only say that the stanzas are self-contained units and that the content of the last three in the manuscript requires no particular arrangement. In the case of the first, however, the position of the stanza is justified by the one-line nature introduction. The assumption here is that the work is a cycle of *Sprüche* which treat the same general subject, but have no specific relationship to each other.

The mood for the first *Spruch* is established by a reference to nature in the opening verse, just as the mood of a minnesong is set by the traditional nature introduction. It is a beautiful day, and the singer hopes that He who rules over the wonders of creation will so care for him that he may know bliss and may atone for his great guilt. He knows that God can help him to preserve his soul, recover from sin, and gain divine grace. There follows a series of prayers and the reasons behind them, which make up a catalogue of petitions. The singer asks for a constant spirit, a good end to his life, God's favor, a happy soul, a sweet death, and escape from hell. He prays that the Pure One grant his request so that he may share the highest joy and, when he leaves his family, may find friends who will welcome him joyfully to heaven, where he may be called a blissful servant of his Master. The frame of mind, reflecting God's beautiful day, is one of reverent confidence, and there is nothing to indicate that the singer's guilt is anything more than that shared by all humanity. The cataloguing effect is achieved particularly by the repetition of *daz ich, daz ez, daz mir*, and *daz mich*. These appear eleven times and introduce fourteen subordinate clauses.

The prayers in the first *Spruch* are voiced indirectly as a thoughtful soliloquy. Those in the second are addressed to God directly, giving a stronger impression of immediacy. The singer laments that he has sinned all of his life and has very seldom felt remorse. He asks God for His mother's sake to grant him a sympathetic hearing. He believes that God's suffering on earth and His divinity will help him turn from his sins and atone for them during his lifetime. The singer prays that his will may be strengthened so that his soul may gain eternal bliss. He desires such an unchanging mind that the devil, who sets many snares for God's children, cannot lead him astray. In conclusion, he asks for God's aid that we all may be found without sin, according to His will. Although the singer refers to his own sins and repentance, the *Spruch* has throughout a general, almost congregational tone, which is underscored at the end by the shift to the first person plural. Once more there is no despair, but complete confidence in the availability of divine assistance. The cataloguing effect — not quite as pronounced as in the preceding *Spruch* — is again emphasized by the frequent repetition of the conjunction *daz*.

The following *Spruch* also makes a direct appeal. The singer prays that God, the source of all compassion, may preserve and waken him before the time of judgment. He wants help to make himself right with Christ and to learn to love Him with all his heart. If this hope is fulfilled, he will be happy. If he has lost God's grace by breaking His commandment, he seeks full pardon because of the Trinity, the resurrection, God's love for His mother, and her supplication. He asks assistance not only for himself, that he may escape his sins, but for all who, in hope of heaven, wish to find God. There is a marked similarity to the previous stanza: God is addressed directly, reference is made to the intercession of Mary, and a personal appeal is broadened in the last verse to include all penitent humanity. The author calls attention to his cataloguing by his oft repeated *durch*, "because of."

The last *Spruch* in the cycle differs considerably from the others. It is not a prayer, but a sermon, and it begins as well as ends with the universal "us." To save us, God suffered pain and was hanged on a cross. His death averted that of the singer, who alas, easily forgets this great sacrifice. Nevertheless, God comes to console him when he calls. A pure maid bore a Child Who never sinned and now lives in heaven, and He takes there the best of those who have received His name in baptism. God well knows what the flesh will do if it grows old without baptism, and it is not good for the soul. God is the Highest, who rules over all things; He is the Father, the Son, and will become a lion, a sheep, a fire, a salvation, according to our individual deserts. Although the *Spruch* represents a different type of religious verse, it shares a number of elements with the others in the cycle. It cites the guilt both of the singer and humanity in general, mentions Mary, emphasizes the forgiving nature of divinity, and employs cataloguing to underscore a specific point — this time without the repetition of a particular word. The mood here, as in the preceding *Sprüche*, is marked by a thin curtain of solemnity which does not quite conceal a confident, even light-hearted optimism.

The overall impression which the cycle makes is certainly not that of personal confession and remorse. The singer is only a spokesman for his audience, and his sin and guilt are representative of theirs. Although the didacticism consists for the most part of very simple Christian doctrine, the poet is careful in each of the stanzas to present a theological aspect of the working of divine grace with which few laymen of that time or this would have been concerned. The singer never asks for God to direct his actions, but to direct his will, for only through our own volition can we be saved. If the Jena stanzas were indeed composed by Tannhäuser, they support the possibility that the poet was a cleric.

The Jena poem is as important for the melody to which it is written as for its own sake. Assuming that the work is Tannhäuser's, the melody is one of two by him which are extant. Its composition reinforces the impression made by the music of *Leich* IV and the examination of the versicles of the other *Leiche*, which is that Tannhäuser always attempted to get maximum use of a melodic theme or phrase by repetition and variation. The music of the *Abgesang* shows an interesting re-use of motives and phrases from the *Stollen* and from the first part of the *Abgesang* itself, fitted together in a mosaic-like pattern. The form of the entire song is:

$$\underbrace{\text{ABCD}}_{\textit{Stollen}} \quad \underbrace{\text{ABCD}}_{\textit{Stollen}} \qquad \underbrace{\text{EFG EFG' AG''HI AG''HJ.}}_{\textit{Abgesang}}$$

The third phrase (C) ends with a descending fifth which reappears as the cadence of lines 11, 16, and 20 (G and the two appearances of G''). The whole of line 4 (D) is incorporated into the long closing line (J), making the closing quatrain begin and end like the *Stollen* melody, but using material from the *Abgesang* in the middle. The treatment of the material introduced in line 11 is quite ingenious (G, G', and G''). Lines 11 and 14 (G and G') begin alike but end differently. G'' (lines 16 and 20) begins with a new *Auftakt* and adds one ornamental note, but ends with the same cadence as G (line 11). The repeated sections reflect the poetic form, which uses a new meter and rhyme scheme for the verse triplet with which the *Abgesang* begins. The whole form resembles the structure of a *Leich*.[78]

His *Sprüche* reveal that Tannhäuser shared the strongly didactic tendency of his age. The first cycle begins with the narrator giving a simple account of his homelessness, unencumbered by any moralizing. In the second *Spruch*, however, he admits that his plight is partly his own fault, that he is suffering from his own mistakes. The third in the cycle develops this theme into allegory as he lists the traits which would build the house of his character. The fourth *Spruch* teaches geography as it parodies the songs of those who claim to have traveled widely. And the good advice of the last *Spruch*, which instructs in court etiquette, is not nullified by its somewhat ironic tone. A similar mixture of humor and didacticism permeates the second *Spruch* cycle, for what begins as a parody of crusade songs, ends as a picture of the life of Everyman, buffeted from place to place by the winds of fate. In the first *Spruch* of the third cycle the narrator reports on the political situation of the Empire, and in the second informs his hearers of the best subjects for song. In the next three he tells of the property he lost through his own extravagance, and thus presents by inference a picture of the transience of earthly possessions. The last *Spruch* of the series, with its description of the run-down estate, is a humorous sketch of the situation of an impoverished nobleman, but it is also an allegorical representation of the vanity and corruption of all worldly things. It would be a mistake, however, to assume that the first three *Spruch* cycles, like the last, were composed primarily for moral or religious edification. What makes them didactic, perhaps at times without the intention of the author, is their humor and the spirit of their age. Humor exposes human failings to the objective scrutiny of reason, which is likely to

---

78 The discussion of the music of the Jena *Sprüche* is taken from Barbara Garvey Seagrave and Wesley Thomas, *The Songs of the Minnesingers* (Urbana and London: University of Illinois Press, 1966), p. 131.

draw general conclusions from specific behavior. And Tannhäuser's age was one which saw all individual phenomena and experience as symbols of universal creation and history.

TANNHÄUSER'S IRONY; HIS SOURCES AND RECEPTION

In his didacticism Tannhäuser shows what is most representative of his times, in his humor he reveals what is most typical of himself. A basic element of his humor is the intent to convey a meaning other than that seemingly expressed. When examining this irony one needs to remember that we are forced to judge the poet through a medium for which he did not compose, the written word. Tannhäuser composed with a performance in mind, one in which the verses themselves often would serve only as a foil for gestures, smiles, and knowing winks that let the audience know how he really felt — or deliberately confused it as to his meaning. This presentation soon disappeared, but one can safely assume that there was a great deal more irony in the original dramatic version than can be reconstructed from the bare text and that it was the more sophisticated, subtle, and unexpected ambiguities and contradictions which have been lost. The chief objects of Tannhäuser's irony were the standard conventions of courtly literature, lyric and epic, and one must therefore assume for his compositions a highly literate audience which was thoroughly familiar with the works of the Hohenstaufen chivalric period. Humor was drawn from the conventions either by violating them with incongruent or incompatible material or by exaggerating them through parody. The first of Tannhäuser's *Leiche* presents incongruence to the point of grotesqueness when it combines a eulogy with a dance and makes Duke Friedrich share the stage with a pretty dancer. A similar mixing of genres appears in the two following *Leiche* with the unexpected consummation of the love of the narrator and his sweetheart, an act not foreign to epic verse, but quite contrary to the minnesong or *Minneleich* tradition. The incongruence of the fourth *Leich* consists primarily in the narrator's comparing his sweetheart with famous queens and goddesses, and then describing her nude form in an affectionate, but quite irreverent manner. Other incongruities appear in the intentional confusion of literary heroes and deeds. The baroque contrast of disparate elements is particularly marked in the fifth *Leich* where, after presenting an imposing list of great men and exotic places, the narrator turns to his own heroic accomplishments on a nearby meadow with his sweetheart. The humorous inconsistency of the following *Leich* is that the narrator promises to name the epitome of all princely virtue, and does not. Incongruence is seen in the last *Leich* not only in the fact that it does not supply answers to its riddles, as many other such songs did, but that it so crowded them together as to make them almost undecipherable. Incongruities in the minnesongs and *Sprüche* include another

45

description of a nude form, a crusader who is more concerned with hard biscuits than God's cause, a *Gehrspruch* from a confessed wastrel, and the picture of the nobleman who has a manor house and estate — both in complete ruin.

Tannhäuser parodies several established literary conventions of the courtly literature of his day and with considerable success. He most frequently attacked the cataloguing tradition by means of which poets satisfied the thirst of their audiences for all sorts of information and established themselves as men of vast experience and erudition. It was also commonly used as a literary device to emphasize a particular point.[79] Tannhäuser exploited this practice with ostentatious registers of meadow flowers, beautiful women of literature, exotic lands, German princes, names of dancers, details of the female form, rules for behavior at court, traits of his narrator's character, cities and rivers, names of winds, topics for songs, causes of the narrator's poverty, and examples of the ruin of the latter's estate. One might even suspect that the long list of the virtues of Friedrich II in the first *Leich* was not entirely free of humorous intent.

Another literary convention which Tannhäuser parodied was the affected adornment of German verse by means of French. Here again he goes far beyond the others, employing their borrowings, bringing in new ones, and in places composing a true *Kauderwelsch*. Tannhäuser's parody is particularly obvious since he uses French words in lyric verse, which till then had been almost free of them. He also sometimes follows a flood of loan-words with a markedly pure German for contrast. His poems contain some seventy French words, among which his favorites are: *amis, bel, clar, creatiure, dulz, fores, massenie, parolle, tschantieren,* and *tschoie,*[80] words which are closely associated with the French pastoral tradition and the highly stylized love affairs of the German Arthurian novels. Since he uses them most frequently in the narrative sections of *Tanzleiche,* just before the German folk dances begin, it is apparent that the poet is inviting comparison of the pretentious borrowings, and the superficial manners connected with them, with native songs and customs. However, as if to prove that there was nothing chauvinistic about his irony, Tannhäuser also subjected the opposing trend, exemplified by Walther's intimate *Mädchenlieder,* to parody. This appears especially in the Christmastide song, which is filled with such endearing, very German diminutives as: *lökkel, mündel, öugel, wengel, kelli, spengel, tökkel, sitüli, suezel, vuezel, beinel,* and *meinel.*[81]

Tannhäuser's most obvious and effective parody appears in the three songs in which he ridicules the concept of service of ladies by listing all of the impossible

---

[79] Roethe, *Die Gedichte Reinmars von Zweter,* pp. 317-18, gives a concise history of the cataloguing technique from Walther to the mastersingers. Paul Lehmann, *Die Parodie im Mittelalter,* 2nd ed. (Stuttgart: Anton Hiersemann, 1963), p. 103, supplies an example of the citing of a long series of names of people in a medieval Latin work as a humorous device.

[80] Walter Sandweg, *Die Fremdwörter bei Tannhäuser* (Diss. Bonn, 1931).

[81] Other noncourtly elements in Tannhäuser's verse are treated by F. Mohr, pp. 60-68.

demands the lady fair makes as the price of her favor. Everything is recounted with a straight face, and the narrator, though expressing his grief, gives no indication that he believes her unreasonable. In two of the songs the humor is underscored by a refrain which stresses his eternal affection and constancy. Since the refrain is traditionally a part of joyous songs, its use here by the frustrated lover adds more irony to the situation. This is ridicule not only of the minnesong as such, but also of a basic idea of chivalry. As far as is known, Tannhäuser is the first German lyric poet to parody it directly, although Neidhart and the anonymous author of the goliard song, "Ich was ein chint so wolgetan," present caricatures of *Minnedienst*. But Tannhäuser's laughter was without bitterness or design. He certainly had no such Cervantine goal as the destruction of a false romanticism, for his two summer songs are quite traditional.

Perhaps the key to Tannhäuser's irony lies in the ambivalence of time which has been mentioned in connection with the *Tanzleiche*. His narrator never so loses himself in the memory of his Arcadian adventure that he completely forgets the dance in progress. At the same time the dance does not keep his mind from wandering back to his wonderful experience, the dream-like nature of which is conveyed by foreign words and an idealized milieu. In a similar manner his creator moves back and forth from the world of minnesong and King Arthur — the sphere of courtly literature — to that of thirteenth-century Vienna, sometimes painting the one by the light of the other. The best humor results when romanticism is described by a realist, but the realist must have his romantic side or he will not understand what he sees.

The poet's humor grows out of a realism which is most unusual in the lyric verse of the time. This is seen not only in his interest in the contemporary scene — politics, manners at court, geography — but also in his unique attention to detail. The standard heroine of the minnesong has red lips, a lovely form, and no name. Tannhäuser's heroine is Kunigunt. She too has red lips — and also rather short, curly, golden hair with a silken texture; regular, white teeth; slender fingers; tiny feet; etc. She sometimes wears a peacock hat, a white shawl, a brooch at the throat, and a belt, in addition to the rose wreath with which other ladies of minnesong are decked. When she and the others dance, it is to the music of bugle, drum, fiddle, flute, harp, or tambourine, and the manner in which they dance is rather carefully described. Details particularly abound in the *Spruch-cycle* of the sea. The knights who have remained in Italy spend their time with falconry, hunting with hounds, walking to the fountain, and riding about with ladies to see the sights. Meanwhile, during the five-day storm near Crete, the winds almost drove the hero's ship on a rock, the oars were broken, the sails torn to pieces, and he got seasick. It was no wonder, for in addition to bad weather, his drinking water was stale, the biscuits hard, the meat too salty, the wine mouldy, the peas and beans unappetizing, and the smell from below decks most unpleasant. The unique character of the *Spruch* which lists the narrator's property in Vienna has been mentioned. In the one that follows, the itemizing of the decay of his estate also presents a sharp contrast to the typical medieval generalization.

Tannhäuser's treatment of love has been cited as a significant outgrowth of his realism, and certainly with some justification. However, a distinction must be made between realism and the parody of romanticism. His lovers consummate their love, not because it is the natural thing to do, but because this normally does not take place in the minnesong or *Minneleich*. And the circumstances under which the consummation takes place are by no means realistic. There is no vital eroticism in Tannhäuser's works, his love scenes are idyllic and slightly burlesque. More closely linked to realism is his merry affirmation of the world about him and an indomitable lightheartedness which can joke about poverty, storms, and a homeless life. The situation of his narrator often seems hopeless, but never very serious, which justifies as well as anything else the claim that Tannhäuser is the first genuine realist among the German lyric poets of the Middle Ages.[82] Although the impression of realism that he gives is largely a result of content and attitude, to a certain extent it is also the product of his style. The numerous exclamations, short sentences, comments to the audience and himself, the anaphora and correspondence of verse and grammatical units, even the occasionally irregular and careless rhythm, all lend immediacy and verisimilitude to his work.

Tannhäuser was the most original of the lyric poets of the midthirteenth century and was influential in leading courtly song in new directions. However, much that appears novel in his works is itself a part of traditions which, in some cases, can be linked directly or indirectly to him. Possible connections with the French *pastourelle* and *mal mariée* songs or the goliard seduction songs have been mentioned in connection with the narrative sections of Tannhäuser's second and third *Leiche*. In addition it should be noted that detailed descriptions of feminine charms are not unusual in Middle Latin lyric verse, as, for example, No. 109 and No. 118 of the *Carmina Burana*, nor are catalogues, such as the long register of birds and wild animals in No. 97. And a German song, No. 117a, compares the sweetheart of the singer with a series of goddesses and queens in much the same manner as Tannhäuser's fourth *Leich*. There is also parody: parody of the minnesong in No. 146 and erotic parodies of certain Biblical passages in No. 50.[83] None of these songs resemble those by Tannhäuser to the extent that one can assume a specific influence, but they do indicate a source from which he may have drawn.

Of greater importance to Tannhäuser was the verse of his famous colleagues, Wolfram, Walther, and Neidhart, with whose works he probably was well acquainted. He seems to have been especially interested in Wolfram, for there are frequent references to the characters and places of *Parzival* and *Willehalm*

---

[82] Heinrich, p. 828.
[83] *Carmina Burana*, fols. 60r, 63r, 56r, 62v, 72, 31v-33v.

in his songs. Indeed, all that is distinctive in Tannhäuser's works can be found in those of the older poet. Wolfram's narrator, too, describes himself comically as a knight with an impoverished fief. He, too, makes ironical comments about himself, his situation, and his characters; directly addresses himself, his characters, and his listeners; and skips about in time and place. Like Tannhäuser's narrator, he has a ladylove who is unkind to him and about whom he composes some bitter verse.

Catalogues are as typical of Wolfram as of Tannhäuser. In Book XV of *Parzival*, he lists kings and lands (some invented by himself) as does the latter in *Leich* V, and he gives a register of snakes in Book IX and precious stones in Book XVI which is comparable to Tannhäuser's inventory of flowers in his third *Leich*.[84] When Gahmuret enters Patelamunt and Arthur approaches Schastel Marveile, we are told which instruments are being played, as in the third and fifth *Leiche*. Although Wolfram does not give a catalogue of heroes and heroines of literature like that in *Leich* IV, the total number which he mentions is equally large and indicates a similar pride in his familiarity with contemporary verse.

Both Wolfram and Tannhäuser are humorists, and their chief source of humor is *Frauendienst*. At times the former bitterly attacks this tradition as senseless and dangerous, and relates several tragedies which it has caused: the deaths of Isenhart, Galoes, and Schionatulander, and the suffering of Anfortas. But mostly he treats it with ironical humor, as in Gawan's relations to a series of females. Indeed, the entire Gawan action makes up a *minne* parody that contrasts with the more natural and more idealistic devotion of Parzival and Condwiramurs. In the Obilot episode the *Frauendienst* tradition is distorted to a child's game, amusing partly because of the comic explication of chivalric acts as the product of two beings in one body and partly because the innocent child does not realize the erotic implications of the phrases she uses. The slapstick comedy of the Antikonie adventure is a burlesque of *Frauendienst* from another standpoint, in that its actual goal is revealed, which in the minnesong is veiled. At first sight Antikonie invited the hero's attentions with a *kus ungastlich* and as soon as they were alone they got at the business of lovemaking without any preliminary formalities. The scene in which Antikonie aided her lover by throwing chessmen at the enemy while he fought with a door-bar as a sword and a chessboard as a shield is a caricature of the romantic union of arm and spirit which Gawan had explained to Obilot.

Wolfram's third parody of the *minne* tradition in literature is the episode where Gawan spends the night at Plippalinot's home with Bene watching over his sleep. Even though she would have readily responded to his advances, Gawan ignores Bene and goes to sleep. And the *huote*, in the person of her father, does not try to protect her, but actually encourages a love affair and is disappointed that

---

[84] Albert Leitzmann, ed., *Wolfram von Eschenbach*, Altdeutsche Textbibliothek, 13 and 14, 6th ed. (Tübingen: Niemeyer, 1963, 1965), 770, 1-30; 772, 1-23; 481, 8-10; 791, 1-30.

her virginity has been preserved. The parallel to the dawn song is underscored by the ambiguous comment on Gawan's situation at the end of Book X:

got hüete sîn, sô kom der tac.[85]

The most obvious *minne* parody in Parzival, of course, has to do with Gawan and Orgeluse. His complete devotion puts him at the mercy of an unreasonable lady who enjoys his difficulties. Her request that he fetch a wreath from Gramoflanz' tree, together with the spectacular adventures at Schastel Marveile — certainly a part of Gawan's service for Orgeluse — may well have inspired the fantastic demands made by the heroine of Tannhäuser's *minne* parodies. Other ironical treatments of *minne* by Wolfram appear in his lyric poem, "Ursprinc bluomen, loup uz dringen," where he uses the motifs of the traditional love song to ridicule its shop-worn content,[86] and in his anti-dawn-song, "Der helden minne ir clage," in which he compares the sorrows and dangers of stolen love with the pleasures of marital love. All in all, there is more parody of the courtly song and of the *Frauendienst* tradition in general in the works of Wolfram than in those of any other contemporary or predecessor of Tannhäuser. One can assume that here, as with his catalogues, the latter was influenced by his famous colleague.

Other instances in which Wolfram may have left his mark on Tannhäuser's verse have to do with French words, rules for behavior at court, and riddles. Wolfram was the first Middle High German poet to make liberal use of French borrowings, and he does this on such a scale that one is inclined to believe that he, as well as Tannhäuser, was at times striving for a comic effect. In any event, the latter must certainly have been thinking of Wolfram when he exaggerated this tendency. Indeed, one scholar maintains that Tannhäuser was ridiculing Wolfram and Gottfried specifically.[87] When reading Tannhäuser's *Spruch* in which the wise man gives his son rules to follow in order to be well accepted at court, one thinks at once of the advice of Gurnemanz to Parzival. Not that the two sets of precepts are similar, but because they are the only ones in German up to that time which are tailored especially for a courtly society. Tannhäuser's slightly ironical tone also reminds us of that which Wolfram imposes on Gurnemanz's dry didacticism. The riddle with which Tannhäuser's last *Leich* begins is, as has been noted, the only one of the five which does not appear elsewhere in Middle High German literature. However, two similar riddles are propounded in *Parzival*. In Book IX Trevrizent recounts that an offspring of Adam and Eve deprived his ancestress of her virginity. He then explains that Adam's mother was the earth, which retained its virginity until Cain spilled his

---

[85] Leitzmann, 552, 30.
[86] James F. Poag, "Heinrich von Veldeke's *Minne*; Wolfram von Eschenbach's *Liebe* and *Triuwe*," *JEGP*, 61 (1962), 735.
[87] Bernhardt, p. 95.

brother's blood on it.[88] The difficulty here is, of course, how a virgin could have offspring. In Tannhäuser's riddle it is a matter of how a dead woman could have children. The second riddle in *Parzival* comes in Book XIII where Arnive tells Gawan of a mother who had a child who became the mother of its mother. There are two answers: water and ice, and joy. Following this double riddle is an answer to a third riddle: the ship which is driven by a strong wind moves rapidly, but the man who walks on its deck goes even faster.[89] It was perhaps Wolfram's posing of three riddles in succession which gave Tannhäuser the idea for his *Rätselleich*.

Another riddle-like expression in *Parzival* that is apparently reflected in Tannhäuser's verse is the risqué comment which the narrator makes about the wedding night of Orgeluse and Gawan:

> er vant die rehten hirzwurz,
> diu im half daz er genas,
> sô daz im arges niht enwas:
> diu wurz was bî dem blanken brûn.[90]

The last line recalls Tannhäuser's enigmatic playing with color in stanza two of his first winter song:

> guten trost han ich von ir.
> mehte ich der blanken.
> machen brvn ir roten gris.

If Tannhäuser's verses were borrowed from Wolfram, it is quite possible that they comprise an ironical riddle which conceals a similar, erotic meaning.

The influence of Wolfram on Tannhäuser is largely a matter of viewpoint and style; that of Walther has to do principally with types of songs. Most of Tannhäuser's verse was composed in genres which Walther either invented or popularized among the courtly lyric poets of medieval Germany: courtly songs of natural love, humorous songs, political *Sprüche*, and autobiographical *Sprüche*. Although some of Walther's songs of natural love resemble the French *pastourelle* in that the heroine is a peasant girl, in others he anticipates Tannhäuser either by making her a noblewoman or by ignoring the matter of class. The older poet is, to be sure, somewhat more discreet in telling of the consummation of love, but he too exploits the titillating potential of eroticism. As in Tannhäuser's *Leiche* and minnesongs, this consummation results from mutual desire, rather than a clever seduction. In general, one can say that Tannhäuser's songs of natural love are more courtly than those of Walther.

Tannhäuser probably also learned something about humor from Walther.

---

88 Leitzmann, 464, 11-20.
89 Leitzmann, 659, 23-660, 5.
90 Leitzmann, 643, 28-644, 1.

Judging from the thirteenth-century verse tale, the predominant form of humor at that time was one in which a clever character outwits and takes advantage of a dull one, who is made to appear ridiculous. Walther's humor, however, is more genial, and, like that of Tannhäuser, is based largely on surprising the audience by adding an unusual, incongruous ending to a traditional situation. In "Si wunderwol gemachet wip," Walther presents the highly conventional eulogy of his lady, and it is not until the last line that we discover him to be a Peeping Tom, describing her as she leaves her bath. The idyllc scene and exalted dream of "Do der sumer komen was" is disturbed first by the cawing of a crow and finally by the ridiculous interpretation of the dream. In like manner, his fond hopes of being favored by his lady, in "In einem zwivellichen wan," turn out to be based on nothing more substantial than the child's game of she-loves-me-she-loves-me-not. There are certainly the beginnings of *minne* parody in Walther, and one of his lover's plaints — "Min frouwe ist ein ungenædic wip" — may well have inspired Tannhäuser's second *minne* parody. Especially the line where the narrator says that he would have given the lady stars, moon, and sun, if he could, remind one of the later song. Tannhäuser may also have borrowed some devices for humor from such political satire as Walther's derisive song about Otto IV, "Ich wolt hern Otten milte nach der lenge mezzen," or the advice to Philipp II in "Wir suln den kochen raten."

Since Walther was the only Middle High German lyric poet before Tannhäuser to compose an appreciable amount of political verse, one may safely assume that the older poet influenced the compositions of the younger in this area, at least to the extent that he established the political song as a standard literary form. Actually, however, the two were in complete agreement as to the overriding issue of their time: the power struggle between the Empire and the papacy. It has been noted that Tannhäuser criticized the attempt of the pope to bribe electors and proclaimed his loyalty to the Hohenstaufens. In *Leich* V he also boasted that he had often seen the emperor (Friedrich II), admonished Wenzel I of Bohemia to support the Empire, and objected to the pope's attempt to depose the emperor as king of Sicily. *Leich* VI began its parade of German rulers with a eulogy of Friedrich II and his sons Konrad and Heinrich, and included only one ecclesiastical prince, who was a supporter of the emperor.

Although it would be too much to assume that Tannhäuser borrowed his politics from Walther, one may certainly expect that the latter's example could well have affected Tannhäuser's choice of subject matter. The fact that Walther praised Leopold VI of Austria in several of his *Sprüche* may have inspired Tannhäuser to devote an entire *Leich* to a eulogy of the duke's son, Friedrich II. And when Walther dated the beginning of his misfortunes from the death of Duke Friedrich I, it could easily have reminded Tannhäuser that his own difficulties, which began with the death of the duke's nephew, were equally worthy of recording. The personal element behind his political expression is as controversial in the case of Tannhäuser as with Walther. On the one hand, it has been assumed that Tannhäuser's support of the Hohenstaufen party came from patriotism,[91] on the other hand, he has been damned for being a mere flatterer and opportunist.[92]

Walther's development of the autobiographical *Spruch* to a literary form contributed to his age a type of song which was of particular value to a humorist. For embarrassing jokes on oneself have always made up a considerable part of the repertoire of humor, particularly that of live performance. Tannhäuser seized upon the medium and also some of Walther's content for his own use. When, in "Ob ieman spreche, der nu lebe," the latter tells of the generosity which he was shown in Vienna, one is reminded of Tannhäuser's account of the property in that city which he received from Friedrich. When Walther, in "Der hof ze Wiene sprach ze mir," has the Viennese court recount its decay — the roof is rotten, the walls are cracked, gold, silver, horses, clothing are gone — one recalls Tannhäuser's *Spruch* of the impoverished nobleman. Walther's verses which begin, "Sit willekomen, her wirt," compare the situation of home owner and wanderer and plays with the words, *wirt* and *gast,* as do the first two *Sprüche* in Tannhäuser's first cycle. And his discussion of the different types of songs, in "Ich traf da her vil rehte drier slahte sanc," brings to mind Tannhäuser's poem which lists the things of which he would sing if he had a melody.[93] In both instances the narrator asks assistance with his composition. Echoes of Walther's autobiographical *Sprüche* are heard also in Tannhäuser's minnesongs. The elegy which begins, "Owe war sint verswunden alliu miniu jar," compares the drab present with a happier, more courtly past in nostalgic language quite similar to that of Tannhäuser's second summer song, which possibly was likewise influenced by Walther's "Muget ir schouwen waz dem meien."

Although Tannhäuser's style resembles that of Walther in several ways, they share only one stylistic peculiarity which is sufficiently pronounced to indicate an influence. This is in the use of diminutives. Walther occasionally employs such words as *dänkelin, friedel, fröidelin, frouwelin, trœstelin,* and *zörnelin* in his songs to add an intimate, endearing touch and also perhaps to give the impression of a folksong. Tannhäuser uses diminutives for the same reasons and in addition to achieve an amusing effect. When the narrator of his Christ-

---

91 Siebert, *Der Dichter Tannhäuser*, p. 29; Heinrich Drees, "Die politische Dichtung der deutschen Minnesinger seit Walther von der Vogelweide," *Jahres-Bericht des Gräflichen Stolbergischen Gymnasiums zu Wernigerode* (Wernigerode, 1887), p. 14.

92 Reinhold Becker, rev. of "Die politische Dichtung der deutschen Minnesinger seit Walther von der Vogelweide," by Heinrich Drees, *Literaturblatt für germanische und romanische Philologie,* 9 (1888), 294.

93 One also thinks of the lines in Walther's *Spruch*, "Von Rome vogt, von Pülle künec, lat iuch erbarmen," which read (Lachmann, *Die Gedichte Walthers von der Vogelweide*, 28, 4-9):

zâhiu wiech danne sunge von den vogellînen,
von der heide und von den bluomen, als ich wîlent sanc!
. . . .
sô mac der wirt baz singen von dem grüenen klê.

mastide song has words like *löckel, mündel, wengel, kelli, spengel,* and *sitüli* in his description of the sweetheart whom he addresses so respectfully, the result is ironic humor. Needless to say, Tannhäuser greatly exaggerates this characteristic of Walther, and one might even suspect him of mimicking the *Mädchenlieder* of the older poet.[94] It is significant that no diminutives appear in Tannhäuser's relatively traditional summer songs or in the *minne* parodies. His inclination toward cataloguing may have been reinforced by his familiarity with Walther's songs, although this trait is not nearly as strong in the latter's verse as in that of Wolfram.[95]

Neidhart, the last of those who made a significant impact on Tannhäuser's works, was, like Walther, a predecessor of the younger man as court singer in Vienna and thus was connected to him by similar cultural traditions. Critical opinion differs greatly as to the extent of his influence on Tannhäuser, varying from the claim that the latter was little more than an imitator to the doubt as to whether his verse was in any way significantly affected by Neidhart.[96] The probable answer to the question is that Tannhäuser received considerable inspiration from the older poet, but that his aims, point of view, and manner of composition were so different that their works have only a surface similarity. Both men were primarily humorists, and their chief source of humor was the parody of the conventional minnesong. Neidhart moves the scene to the village green or village tavern, substitutes a rustic maiden for the courtly lady, and brings in a cast of rough and pretentious country bumpkins to fill the role of the formerly nebulous *nidære* and provide an amusing incident. Tannhäuser's milieu, when it is described, is an ideal Arcadian one, and his characters are essentially classless. Neidhart's humor is basically malicious, and consists of ridiculing either his peasants or his impoverished knight-narrator or both. Tannhäuser's humor is more benevolent and literary, consisting largely of the ironical treatment of the poetic convention itself, and the butt of his jokes — where there is one — is likely to be his audience and the formal, ceremonious culture of which it was a part. The common denominator in their work is the dance, for which practically all of Neidhart's verse and most of Tannhäuser's was composed. And it is in the combination of narrative and comments on the dance itself that the significant influence of Neidhart is seen. From him Tannhäuser learned both how to form smooth transitions from one to the other and how to mix the two so as to produce a

---

94 Neidhart also employs many diminutives, but he does not use them quite as Walther and Tannhäuser do: to emphasize the contrast between intimate and more formal expression.

95 Examples of Walther's catalogues are found in the *Spruch,* "Die wisen ratent, swer ze himelriche welle," where six highwaymen on the path of life are listed, and in the *Spruch,* "Ich muoz verdienen swachen haz," which names six counsellors.

96 Among those who stress Tannhäuser's dependence on Neidhart are Meyer, pp. 62-63; Reuschel, p. 654; and F. Mohr, pp. 60-62. Conversely, Siebert, *Der Dichter Tannhäuser,* pp. 32-33; and Ehrismann, pp. 265-66, do not think the influence of Neidhart on Tannhäuser was significant.

humorously incongruous effect. This exploitation of the grotesque he got from Neidhart, but Tannhäuser's grotesqueness is more refined and less striking. The same thing can be said of his other violations of the conventional minnesong tradition. When he refers to parts of the female form which are not mentioned in the older courtly lyric and when he tells of sexual intercourse, he does so to surprise, rather than to shock his audience. Such references in Neidhart's songs are often intentionally crude, in keeping with his unpolished characters. Tannhäuser makes no use of dialogue, which is so important in many Neidhart songs, but he does add to the folksy nature of his dance *Leiche* by speaking of the dancers by first name or nickname or by addressing them directly — devices characteristic of the older poet.

One of Tannhäuser's compositions, his first *Leich*, was apparently directly inspired by a Neidhart song ("Owe, lieber sumer, diner süeze bernden wünne") in which Duke Friedrich II is praised as the last refuge of courtly joy. Both works are divided into eulogy and dance sections and have several minor motifs in common.[97] In most respects, however, they are quite different. Neidhart's crusade song and Tannhäuser's first *Spruch* cycle also have several elements in common: they stress the pleasures left behind, the difficulties of the pilgrimage, and the sea which separates the narrator from his homeland. But one takes the form of a message to sweetheart and friends and the other that of a soliloquy on the nature of life.

One critical opinion states that Neidhart's influence on Tannhäuser was negligible and that the similarities in their works are the result of the effect of the folksong on both of them.[98] Others also assume that Tannhäuser drew extensively from this source for his dance *Leiche* and dance songs. This school of thought believes that the folksongs which accompanied dancing in the thirteenth century were humorous, rather uncouth, and openly erotic;[99] their form was supposedly quite simple and their rhythm somewhat irregular. And Tannhäuser's frankness in sexual matters, his uncomplicated strophic patterns, and the occasional dactyls in his iambic lines are assumed to be a part of this folksong heritage. Such Tannhäuser conceits as that which associates the joy of the dance with spring and love and that which insists that only the happy should come to the dance are likewise attributed to the folksong. In addition, certain expressions which appear in the dance sections of his *Leiche* and minnesongs may have been standard formulas in the popular dance songs of Tannhäuser's time. These include the summons to the dance, questions as to the whereabouts of the dancers, a roll call of girls' names, the invitation to be happy, the reference to the end of the

---

[97] Edmund Wiessner, "Die Preislieder Neidharts und des Tannhäusers auf Herzog Friedrich II. von Babenberg," *ZfdA*, 73 (1936), 128.

[98] Siebert, *Tannhäuser: Inhalt und Form*, p. 13.

[99] F. Mohr, p. 62, and Siebert, *Tannhäuser: Inhalt und Form*, p. 12. However, J. Wahner, in a review of Siebert's book in *ZfdPh*, 28 (1896), 385, maintains that the "indecente Schilderung der Reize der Geliebten" was as foreign to the folksong as to the courtly minnesong.

dance, an admission that the dancers are displeased that it should end, calls of "heia hei!", and the assertion that a fiddle string or bow has broken.[100]

It is highly probable that Tannhäuser's dance sections were significantly influenced by the popular dance songs of his day, and it is even likely that he introduced the most typical folk expressions as an ironic contrast to the formal language of the courtly minnesong. However, in estimating the effect of the folksong on Tannhäuser's verse, one must not overlook the fact that no thirteenth-century folksongs are extant. Indeed, all that we surmise about their nature is based on that material in the songs of Tannhäuser, Neidhart, and others which to modern ears sounds folksy.

The important sources from which Tannhäuser drew were Wolfram, Walther, Neidhart, and the noncourtly dance song of his day. In addition, he is said to have borrowed from Bruder Wernher, Herger, Neifen, Raumsland, Sigeher, and Veldeke,[101] but these poets certainly contributed little, if anything, to his art. The influence which Tannhäuser exerted on later poets, although no doubt considerable, is more difficult to determine. The mere existence of such an unrealistic literary convention as *Frauendienst* is an invitation to parody, and one probably should not assume that all of the numerous *minne* parodies which followed those of Tannhäuser were inspired by him. The courtly songs which tell of the consummation of love and those which give risqué descriptions of feminine charms might also have had other models than his songs. However, the style which characterizes Tannhäuser's treatment of these and other matters is sufficiently unique for his time that one can in some cases detect specific influences.

The most significant influence of Tannhäuser's verse can be seen in the dance *Leiche* of the priest and nobleman Ulrich von Winterstetten, one of the most prolific of all the minnesingers. Although highly talented with respect to metrics and rhyme, Ulrich lacked originality in subject matter and borrowed quite freely from other poets, especially Walther, Wolfram, and Tannhäuser. Three of Ulrich's five *Leiche* are traditional *Minneleiche* which present in many variations the lover's lament. They contain nothing to indicate that they were sung to dancing, but they may have been. The other two (III and IV) are dance *Leiche* in Tannhäuser's manner, with nature introductions, references to the dance, admonitions to the dancers to be happy, a roll call of the girl dancers, the cry, "heia hei," and the breaking of the fiddle string. The main change is that Ulrich substitutes a declaration of love and a lover's lament for Tannhäuser's narrative. Other differences are that Ulrich preserves the tradition of conventional *minne* and includes no consummation of love, irony, or parody. Nevertheless, the lament is not very sad and the overall mood is lighthearted, in keeping with the occasion.

---

100 Siebert, *Tannhäuser: Inhalt und Form*, pp. 16-21; F. Mohr, p. 62.
101 Wolff, p. 359, mentions Wernher and Herger; Wallner, rev. of *Der Dichter Tann-häuser*, by Johannes Siebert, p. 177, lists them and the others.

Although Ulrich's debt to Tannhäuser for his dance *Leiche* is generally recognized, one critic attributes the similarities to the hypothetical formulas of folksongs.[102] However, since the works of the two share distinctive words and phrases which have nothing to do with standard formulas, one must assume that one was directly influenced by the other. In his third dance *Leich* Ulrich, who uses almost no French, employs an unusual French word which appears in a Tannhäuser dance *Leich*. Also in the third *Leich* Ulrich adds to the motif of the breaking string by saying that his heart will break with it, and in his fifth *Leich* — which does not mention dancing — the heart replaces the string and breaks as he cries, "heia hei!" However, the connection between heart and string is already established in Tannhäuser's third *Leich* when the narrator speaks of his deeply wounded heart just before the fiddle string breaks.

Ulrich borrowed from Tannhäuser not only for his *Leiche,* but also — to a lesser degree — for his songs. In the latter's first *minne* parody, the lady fair desires the grail; in Ulrich's Song II, she is said to be as desirable as the grail. Tannhäuser's second *minne* parody has in its refrain the lines: "Ich han den mv̊t. swc si mir tût. dc sol mich alles dunken g v̊t"; while the refrain of Ulrich's Song V goes: "Mîn frouwe ist guot, swie sî doch tuot mich ungemuot." And Tannhäuser's favorite description of his lady, "ir zimt wol dc lachen," frequently characterizes that of Ulrich, most closely in the lines of Song XVIII: "Wer gesach ie frouwen lîp/ der ir lachen alsô wol gezæme?"[103] Many other verbal parallels can be seen in the works of the two poets.

A second thirteenth-century poet who was in some respects a pupil of Tannhäuser was the wandering minstrel, Meister Boppe. Their relationship is especially apparent in the latter's single minnesong, a parody which imitates Tannhäuser's second *minne* parody, using the same format, including some of the same impossible tasks, and even beginning with the same line: "Min vrouwe diu wil lonen mir." One has the impression that the composition is a parody of a parody, that the poet assumes his audience knows Tannhäuser's song and is attempting to show he can think of even more fantastic demands for the lady to make. A more significant influence on Boppe's verse, however, is seen in his use of repeated, parallel phrases and of catalogues, literary devices which are developed to a distinctive trademark of the author. One of his *Sprüche* begins eight successive clauses with "ob"; a second starts ten clauses with "barminge"; another begins thirteen phrases with "durch"; a fourth introduces sixteen clauses with "die milte"; and a fifth uses "die kerge" as the subject of seventeen clauses in an eighteen-line stanza. Other *Sprüche* employ parallel repetition to a lesser, but still noticeable extent. Boppe's catalogues are even more imposing, and sometimes resemble those of Tannhäuser in content as well as in method. His *Spruch* I, 22[104] presents a long list of the virtues and talents of famous men —

---

102 Kuhn, p. 110.
103 Kraus, *Deutsche Liederdichter des 13. Jahrhunderts,* I, 513, 515, 531.
104 The designations of Boppe's *Sprüche* are those appearing in Friedrich von der Hagen's

Solomon's wisdom, Absalom's beauty, Virgil's magic, etc. — which are worth less to him than the affection of his sweetheart. This recalls Tannhäuser's fourth *Leich* and its register of the beautiful women of history and literature who were no better endowed than his loved one. In *Spruch* I, 25, Boppe counts off the European lands from whose princes he has received no pay, and then names two from whom he has hopes of support. One thinks at once of Tannhäuser's sixth *Leich*, which parades the living and dead rulers of Central Europe, grades them on their generosity, and ends by promising to name the one of those living who most deserves praise. Boppe's *Spruch* I, 26 lists the nationalities of mighty kings of Europe, Asia Minor, and North Africa, as does Tannhäuser's fifth *Leich*. Also reminiscent of this *Leich* is Boppe's *Spruch* I, 24, which recites the thirty-seven lands (sometimes incorrectly) whose kings were slain by Joshua. Among many other Boppe catalogues are a list of the virtues of Charlemagne, an inventory of God's creation, and a flood of terms of abuse which are directed at an adversary.[105]

In addition to *minne* parody, repetitions, and catalogues, the influence of Tannhäuser on Boppe can be seen in the latter's tendency to mix truth and fiction by inventing birds, animals, precious stones, mountains, and lands. Boppe's exploitation of his own poverty for humor in *Spruch* IV also reminds one of the older poet, especially since he gives a long list of improbable happenings which will come to pass before his poverty is alleviated.

The works of a number of other thirteenth-century poets contain echoes of Tannhäuser. The Viennese merchant, Jans Enikel, praises Duke Friedrich in his *Fürstenbuch* with language drawn in part from Tannhäuser's first *Leich*. Several of Konrad von Würzburg's nature introductions, especially that of Song XXI, are based on Tannhäuser's Song VIII. Both the nature introductions and the natural love of the songs of Count Konrad von Kirchberg remind one of Tannhäuser, as does also the summons to the dance, the listing of the given names of fifty-three girl dancers, and the question as to the whereabouts of dancers in his Song V. In addition, Steinmar and Marner,[106] Taler, Friedrich der Knecht, Neune, Johannes Hadlaub, Duke Johann von Brabant, and Duke Heinrich von Anhalt[107] are said to have been influenced to some extent by Tannhäuser.

Also poets of the late medieval period were familiar with Tannhäuser's verse. The fourteenth-century Meister Altswert copied his style and used some of his subject matter. And mastersingers of the fifteenth and sixteenth centuries reworked

---

Minnesinger: Deutsche Liederdichter des zwölften, dreizehnten und vierzehnten Jahr-hunderts, 5 vols. (1838-61; rpt. Aalen: Otto Zeller, 1963), II, 377-86.

[105] A survey of the subsequent development of cataloguing among the later minnesingers and the master singers is given by Roethe, *Die Gedichte Reinmars von Zweter*, pp. 317-18.

[106] Siebert, *Tannhäuser: Inhalt und Form*, p. 97.

[107] Oehlke, pp. 42-45.

the first of his *minne* parodies (IX) and the first, second, and fourth *Spruch* of his first *Spruch* cycle (XIII).[108] A mastersong lists him as fourteenth among the old masters, and a citizen of Magdeburg in 1558 places him nineteenth in a long register of medieval poets.[109] The *Kolmar Liederbuch* contains four songs in "Tannhusers haupt ton od gulden tone."[110]

By the end of the sixteenth century Tannhäuser, together with the rest of the Middle High German poets, was forgotten and remained so for two centuries. When he and the others were finally discovered, it was not by performers seeking to expand their repertoires, but by scholars and writers, who were intent on creating a medieval past according to preconceived, Romantic ideas. They believed the unselfish service of ladies to be not only the dominating literary motif of the secular medieval lyric, but also a significant factor in the actual life of upper-class society. These scholars missed the clever, erotic ambiguity in the language of courtly *minne*, and it took on for them an idealized quality which originally it never had, even in the verse of such an anemic theorist as Reinmar von Hagenau. They could forgive Walther his so-called *Mädchenlieder*, because the love stories in these songs transpired — they maintained — in a noncourtly setting and formed, in essence, folksongs. Even Neidhart could be tolerated, because his specifically peasant milieu removed him from the courtly scene. However, Tannhäuser, with his outspoken parody of *minne*, his frankness in sexual matters, and his failure to place his "excesses" in a markedly peasant society, could neither be misunderstood nor forgiven. Irony and humor were qualities which the interpreters of the Middle Ages had not sought and did not wish to find, and Tannhäuser, when not completely ignored, was branded as a decadent and uninspired composer of vulgarities and obscenities.

This evaluation of the poet prevailed throughout the nineteenth and well into the twentieth century, with criticism of his verse usually turning on its lack of idealism and alleged immorality. In 1869 Joseph Haupt damned Tannhäuser as a talentless composer of mechanical jokes,[111] and some three decades later Richard Meyer maintained that it was precisely his poetic limitations which had made him a humorist, that what had ended in parody had begun as an awkward imitation of the masters. Tannhäuser was called a true epigone of medieval Romanticism, a thoroughly prosaic person who lacked the "inner form" of the true poet (*Dichter*).[112] A similar insistence on measuring Tannhäuser according to the conventions which were the object of his irony continued on into the twentieth century. He was castigated for a lack of moral force even when granted poetic talent,[113] and criticized for incoherency when that was

---

108 These are printed in Siebert, *Der Dichter Tannhäuser*, pp. 227-31.
109 Hagen, IV, 888, 892.
110 Ludwig Uhland, *Schriften zur Geschichte der Dichtung und Sage*, IV (Stuttgart: Cotta, 1868), 259-86, gives an account of the mastersingers' use of Tannhäuser's *Töne*.
111 Haupt, p. 315.
112 Richard M. Meyer, "Tannhäuser," *ADB*, LXXIII, 386.

the particular effect for which he had striven. As late as 1934 Anton Wallner was suggesting that Tannhäuser's reputation among his contemporaries and with the mastersingers must have been based, not on his verse, but on his melodies.[114]

But Wallner was behind the times, for others had begun to realize that courtly *minne*, either as cultural ideal or as mere literary convention, was too insubstantial and limited to dominate the medieval love song indefinitely. And some scholars had come to see that much of the best of medieval literature is amusing and should be judged by criteria specific to humor. In 1913 Ferdinand Mohr correctly indicated Tannhäuser's position in the history of lyric verse when he classed him with Walther and Neidhart as one of the three most original and versatile poets who undertook to revitalize the old courtly minnesong with new elements.[115] And in 1931 Werner Lennartz protested that Tannhäuser's parody was not the coarse expression of inordinate presumption, but a fine smile of irony, carefully shaped and superior, which springs from his lines now that we can see what the experiential world of the minnesong was really like,[116] Soon afterwards Johannes Siebert expressed the general view of recent scholarship when he asserted that we would have to rank Tannhäuser higher than previously now that we had to judge him as the representative of new sentiments and a new attitude toward reality, rather than as an imperfect epigone of courtly art.[117]

The tools of Tannhäuser's irony were not unusual, and its sources were the obvious ones: the works of the most popular epic poet and the two most popular lyric poets of the medieval period. However, he was no mere imitator, for what he borrowed was worked into an art which was intrinsically his own. Tannhäuser was an innovator in several respects. He composed the first direct parodies in lyric verse of the idea of service of ladies; his were the first songs with a courtly milieu — except the dawn songs — to give a frank account of love's fulfillment; he initiated the use of repetition and catalogues as a deliberate stylistic device in lyric verse; and he was the first — as far as is known — to discuss the quality of food and drink in a song. If one were to assume that all *minne* parody, glutton songs, and drinking songs stem from him, then his impact on the lyric verse of the later medieval period was equal to that of Walther and Neidhart. And even if one considers only those works which show more specific influences of Tannhäuser, it is still apparent that his songs were in circulation for several centuries. In the modern period, his irony was offensive to the early, Romantic scholars of the minnesong, but it eventually found acceptance and appreciation. Nevertheless, the imprint which Tannhäuser left on modern literature was the result of a legend rather than of his verse.

---

[113] Rottauscher, p. 39.
[114] Wallner, rev. of *Der Dichter Tannhäuser*, by Johannes Siebert, p. 177.
[115] F. Mohr, p. 68.
[116] Werner Lennartz, *Die Lieder und Leiche Tannhäusers im Lichte der neueren Metrik* (Diss. Cologne, 1931), p. 53.
[117] Siebert, *Der Dichter Tannhäuser*, p. 38.

THE MEDIEVAL LEGEND

The Tannhäuser legend grew out of a ballad of unknown authorship which was composed shortly before or after the poet's death, probably in the decade from 1264 to 1274. The poem is one of a group of medieval works that treat fictional incidents in the lives of certain minnesingers. In the song, "Vom edlen Möringer," the Ulysses-Penelope theme is transferred to Heinrich von Morungen, who returns home just in time to forestall the marriage of his wife to another poet, Gottfried von Neifen; in "Vom Brennenberger," Reinmar von Brennenberg becomes the hero of the well-known story in which a lady is made to eat the heart of her dead lover; in "Der Welt Lohn," Wirnt von Gravenberg is so disturbed by a meeting with Dame World that he gives up all worldly activity and goes on a crusade to strive for the salvation of his soul; Walther, Wolfram, and Reinmar von Zweter take part in the singers' contest in "Der Sängerkrieg auf der Wartburg"; and Neidhart appears as the central figure in a long series of amusing songs and dramatic sketches.

The best known version of "Das Lied von dem Tannhäuser" is a song of twenty-six four-line stanzas[118] which tells of a knight who is living in Venus Mountain, surrounded by every pleasure, when he is overcome with remorse. He leaves and journeys to Pope Urban IV to obtain absolution, but is told that he will no sooner expiate his sin than will a dry staff in the pope's hand begin to grow. Sorrowfully he returns to the Venus Mountain, and three days later green leaves appear on the staff. Messengers are sent to look for the knight, but he cannot be found and the pope is damned. This first appeared in print in a Nürnberg broadside of 1515.

The great mass of scholarship which has attempted to show that the Tannhäuser ballad in its variant forms is the product of one or another folk tradi-

---

118 Subsequent references will be to Text D, John Meier, ed., *Deutsche Volkslieder: Balladen* (Berlin & Leipzig: Walter de Gruyter, 1935), pp. 145-46. In a study of this version, Selma Hirsch, "Die älteste Gestalt der Ballade vom Tannhäuser," *Jahrbuch des Vereins für niederdeutsche Sprachforschung*, 56-57 (1930-31), 194-204, states that it is the oldest of the variants, but that it consisted of only twelve stanzas in its original form and that the additional stanzas were included by a later poet. Her reasoning, based essentially on the belief that the "added stanzas" are either repetitious or introduce extraneous elements, is fallacious. Succinctness is a rather uncommon quality in Middle High German narrative verse. Meier includes a version of the ballad which appears in a manuscript of the mid-fifteenth century, but it is apparently not as old as that of the broadside.

tion[119] has failed to consider fully the implications of the historical references in the poem. It speaks of an obscure pope who ruled for only three years and of a poet who is mentioned by no contemporary, is referred to in no official document, and is known only by a descriptive title which he assumes in several poems but which may not have been his real name. The two men were contemporaries and probably died within three or four years of each other.[120] That the ballad should preserve their chronological relationship to each other indicates the following: that the legend was preceded by the ballad, that the original version was essentially the same as the Nürnberg broadside, and that it was the work of a thirteenth-century poet. He drew from the most obvious of sources, for everything he treats can be found in the songs of or in references to Walther von der Vogelweide.[121] The first two stanzas of the ballad introduce the hero and the wonders of the Venus Mountain, a paradise of beautiful women and love which appears frequently in the writings of the late medieval and early modern period. The earliest reference in German literature to such a place is in *Tristan*, a work with which the author of the ballad may well have been familiar. In his famous literary review Gottfried links the realm of Venus to Walther.[122]

After the introduction the narrative proper of the ballad begins abruptly with an argument between Tannhäuser and Venus. In the first five exchanges the speakers address each other by name the first three times, but not the following two. The altercation closely parallels that between Walther and Dame World in his song which begins: "Frô Welt, ir sult dem wirte sagen."[123] Here, too, the first three exchanges, but not the last two, are introduced by the name of the adversary. Venus starts the argument in the ballad with a reminder of her affection: "Herr Danheüser, ir seyd mir lieb, daran solt ir mir gedencken!" Dame World uses a similar approach with Walther: "gedenke wie ich dirz erbôt, waz ich dir dînes willen lie." Venus then brings up an oath with which

---

[119] The most complete accounts of the literature on the Tannhäuser Ballad are contained in Philip Barto, *Tannhäuser and the Mountain of Venus* (New York: Oxford University Press, 1916) and Otto Löhmann, "Die Entstehung der Tannhäusersage," *Fabula*, 3 (1960), 224-53.

[120] Urban IV died in 1264. References to contemporary people and events in Tannhäuser's poems do not go beyond ca. 1265. He may have died in that year.

[121] The discussion of Walther and the ballad is drawn largely from J. W. Thomas, "Walther von der Vogelweide and the Tannhäuser Ballad," *Neuphilologische Mitteilungen*, 74 (1973), 340-47.

[122] Ranke, ll. 4801-15.

[123] Lachmann, *Die Gedichte Walthers von der Vogelweide*, 100, 24-101, 22. Zander, p. 31, mentions the similarity between Walther's song and the 1515 version of the ballad, but does not suggest an influence of one on the other. Neither does Hermann Güntert, *Kalypso* (Halle: Niemeyer, 1919), although he suggests (p. 104) that the thirteenth-century version of the Tannhäuser legend may have had Dame World as the temptress, rather than Venus. So, too, does Golther, "Tannhäuser in Sage und Dichtung," p. 22.

her loved one is supposed to have bound himself to her: "Ir habt mir einen aydt geschworen," which recalls the obligation which Walther had incurred and paid: "mîn grôziu gülte ist abe geslagen." Dame World also alludes to a bond between herself and the poet when she tells Walther: "sô dû mir rehte widersagest, sô wirst dû niemer wol gemuot." In their replies, Tannhäuser denies and Walther renounces any obligations to their respective temptresses, but the latter persist. Venus says: "Herr Danheüser, wie redt ir nun? Ir solt bey mir beleyben," while her counterpart asserts: "Walther, dû zürnest âne nôt: dû solt bî mir belîben hie." In rejecting the offer of a beautiful woman for his own, Tannhäuser expresses a fear of eternal punishment: "So müst ich in der helle glut auch ewigklich verbrinnen," as does also Walther in a similar context: "dîn zart hât mich vil nâch betrogen." A fear of damnation is likewise implied in Walther's comment on his host: "swer ime iht sol, der mac wol sorgen," as well as in his statement that he would be happy to return, "wan deich fürhte dîne lâge, vor der sich nieman kan bewarn." In their next exchange Venus and Tannhäuser speak of the joys of love as symbolized in the former's red lips, which recalls Walther's remark about the affection of Dame World: "wand er vil süezer fröiden gît." And Tannhäuser's cry, "Was hilffet mich ewer roter mundt? Er ist mir gar unmere," expresses the same thought as Walther's more restrained "Frô Welt, ich hân ze vil gesogen: ich wil entwonen, des ist zît."

The strife between Tannhäuser and Venus reaches a climax when he calls her a she-devil and she objects to such abuse: "Ir seyt ein Teüffellinne!" "Herr Danheüser, was redt ir nun, das ir mich günnet schelten?" Walther too refers to the diabolical nature of his antagonist and vows to speak abusively of her from then on: "doch was der schanden alse vil, dô ich dîn hinden wart gewar, daz ich dich iemer schelten wil." In desperation Tannhäuser prays to Mary for aid: "Maria mutter, reyne maydt, nun hilff mir von den weyben!" Walther's final words are also expressed as a prayer: "got gebe iu frowe, guote naht." In his *Leich*, however, he has a passage which resembles Tannhäuser's cry more closely. He speaks of Mary as "der reinen süezen maget," and entreats: "Maget und muoter, schouwe der kristenheite nôt, dû blüende gert Arônes."[124] Venus now agrees to let Tannhäuser go and asks a favor: "Her Danheüser, ir solt urlaub han, mein lob das sol ir preysen, wo ir do in dem landt umbfart." Dame World, in giving Walther leave to depart, also makes a request: "Sît ich dich niht erwenden mac, sô tuo doch ein dinc des ich ger: gedenke an manegen liehten tac." Both ladies are apparently inviting the poets to compose songs in their honor.

The last statement of Venus as Tannhäuser leaves, "Nembt urlaub von dem Greysen," has no connection with the preceding content and has evoked considerable speculation. It has been suggested that the reference is to dwarfs in the

---

124 Lachmann, 3, 28-4, 4.

mountain,[125] to King Arthur,[126] to the legendary Eckart,[127] to the pope,[128] to Wotan,[129] and to old men in general.[130] Assuming that the author of the ballad was familiar with Walther's song, the words are quite clear. The "Greyse" is the "wirt" to whom the poet has made a final payment and who has no further claim on him. Both terms were well known to medieval theology: St. Paul refers to the "old man" as the symbol of humanity's carnal nature, while there are many Biblical allusions to Satan as the lord, or "wirt," of this world. After the final remark by Venus, Tannhäuser leaves the mountain, "in iamer und in rewen," and determines to journey to Rome and seek readmission into the family of Christianity through the intercession of the pope. His goal is the same as that of Walther when the latter says: "Ich wil ze hereberge varn." Both wish to return to their spiritual home.

At this point the ballad becomes the story of a penitent sinner and Walther's "Frô Welt" comes to an end. However, several other poems by Walther may have supplied the subject matter for the second half of Tannhäuser's adventures. One song tells of a contrite sinner who hopes to atone for his transgressions and save his soul by going on a crusade.[131] In another the singer declares that it is time for penitence, and prays that he may be made pure before his soul is lost.[132] A third expresses the main theme of the ballad — that God will always forgive the repentant sinner — in the lines: "swen si [die Welt] nû habe verleitet, der schouwe sînen trôst: er wirt mit swacher buoze grôzer sünde erlôst."[133] Tannhäuser travels to Rome, but finds that the pope takes a most un-Christian attitude with respect to the forgiveness of sin. One thinks at once of Walther's attacks on the latter, such as: "sîn süener mordet hie und roubet dort, sîn hirte ist zeinem wolve im worden under sînen schâfen,"[134] or "seht wie iuch der bâbest mit des tievels stricken seitet."[135]

The pope declares that the dry staff in his hand will send forth leaves before Tannhäuser will receive God's grace, whereupon the knight sadly departs, saying: "Maria mutter, reyne maydt, muss ich nun von dir scheyden?" Thus, for the second time, he addresses Mary in the words of Walther's *Leich*. When we remember the following designation in the *Leich*, "du blüende gert Arônes," the origin of the staff miracle in the ballad becomes apparent. Earlier Tannhäuser

---

[125] Arthur Remy, "The Origin of the Tannhäuserlegend," *JEGP*, 12 (1913), 50.
[126] Philip Barto, "The German Venusberg," *JEGP*, 12 (1913), 296.
[127] Richard M. Meyer, "Tannhäuser und die Tannhäusersage," *Zeitschrift des Vereins für Volkskunde*, NS 21 (1911), 1-31.
[128] Elster, p. 9.
[129] Adolf N. Amman, *Tannhäuser im Venusberg* (Zürich: Origo, 1964), pp. 131-32.
[130] Fernand Desonay, "Der italienische Ursprung der Tannhäuser-Sage," *Universitas*, 3 (1948), 149-61.
[131] Lachmann, 76, 22-78, 23.
[132] Lachmann, 122, 24-123, 40.
[133] Lachmann, 124, 39-40.
[134] Lachmann, 33, 29-30.
[135] Lachmann, 33, 2.

prayed to Mary for aid, now he regrets being cut off from her, soon — in the form of the dry staff — she will send forth green leaves and thereby announce his salvation. Of course, the author might have got this symbol of Mary elsewhere, for it had appeared in German verse nearly two hundred years previously in the "Marienlied von Melk," but the fact that the designations of "pure maid" and "mother" appear in both works in connection with a blooming staff makes it seem likely that the ballad drew from the Leich.[136] Tannhäuser returns to the mountain and Venus, who greets him affectionately. The idea of the return may have been suggested by the passage where Dame World invites Walther to come back "niuwan sô dich der zît betrâge," and the latter confesses that he would very much like to if he were not afraid of her snares.

It is a mistake to assume, as many critics have done, that the author of the ballad intended Tannhäuser to be damned at the end;[137] the witness of Mary — the blooming staff — is unequivocal. However, a second sin has been committed and must be punished, and that is why Pope Urban is damned. He is the cause of the sin and receives the punishment which otherwise would have been Tannhäuser's. The logic here was as clear to an audience of the thirteenth century as was that of the vicarious atonement of Christ. In both instances there is an appeasing of divine justice by means of a substitute. However, the damnation of a pope is a serious matter, and some modern scholars have been reluctant to believe that a medieval poet would have given the ballad such a conclusion. They have

---

136 The Tannhäuser ballad provides a transition in the evolution of the blooming staff as a literary device. The development begins, of course, with the account in the fourth chapter of the Book of Numbers. In the Middle Ages religious writers adopted it as a designation for Mary (virga Aaron florida). The Tannhäuser ballad employed it as a symbol of Mary and also of forgiveness. Later writers and legends — influenced by the ballad, but ignorant of the dual symbolism — used the blooming staff only as a sign of forgiveness. H. Holland, in Geschichte der altdeutschen Dichtkunst in Bayern (Regensburg: Friedrich Pustet, 1862), pp. 508-10, tells of a rose-bearing staff in connection with the pardoning of a Herr von Schnewburg and refers to other legends in South Germany and Austria in which blossoming staffs appear. Viktor Junk, in Tannhäuser in Sage und Dichtung (München: Beck, 1911), pp. 17-18, gives an account of a Swedish water spirit whose salvation is made evident by a blooming staff. A heroic source of the motif is given by Haupt, pp. 315-22, who maintains that the Tannhäuser ballad was a product of heroic legend and that the staff was the spear which Dietrich threw at Wittich in the Vilcinasaga.

137 All of the scholars who have expressed an opinion on the matter have assumed that, in the earliest form of the ballad, Tannhäuser was damned. But folk interpretation, as indicated by changes in the ballad through oral transmission, has assessed the matter quite differently. The version which Heinrich Kornmann gives in Chapter 14 of his Mons Veneris: Fraw Veneris Berg (Frankfurt: Fischer, 1614) says that Tannhäuser will remain in the Venus Mountain until Judgment Day and that God will then decide his fate. Later variants make it clear that Tannhäuser is redeemed.

considered the damnation to be a later addition, a product of the Reformation.[138] But Walther proves that a thirteenth-century singer could suggest such a thing and once more supplies a possible inspiration for the ballad writer. When Pope Innocence III announced the excommunication of Otto IV, Walther reminded the pope of his proclamation during the coronation of the emperor and implied that the former was damned by his own words: "ir sprâchent 'swer dich segene, sî gesegent: swer dir fluoche, sî verfluochet mit fluoche volmezzen.'"[139]

The appearance of Urban IV and Tannhäuser together in the ballad is convincing evidence that the work was composed, largely in its present form, by a thirteenth-century poet. The fame of Walther at that time was such that it is easier to believe that the unknown author of the ballad was familiar with his verse than that he was not. Therefore, when the ballad treats the same material in the same general manner as do songs by Walther, the assumption is that one was influenced by the other. To be sure, much of this material did not originate with Walther and the anonymous poet could have got it from other German or Latin sources. However, in none of these is the treatment so similar to that of the ballad as in Walther's poems. Indirectly, these poems provide the first German description of a Court of Venus. Directly, they supply the argument between hero and temptress, the identity of the "Greyse," the theme of the penitent pilgrim and the boundless mercy of God, the figure of the un-Christian pope, the symbol of the blooming staff, the idea of a return to the temptress, and the damnation of the pope.

Although the Tannhäuser ballad treats two historical, contemporaneous people and draws largely from poems which have a theological, rather than mythological background, it is quite possible that the composition of the poem was influenced to a limited extent by folklore. Certainly the motif of the relationship between a mortal and a divinity, the Ulysses-Calypso theme, was as popular then as later. There were doubtless many tales of men and fairies that may have colored the narrative, and the classical Venus may have been only a pseudonym for the German mountain spirit, Holda, or the goddess Freia. The author might also have been aware that, according to certain myths, the entrance into a realm of earth spirits was symbolic of death, and the return only a vain attempt to rejoin the living. And he certainly knew the broad implications of the sojourn in the mountain with regard to the conflict between Christianity and the pagan past. However, if the anonymous author of the ballad was typical of thirteenth-century writers, he was a sophisticated artist, strongly rooted in a Judeo-Christian culture, who composed for a refined and courtly audience which felt as remote from a primitive mythology as does the modern audience. As a basis for interpreting the work, mythology can safely be ignored.

---

[138] Junk, p. 18; Barto, *Tannhäuser and the Mountain of Venus*, p. 103; Löhmann, p. 248; Hermann Schneider, "Ursprung und Alter der deutschen Volksballade," *Vom Werden des deutschen Geistes: Festgabe Gustav Ehrismann*, eds. Paul Merker and Wolfgang Stammler (Berlin and Leipzig: Walter de Gruyter, 1925), p. 121; and others.

[139] Lachmann, 11, 13-15.

A second approach to an understanding of the author's intent is to assume that he identified Venus with her literary prototype, Walther's Dame World.[140] The narrative then would present an allegorical conflict between Christianity and the pleasures (evils) of the flesh — certainly a topical theme. But difficulties immediately appear: thirteenth-century secular literature on the whole did not make this identification, and the true villain is not Venus, but the pope. Actually, at the time of the ballad's composition, Venus — when she was not the classical goddess — could be only one thing: *minne.* This is clear, especially in light of the famous Venus journey in Ulrich von Liechtenstein's *Frauendienst.* The story of the ballad is simply that the hero feels remorse because he has devoted himself exclusively to Venus (courtly love) and the pleasures of the Venus Mountain (the chivalric life) and turns to the Church for the remission of his sin. However, the Church leadership has so emphasized asceticism that it has forgotten a fundamental teaching of Christianity, that God has infinite capacity to forgive. The pope, therefore, becomes guilty not only of driving a repentant sinner away from the means of salvation, but also of excessive pride in presuming to limit the power of God.

The goal of the classical period of courtly verse — to find a harmonious balance in life between worldly and spiritual values — was never quite attained. And the asceticism advanced by the Church continually crept into the songs of the minnesingers to disturb their attempts to depict a life in which earthly joys did not interfere with the service of God. But Walther, for one, was wise enough to see that the values of chivalry were at variance with the religious doctrines advanced by the Church and said so in the well-known lines of his "Ich saz uf eime steine." As the ideals of chivalry faded during the thirteenth century, the religious emphasis on the ascetic life must have become ever stronger, particularly since the temporal power of the Church increased greatly in this period. The clash between the service of *minne* and the service of God is a basic element in the traditional crusade song, which may have been a model for the ballad with respect to the central conflict and also the theme of departure and return. Another genre which may have influenced its composition — either directly or through Walther — is the dawn song, with the alternating arguments between knight and lady as to whether the former should leave.

One of the most interesting questions which the ballad poses is that of the relationship of its hero to the minnesinger. And the answers which scholars present vary widely. Some of those who support the theory that the work evolved from a primitive myth maintain that the fictional Tannhäuser is not the same as the historical one. Others of this school say that they are identical, but that the legend had taken definite form before the minnesinger's time, and that his name was lent to the hero because of similarities between the two with respect

---

140 Güntert, p. 102, says: "In der Dichtung des deutschen Mittelalters sind *Venus* und *Frou Werlte* identisch," but he would not be able to support this statement with examples from the thirteenth century.

to character or situation. Among the ones who assume that the ballad preceded the legend there is a difference of opinion as to whether the work was composed specifically about the minnesinger or whether he became the hero more or less accidentally. Several even suggest that the ballad reflects incidents in Tannhäuser's life. The theory has been advanced that Tannhäuser, after a life of debauchery, was seized with remorse and actually made a pilgrimage to Rome, and that he returned to his evil ways when refused absolution by the pope.[141] Another scholar develops this idea further and reconstructs the following chapter in the life of the minnesinger as a source for the ballad. While on his crusade he came into a remote region of Asia Minor, was there involved in a love affair with a Mohammedan princess, and remained for a year or more. Satiety and repentance led him back to the Church and he made a pilgrimage to Rome, where he was rejected by the pope. An outcast from Christianity, he returned to the Orient and his Mohammedan sweetheart and was never seen by Westerners again. Since the hero not only neglected his holy mission as a crusader, but even consorted at length with an enemy of Christianity, the hardness of the pope's verdict was understandable. It is proposed that the name Frene, by which the heroine is known in another version of the ballad, was the name of the princess and that her court may have been in a castle on a mountain.[142] A third scholar suggests that the ballad grew out of a boast by the minnesinger that he had been in the Venus Mountain and enjoyed the love of its queen;[143] a fourth, that it is an attack on the pope for having excommunicated Tannhäuser because of the latter's anti-Roman political leanings.[144]

More conservative scholarship restricts itself to Tannhäuser's works in seeking to explain the connection between minnesinger and ballad. They portray a man who demands a joyous affirmation of life, who describes merry dances, who tells of his enjoyment of love's delights, and all in all reveals a livelier sensuousness than do his contemporaries — who, however, in later songs, laments his fate and blames himself for his grievous situation. Such a figure could readily become a symbol for a way of life that an ascetic Church deplored and a suitable servant and victim of a heathen goddess of love. For the pious he could be a notorious representative of wantonness; for the more sympathetic, an example of a new literary type: the noble sinner. In addition to the character of the narrator, Tannhäuser's verse contains other elements which may be reflected in the ballad. His Leiche and songs refer three times to Paris and Venus, and his name might well occur to a poet who was seeking a contemporary figure as an associate of the goddess. The beautiful girl of whom he sings and the love-making in the forest could also have supplied the germ for the Tannhäuser-Venus relationship. The

---

[141] Zander, p. 18, cites the seventeenth-century scholar, Melchior Goldast, as having made this suggestion. It was also advanced by Bernhardt, p. 103.

[142] Zander, p. 31.

[143] Rottauscher, p. 45.

[144] Erich Schmidt, "Tannhäuser in Sage und Dichtung," Nord und Süd, 63 (1892), 183.

many difficult tasks of the *minne* parodies, including the obtaining of the apple of Paris, may have inspired the seemingly impossible condition set by the pope for the salvation of the knight: that the staff should green. And the *minne* parodies might have been connected to the strife between the knight and *minne*-Venus at the beginning of the ballad, at least to the extent of giving a name to the hero.

An unusual feature of the ballad is the harsh and nondoctrinal position taken by the pope with regard to the penitent sinner. However, one does not need to look beyond Tannhäuser's works for an explanation of it. Urban IV followed the policy of his predecessors in attempting to destroy the power of the Hohenstaufens. He forbade under threat of excommunication the election of Konradin, the grandson of Emperor Friedrich II, to the throne of Germany, and excommunicated Friedrich's son, Manfred, offering Manfred's kingdom of Naples and Sicily to Count Charles of Anjou. The latter action in particular aroused anger throughout Germany. Although Tannhäuser's verse is much less political than is Walther's, still there is no question as to his Hohenstaufen sympathies. And the composer of the ballad, who was certainly no friend of the pope, may well have been aware of Tannhäuser's politics when he tells of the un-Christian treatment of his hero. Since it is above all the story of a penitent, the ballad especially calls to mind the *Spruch* cycle under Tannhäuser's name in the Jena Manuscript. The resemblances are, for the most part, quite general; both contain a confession of sin, emphasize the limitless power of God to forgive, and stress the role of Mary as an intermediary. However, one stanza of the ballad shows some verbal similarities to lines in the cycle.[145] Those who believe the Jena *Sprüche* authentic assume that they influenced either the composition of the ballad or the choice of hero, while scholars who consider them spurious maintain that they were attributed to Tannhäuser because of the ballad. The penitent songs of later centuries which were ascribed to the minnesinger reveal the influence of both Jena *Sprüche* and ballad.

Probably not the least of the reasons why the minnesinger became connected with the ballad is his name, Tannhäuser: the forest-dweller. For forests are in mountains, and both are the homes of supernatural beings and enchanted courts like that of the Venus Mountain. The name Tannhäuser could summon up a host of dark and mysterious impressions for thirteenth-century listeners, and invite all sorts of allegorical interpretations. They knew tales of men who had been

---

[145] Meier, p. 146:
Ach Babst, lieber herre mein,
Ich klag euch meine sunde [sic],
Die ich mein tag begangen hab,
Als ich euchs wil verkünde.
Holz, I, 75:
Ich kvnde dich herre myne klage.
. . . .
Ich habe gesvndeget myne tage.

enticed into the forests and mountains by evil spirits and associated these regions with the mythological past. A Tannhäuser was certainly a proper companion for a heathen goddess, and the name might even have furnished the initial idea from which its author developed the ballad. The aptness of the name has caused some to look beyond the minnesinger in seeking the archetype of the ballad hero. One theory holds that Venus and her knight have nothing to do with either classical mythology or thirteenth-century history, but evolved from two figures of the Vilcina saga: Fria and Wittich, whose name means "forest dweller," or Tannhäuser, and who once lived in a mountain with dwarfs.[146] Another conjecture is that in German mythology the name was a designation of a wind demon who sometimes left his forest home to visit the goddess of love.[147] A third theory is that the name was derived from "Wotanhäuser," and is connected with the mountain where Wotan and his wife Freya (goddess of love) dwelt. The knight, accordingly, was originally called "The Wotanhäuser" because he forsook Christianity to return to the heathen gods of the Germanic past.[148] Such hypotheses are not tenable as they have been presented: as explanations of the origin of the ballad. But they may have a certain validity in explaining the manner in which the author reworked Walther's material and the choice of a name for his hero.

Further proposals concerning the name of the hero of the ballad agree that it came from the minnesinger, but claim that the minnesinger was substituted for an earlier hero. One scholar maintains that a Flemish version is older and that the name of its hero, Daniel, was changed during the Reformation to Tannhäuser because of the latter's opposition to the pope and the similarity in sound.[149] A second critic compares the content of certain songs by Heinrich von Morungen and the character they portray with the ballad and suggests that he was the original hero, whom tradition had confused with a colleague.[150]

Considering the many theories regarding the origins and sources of the Tannhäuser ballad, it is a little strange that there has been almost no speculation as to who the author might have been. The only suggestion made was advanced by a seventeenth-century scholar who believed that it was the minnesinger Tannhäuser himself.[151] Modern critics have not taken this opinion seriously, and perhaps should not. It nevertheless has something in its favor. Although several contemporary scholars have recognized that the situation of the hero of the ballad is not as hopeless as was thought by those of the past century, criticism has completely ignored the ironic humor of the conclusion of the ballad. The

---

[146] Haupt, p. 320.

[147] Edm[und]. Veckenstedt, "Tanhäuser [sic], ein Dämon des Windes," *Das Magazin für die Litteratur des In- und Auslandes*, 111 (1887), 73-75.

[148] Adalbert Rudolf, "Tanhäuser [sic]," *Archiv*, 68 (1882), 51.

[149] Barto, *Tannhäuser and the Mountain of Venus*, p. 103.

[150] Carl von Kraus, ed., *Heinrich von Morungen* (München: Bremer, 1925), pp. 117-19.

[151] Zander, p. 15.

hero has the best of everything, although he may not know it. He enjoys all the physical pleasures which the Venus Mountain can offer without jeopardizing his soul in the least, for no less a person than the pope has been damned in his stead. Few besides Tannhäuser would have thought of such a solution. However, the form of the ballad is unlike that of any poem ascribed to Tannhäuser and weighs against his authorship.

The damnation of the pope was soon lost during the diffusion of the ballad into folk mythology. The most tenacious element was the Venus Mountain, and it was primarily through this that the ballad affected the writings of the late medieval period. Although Gottfried's reference to the Venus Court was considerably earlier, the location of the court in a mountain occurred first in the ballad, and it can be assumed that, as far as Germany is concerned, the Venus Mountain theme is a product of the ballad. The incidence in extant medieval literature of the motif in its purest form has been recorded,[152] and its significance for the period would be relatively easy to evaluate if one were to ignore the existence of similar motifs in Western literature. But there are many of these, and one must consider the likelihood of interaction and interdependence as well as the possibility that similar stories may have no historical connection with each other. For wherever there are caves, there are reports of fantastic wealth and splendid assemblages in them; where are myths of supernatural beings, there are tales of human association with them. Equally universal is the idea of an enchanted realm in which each physical desire is satisfied. Such a domain is the paradise of amorous pleasure in the Celtic legend of Morgain la Fée, which has been linked to the Tannhäuser Venus Mountain.[153] Another is Avalon to which the sorely wounded Arthur was borne, to dwell for ages with the beautiful elfin ruler, Argante. A third is the fairy island to which the infant Lancelot was carried, so that he might later serve its queen. Of particular interest with respect to the Venus Mountain is the story of Thomas of Erceldoune who, according to a Middle English poem and a Scottish ballad, was enticed by a queen of fairies into an underground paradise. Thomas, like Tannhäuser, was a thirteenth-century poet, and it has been maintained that poem and ballad were preceded by a Celtic legend which was the source of the German song.[154] A like claim has been made for the Swan Knight legend,[155] also of Celtic origin. This tells of a knight who comes from a wondrous realm where every desire is fulfilled, marries the queen of a troubled country to which he brings peace and stability, and abruptly returns to his homeland. The chief elements — land of enjoyment, departure and un-expected return, and association with a queen — appear in the Tannhäuser ballad, although in a quite different context. Despite obvious similarities, it is

---

152 Especially throughout the books by Barto and Amman.

153 Roger S. Loomis, "Morgain la Fée in Oral Tradition," *Romania*, 80 (1959), 337-67.

154 Alexander Krappe, "Die Sage vom Tannhäuser," *Mitteilungen der schlesischen Gesellschaft für Volkskunde*, 36 (1937), 106-32; Löhmann, pp. 224-53.

155 Barto, *Tannhäuser and the Mountain of Venus*, p. 71.

most unlikely that these legends had any more than a peripheral effect on the composition of the Tannhäuser ballad because of the close parallels between it and the well-known songs by Walther. It is also improbable that the Celtic legends significantly affected the subsequent occurrence of the Venus Mountain theme. For the popularity of the ballad was such as to indicate that its influence was predominant here, and perhaps may even be traced in the development of some allied motifs: the Melusine, Lorelei, and Undine material, and that dealing with subterranean palaces where intruders fall into a long-lasting sleep.

Medieval writers describe the Venus Mountain and the life there in various ways and from widely differing points of view. Some make it a den of iniquity and continued orgy. Others depict an existence which is quite proper although devoted entirely to pleasure, with music, story-telling, dancing, and other forms of social entertainment. This is what appears in Heinric van Aken's verse novel of the early fourteenth century, *Margarete van Limburg*, when Margarete's brother, Heinrich, spends two years in the castle of Dame Venus during his many adventures. A similar merry and innocent life is revealed in the second half of the century in Meister Altswert's, "Der Tugenden Schatz," when a dwarf leads the poet into the Venus Mountain and shows him the varied entertainment of its inhabitants. Here, as well as in other verse tales of Altswert which tell of Queen Venus, she is simply the embodiment of *minne*. The poet obviously knew Tannhäuser's songs as well as the ballad: he employs to an exaggerated degree the latter's cataloguing technique, describes from head to toe a lovely, curly-headed blonde to whom he makes love on the edge of the forest, and uses many phrases which are characteristic of Tannhäuser. A third narrative of the fourteenth century, the Italian novel, *Guerino* (1391), by Andrea dei Magnabotti, has more of the elements of the ballad, even though the heroine is called a sibyl rather than Venus. Soon after Guerino enters the sibyl's mountain he sees an inscription which says that whoever remains inside for more than a year must stay until Judgment Day, and then be eternally damned. The many pleasures of the subterranean realm and the charms of its queen — who is not only a prophetess, but also a goddess of love — almost cause him to delay too long. But he discovers the diabolical nature of the society in the mountain, leaves at the last moment, and goes to the pope, from whom he receives absolution for having consorted with a witch. Here, as in the ballad, one finds the pleasure palace in the mountain, the evil temptress, remorse, the pope, and the escape from damnation.

There is little mention of the Venus Mountain in the extant literature of the fourteenth century, but the references to it during the following two centuries — about fifty in number — indicate that it was a popular subject for singers and storytellers. One of the more important fifteenth-century treatments of the subject matter of the ballad also chooses the Italian mountain of the sibyl as a setting. This is a novel of education, *La Salade* (ca. 1440), which the Provençal Antoine de la Sale wrote for the edification of his pupil, Jean d'Anjou, the son of King René of Naples and Jerusalem. One of the stories which de la

Sale relates is of a trip that he took to the region of Monte della Sibilla where he learned the tale of a German knight who had remained in it almost to the end of the allotted year. He then tears himself away and, filled with guilt, hurries to Rome to obtain absolution. The pope delays his decision, and the knight's page, who has greatly enjoyed the life in the mountain, tells his master that they are about to be tried for heresy. Despairing of forgiveness and wanting to at least save his life, the knight returns to the sibyl queen. The pope regrets his hesitation and sends out messengers to tell the knight of his absolution, but it is too late and he cannot be found.[156] Although the author does not mention the *Guerino* novel, he was certainly familiar with it. Additional features — the German hero, the failure of the pope to grant absolution, and the return to the magic realm — indicate that he also knew some form of the ballad. The works by Magnabotti and de la Salle were apparently the basis for a Czechish version which first appeared in the sixteenth century.[157]

A third witness to the existence of some sort of Tannhäuser legend in fifteenth-century Italy appears in an account in the *De nobilitate et rusticitate dialogus* (ca. 1456) of the Zurich canon Felix Hemmerlin. The author claims that while he was in Bologna he saw a Swiss peasant who confessed to the pope that he and two German companions had lived with evil spirits in the mountains. At the end of a year, he had left, but the others had not been able to tear themselves away from the women there. Through the intercession of the canon, the peasant received absolution from a confessor designated by the pope.[158]

At about the same time as Hemmerlin's dialogue, a German verse novel appeared which was set in the Venus Mountain. This was *Die Mörin* (1453), by Hermann von Sachsenheim. While walking in the forest, the narrator is seized by the legendary Eckhart and a dwarf and carried into the wondrous land of Venus to answer charges that he has been inconstant in love. The prosecutor is a Moorish girl, the defense attorney is Eckhart, and the judge is King Tannhäuser, a Frankish knight who had entered the realm some time before and had become the husband of Queen Venus. After a lengthy trial the narrator is permitted to return home. There are other elements in the novel beside the figures of Tannhäuser and Venus which recall the ballad. The debate between the Moorish girl and Eckhart reminds one of the argument between Tannhäuser and Venus, and there are several appeals to the Virgin Mary which resemble those in the ballad. There are also similarities in style and content to the works of the minnesinger: the

---

156 Beginning with Gaston Paris' essay on the Tannhäuser legend in his *Legendes du moyen age* (Paris: Hachette, 1903), pp. 111-49, a school of thought has developed which maintains that the legend began in Italy and cites the works by Magnabotti and de la Sale as evidence. It includes Otto Denk, Fernand Desonay, Heinrich Dübi, Friedrich Kluge, Kristoffer Nyrop, and Marjatta Wis.

157 Werner Söderhjelm, "Eine tschechische Version der Reise ins Sibyllenparadies," *Neuphilologische Mitteilungen*, 10 (1908), 72-88.

158 An account of Hemmerlin's report appears in Remy, p. 36.

nature introduction to the novel, the ironic humor which pervades it, and the baroque display of literary and geographic allusions. The eternal spring of the land of Venus and the pronounced *minne* parody of the joust in honor of Lady Infamy likewise are indications that Hermann was as familiar with the works of the poet as with the legend. In contrast to the heroine of the ballad, there is nothing diabolic in the character of Queen Venus.

It cannot be assumed, however, that the heroine of the Tannhäuser legend was gradually losing her witch-like nature, for in the same year the manuscript of *Die Mörin* was completed another appeared which shows her in the traditional role of evil seductress. It contains a mastersinger duet between Venus and Tannhäuser, who wants to leave her and return to the upper world. The argument follows that in the ballad for the most part, but has been expanded by the introduction of new material.[159] Later in the century a similar dramatic dialogue was recorded in which the role of Venus is assumed by Dame World, who, when convinced that Tannhäuser will leave her, recommends that he go to the Venus Mountain, the queen of which will receive him with open arms.[160] In the same manuscript as the mastersinger duet is a song, entitled "Tannhusers tagwise," in which the hero offers a morning prayer to Mary. He confesses the sin to which beautiful women have led him, recounts the events of Christ's passion as assurance that he will be forgiven, and proclaims his faith that Mary will help him escape the devil. There is no mention of Venus or a Venus Mountain, and only the appeal to Mary recalls the ballad. The "tagwise" was apparently inspired by the *Sprüche* attributed to Tannhäuser in the Jena Manuscript.

The wide variety of references to and treatments of the Venus Mountain motif during the fifteenth century show that a broad legend had developed which gave considerable latitude to poets in their interpretations of the characters and situations of the main figures. At the same time it is clear that the original ballad, with few, if any changes, enjoyed widespread popularity. In this respect a report by the Franciscan monk, Felix Faber, is important. In his *Evagatorium in Terrae Sanctae, Arabiae et Egypti Peregrinationem* (1483), he tells of a Venus Mountain on Cyprus which, he maintains, is the original one from which all the others had received their names, including the mountain near Rome. With regard to the latter, he tells of what he calls a foolish rumor that the goddess was living inside with a retinue of men and women. He also relates of a song which apparently was sung by the people throughout Germany and dealt with a noble Swabian, named Tannhäuser, from the Tannhäuser

---

159 This song and "Tanhusers tagwise" are included in Johann Georg Grässe, *Der Tannhäuser und Ewige Jude*, 2nd ed. (Dresden: Schönfeld, 1861), pp. 33-40 and Barto, *Tannhäuser and the Mountain of Venus*, pp. 224-30.

160 "Der Thanhauser," in *Fastnachtspiele aus dem fünfzehnten Jahrhundert*, ed. Adelbert von Keller, Bibliothek des literarischen Vereins in Stuttgart, 46 (Stuttgart, 1858), 47-53.

estate near Dünkelspüchel. He was said to have spent some time in the mountain with Venus before becoming penitent and going to the pope to confess. He was refused absolution, went back to the mountain, and was never seen again. He was supposed to be living there in sensual pleasure until Judgment Day.[161] Faber's designation of the rumor about a Venus Mountain as foolish is representative of many comments of the late fifteenth and the sixteenth century, for the Venus Mountain apparently had become something of a symbol of popular superstition. The chief satirists of the period — Sebastian Brant, Thomas Murner, and Johann Fischart — ridiculed the credulity of those who could believe in such a thing.

The appearance of the ballad in print in 1515 greatly contributed to its spread, and the many subsequent printings of the sixteenth century bear witness to its popularity. Some had a music score in addition to the text, and a few were accompanied by illustrations. Low German translations were made, one of which has received considerable critical attention.[162] The first scholar to pass judgment on the ballad did so soon after its publication. This was Johann Turmair (Aventinus) who, in accordance with his predilection to finding significant places in history for legendary characters, identified its hero with a Gothic king, known to the Greeks as Thanauses, and did not mention the thirteenth-century minnesinger.[163] Since Turmair referred to it as an old song, he apparently knew it before it was printed.

The Nürnberg broadside also may have caused Hans Sachs to become interested in the Tannhäuser material, for just two years after it appeared he wrote his Shrovetide play, "Das Hoffgesindt Veneris." If so, he too must have been familiar with a general tradition, because the play contains nothing of the ballad except the Venus Mountain theme. As in *Die Mörin*, "the faithful Eckhart" has an important role. Probably due to his activity as defense attorney for Hermann's narrator, he has become a type character, the voice which warns against the

---

161 Bibliothek des literarischen Vereins in Stuttgart, 4 (1849), p. 221: "Unde de hoc carmen confictum habetur, quod manifeste a vulgo per Alemanniam canitur de quodam nobili Suevo, quem nominant Danhuser, de Danhusen villa prope Dünckelspüchel. Hunc fingunt ad tempus in monte cum Venere fuisse, et cum poenitentia ductus Papae fuisset confessus, denegata fuit sibi absolutio, et ita regressus in montem nusquam comparuit, et in deliciis vivit, ut dicunt, usque ad diem judicii." On the basis of Faber's report, Reuschel, p. 659, theorizes that the historical Tannhäuser may have been shipwrecked at Cyprus and that his presence there, on the island of Venus Anadyomene, may have given birth to a legend from which the ballad came. The assumption of a shipwreck is based on Tannhäuser's *Spruch* about the winds at sea.

162 Barto, *Tannhäuser and the Mountain of Venus*, p. 102, maintains that a Flemish version which appeared in 1544 gives the ballad in its oldest form. The hero's name here is Daniel and was taken, Barto suggests (p. 145), from the protagonist of Stricker's Arthurian epic, *Daniel von dem blühenden Tal*. According to this theory, the hero has no connection with the minnesinger.

163 Uhland, II (1866), 230.

danger of associating with Venus.[164] Eckhart follows the prologue on stage and cautions everyone that Queen Venus is coming and is intent on increasing the number of her retinue. Tannhäuser then appears and introduces himself as a famous Franconian knight who has been captured by Venus' arrows. The other characters, one by one, defy her power, are warned vainly by Eckart, and fall victim to the goddess: knight, doctor, citizen, peasant, soldier, gambler, drinker, virgin, and married lady. At last Tannhäuser begs Venus to set him and the rest free. She refuses, saying that they will be subject to her as long as they live, and she commands the musician to start up the dance, in which all take part. At its conclusion she tells them of the wonderful life of many pleasures in the Venus Mountain and orders them to follow her there. There is nothing diabolic in the character of Venus, who represents only the pangs of love, or in the life in the Venus Mountain which she describes. The dance at the end of the play once more indicates that the verse of the minnesinger has influenced the development of the legend. It is quite likely that Hans Sachs based his work on a lost Shrovetide play which was performed in the early sixteenth century at Colmar in Alsace by a group from the village of Kiensheim.[165]

"Das Hoffgesindt Veneris" is the only work by Hans Sachs which is based directly on the Tannhäuser legend, but several others mention it. Four *Schwänke* composed at mid-century (1545—1559) employ the Venus Mountain motif, and three of them reveal a new aspect of it. In "Der doctor im Venus perg" two Florentine painters tell a young doctor that they go every Whitsuntide to the Venus Mountain to enjoy themselves with the beautiful women there. When the doctor begs them to get him admitted too, they disguise themselves as a fabulous horse-like beast, carry him off at midnight, and throw him into the excrement of a public toilet. In "Das unhuelden pannen" a peasant who blames all of his troubles on witches is told by a travelling scholar how to get the better of them. The peasant tries his hand at magic, and stable boys, masquerading as witches, beat him severely. The scholar supported his claim to a knowledge of black art by saying that he had just come from the Venus Mountain. A maid in "Die sich unsichtbar haltende Magd" has been told by her employer how to make herself invisible, and she walks around nude during a party he is giving, playing tricks on the guests, who pretend they do not see her. A reference at the beginning of the tale to riding on a goat into the Venus Mountain and to the wondrous happenings to be seen there aroused the interest of the maid in magic. In a similar story, "Der pawren knecht mit der nebelkappen," two vagabonds convince a peasant lad that an old hood they have brought from the Venus Mountain can make him invisible, and he gets a beating when he tries to avoid the innkeeper by means of it. They also spoke of strange events in the Venus

---

[164] Eckhart is also associated with the Venus Mountain in *Das deutsche Heldenbuch*, which was written at about the same time as *Die Mörin*.

[165] Wilhelm Creizenach, *Geschichte des neueren Dramas*, 2nd ed. (Halle: Niemeyer, 1923), III, 140.

76

Mountain and claimed to have learned magic there. The hero of the well-known play "Der fahrende Schüler im Paradeis" introduces himself as a man of unusual talents by saying that he not only has read much in books, but has also been in the Venus Mountain.

"Der doctor im Venus perg" depicts the Mountain as we have seen it before, as a place of beautiful women and sensual pleasure; presumably a locality of ill repute, since the doctor at first believes the strange steed to be the devil. In the three other *Schwänke* and the play, however, the eroticism usually connected with the Venus Mountain is lacking, and it has become a place of black art, a school for magicians. It has been suggested that this element of the Tannhäuser legend was borrowed from the Italian folklore surrounding a mountain north of Rome.[166] The superstitions which were beginning to collect about the Brocken in the Harz Mountains may also have contributed something. Another development of the Venus Mountain myth in the fifteenth and sixteenth centuries made it a place where treasures of gold and jewels were to be found. As such it became a convenient shield for thieves, who could offer stolen valuables for sale and say that they had been got from the Venus Mountain. A Nürnberg trial report of 1587 tells of one who vainly used this excuse for the possession of considerable money. Another account indicates that the alibi had been heard long before.[167]

Although the Tannhäuser legend continued to be mentioned in passing, no other significant literary use of it was made in the sixteenth century. At the beginning of the seventeenth century it was discussed by the historian Melchior Goldast, who was the first to rediscover the medieval minnesong. He reported that the ballad was sung everywhere, and expressed the opinion that the minnesinger was the author and had composed it as a part of his pro-Hohenstaufen politics to discredit the pope. Goldast interprets the Venus Mountain of the ballad, not as the dwelling of a goddess, but simply as a house of ill repute.[168]

More about the legend appeared a few years later in Heinrich Kornmann's *Mons Veneris, Fraw Veneris Berg* (1614), which contains a collection of what classical and medieval writers have said about the goddess Venus and her court, as well as that which the author gathered himself on his many journeys. Among the latter accounts is one he heard in Asia Minor about a traveler who, attracted by the sound of music, finds a door in a mountain, enters, and sees a festive throng. Someone brings him wine, which he is afraid to drink. He pours it out and runs off with the cup. Two reports are of interest in that he connects the Italian sibyl and the Melusine legend with the Venus Mountain motif. The sibyl, so he has heard, lives in a mountain cave and changes once a week into a snake. A watch has been placed near the entrance to prevent people from

---

[166] Reuschel, p. 657.
[167] Gerhard Eis, "Die Tannhäusersage bei Gaunern und Walen," *Archiv*, 191 (1955), 221-23.
[168] Zander, p. 18.

going in. Melusine, without the knowledge of her husband, changes every Saturday into a dragon. When he happens to find her in this form, she leaps out the window, flies three times around the castle, and disappears forever. Kornmann's other contemporary reports which have to do with the Tannhäuser legend include references to Venus caves in Switzerland and Sweden. He also quotes the ballad, but in a form which appears to have been deliberately altered. Instead of damning Urban IV at the end, it says that no priest should drive a sinner to despair, for his sins can be forgiven if he repents and does penance.[169]

Although Kornmann attempted to completely exhaust his subject, there were doubtless many Venus Mountain stories being told at his time which he missed. One of them appears in a Latin letter of the year 1608 in which a physician writes of the visit of a boy to the Venus Mountain and of the latter's report on what he saw.[170] The *Mons Veneris* represents the high point in the history of the medieval Tannhäuser legend, and the interest in it gradually declined throughout the rest of the century. There were a few more printings of different versions of the ballad, a decreasing number of references to the Venus Mountain, and then almost complete silence, which was to continue a hundred years. The last significant developments before the lacuna were the appearance of a song which treated the material of the ballad in a monologue by the hero and the emergence in 1689 of a Danish variant.[171]

The medieval Tannhäuser legend may have been influenced by German mythology, but its immediate source was a song composed about the time of the minnesinger's death, a ballad which drew heavily from several works by Walther. We cannot know how Tannhäuser happened to become its hero, but his evocative name, his emphasis on sensual joy, his expressions of regret for a prodigal life, and his anti-papal politics may have been contributing factors. As a legend grew out of the ballad, the pope was largely discarded and the figure of the penitent became dim, for it was the Venus Mountain which captured the popular imagination. This was a paradise of splendid courtly life, limitless wealth, and all sorts of sensual pleasures. For many it was simply a castle in the sky with no dangerous connotations; some thought of it, however, as a forbidden realm where those who entered might well lose their souls; others made it a school of black magic; some considered it primarily as a source of treasures. There are indications that the legend was colored by the works of the minnesinger. The carefree life in the Venus Mountain, the frequent references to dancing, the occasional detailed descriptions of feminine beauty, and the use of certain stylistic devices lead one to believe that some of those who made literary use of the legend were familiar with the works of the poet.

---

169 Heinrich Kornmann, *Mons Veneris* (Frankfurt: Fischer, 1614), chapters 14, 16 and 27.
170 Otto Böckel, "Zur Sage vom Venusberg," *Alemannia*, 13 (1885), 141-42.
171 Kristoffer Nyrop, *Tannhäuser i Venusbjaerget* (Copenhagen: Gyldendalske, 1909), p. 18.

When the German Romanticists at the end of the eighteenth century began to revive and revise the Middle Ages, they seized enthusiastically on the Tannhäuser legend and made it one of their most popular subjects. Tieck was first, with his tale, "Der getreue Eckart und der Tannhäuser" (1799), in which *Märchen* and mania are interwoven in a characteristically Tieckean manner. The young nobleman, Tannhäuser, leads a moody and troubled youth until disappointment in love drives him past the warning ghost of the heroic Eckart and into the forbidden Venus Mountain, a place of continuous pleasure, so intense as to be almost painful. At last the blind discontent which brought him there leads him out. He is surfeited with joy, desires a rest from pleasure, and wishes to experience again the diversion of occasional pain. But, once in the world outside, he is overcome with remorse and journeys to the pope for absolution, which the latter will not and cannot grant. Deranged, Tannhäuser declares he is returning to the Venus Mountain, murders his former loved one, and disappears forever. Tieck's treatment of his material foreshadows that of other modern writers. Tannhäuser has become the archetype of the Romantic hero: estranged from society and himself, driven by nameless longings, more at home with pain than with joy, and hovering on the brink of madness. The Venus Mountain has a three-fold ambiguity. It represents nature and the epitome of beauty and natural joys; it is the essence of evil and all that is forbidden; it is as much a product of emotional delirium and mental confusion as of magic. One figure in Tieck's story, an unnamed, ghostly minstrel whose enchanting music draws people into the mountain, may be based on the minnesinger.

There is nothing in "Der getreue Eckart" to indicate the author's exact sources, but the Tannhäuser ballad was soon available, for in 1806 it was included in the folksong collection, *Des Knaben Wunderhorn*.[172] The version printed here was the bowdlerized one of Kornmann, which perhaps explains why many modern variants do not mention Pope Urban IV. However, the content of the original ballad became known in 1816 when it was retold in prose in Grimm's *Volkssagen*. Tieck's *Märchen*, *Des Knaben Wunderhorn*, and Grimm's *Volkssagen* were among the most popular and influential works of the Romantic period, and through them the legend and the ballad received wide attention. Goethe speaks of the "großes christlich-katholisches Motiv" of the ballad in a review (1806) of *Des*

---

172 The ballad had appeared in a lesser known collection a year earlier.

Knaben Wunderhorn. Brentano includes Tannhäuser as a secondary character in his *Romanzen vom Rosenkranz*, which also treats the theme of sin and atonement and has as its central symbol a variant of the blooming staff. Moreover, he planned to write for Carl Maria von Weber an opera text, "Der Venusberg," which would be about Tannhäuser. E. T. A. Hoffmann brings together the legends of Tannhäuser and the Wartburg singer contest when he has the devil, Nasias, sing of the ecstatic joys of the Venus Mountain in "Der Kampf der Sänger" (1818). Eichendorff gives a vivid account of an enchanted Venus palace in his "Marmorbild" (1819), and describes the age-old struggle between Christianity and the heathen gods for the soul of a man. Grillparzer's opera text, *Melusina* (1823), which he intended to be put to music by Beethoven, has many elements of the similar Tannhäuser legend. Several minor figures also made use of the Tannhäuser material during the first quarter of the nineteenth century.[173]

The later Romanticists were somewhat less interested in medieval subjects than their predecessors, and it was not until 1835 that the legend again appeared in a significant work. This was a dramatic version by Eduard Duller which was later reworked to form the text of the first opera on the subject, Karl Ludwig Mangolt's *Tannhäuser*. The Duller-Mangolt opera (first performed in 1846) follows the ballad much more closely than does Wagner's, but has some new material: the hero has a sweetheart who is the daughter of the faithful Eckart, and he goes to the patriarch of Jerusalem for absolution instead of to the pope. The work had a great success, but is no longer performed.

Wagner's opera was inspired in part by Heine's poem, "Der Tannhäuser. Eine Legende," which was composed one year after Duller's play. The first of three parts follows the ballad fairly closely in the argument of Tannhäuser and Venus; the second part greatly expands the dialogue between Urban and the hero; the third part — the return to the Venus Mountain — is a humorous account of the latter's journey from Rome to Hamburg which has no connection with the original. In the two sections of the poem which concern us most, Heine modernizes his theme by substituting the Romantic *Dämon* for the medieval sin and guilt. Following Tieck, he has Tannhäuser leave Venus because his soul has become sick from sweet wine, kisses, and laughter, and he longs for bitterness and tears. But he cannot leave his attachment to Venus behind, and the pope soon sees from Tannhäuser's ecstatic and despairing account of his love that he cannot be rescued. Absolution is refused, not from ill will, but because there is no help for one who has so completely become a victim of his passion. He is damned to suffer the pangs of love eternally. It is possible that Heine's unexpected turn to satire in the third part and his cataloging of cities may have been influenced by the *Leiche* of the minnesinger. Another work of Heine which uses the legend

---

[173] For other nineteenth-century treatments of the Tannhäuser legend see especially Dora Koegel, "Die Auswertung der Tannhäuser-Sage in der deutschen Literatur des 19. und 20. Jahrhunderts" (Diss. München, 1922), and Hilda Horowitz, "Tannhäuserdichtungen seit Richard Wagner" (Diss. Wien, 1932).

is the last of four ballet tableaux, called "Die Göttin Diana," which were prepared in 1846. The ballet depicts the love of Diana and a mortal, who is killed in a duel with the faithful Eckart. The final scene takes place in the Venus Mountain amid most luxurious and voluptuous surroundings. Famous lovers and great composers of love verse are there: Helen, Cleopatra, Julius Caesar, Gottfried von Strassburg, Goethe, and others. Venus and Tannhäuser dance a duet in which they seem to scold, entice, and scorn each other, drawn and repelled by an irresistible passion which is not based on respect. All join in the dance when Diana's knight is brought back to life. The duet expresses the same idea of *amour fatale* that is found in "Der Tannhäuser. Eine Legende." The wild dance of Bacchantes at the end, or the choice of the Venus Mountain for a dance scene, may also have been inspired by the verse of the historical Tannhäuser.

Heine's poem has been credited with having revived the interest in the legend, for several treatments of it appeared soon after his work was published. Two of these were songs by Geibel and Friedrich von Sallet, both entitled "Der Tannhäuser," composed in 1838 and 1843, respectively. The former tells of a boy who one summer night wanders into a splendid castle while a dance is in progress. A beautiful woman gives him a cup of wine, which he drinks, and discovers too late that he is in the Venus Mountain and under its spell. The woman seduces him in the garden and he falls asleep. At dawn he awakens, a gray, old man alone in a desolate wilderness. The poem probably owes something to Eichendorff's "Das Marmorbild," but nothing to Heine, for it is quite medieval in outlook. The connection between the Venus Mountain and those caves where sleep is magically prolonged was established much earlier, but this is the first Romantic work to combine the motifs. Sallet's song has a more modern tone. Tannhäuser seeks the eternal fountain which will still all thirst, the water from which young life swells. When he discovers Venus asleep on a mountain, he expects to find in her what he seeks, but cannot achieve the ultimate of bliss. He hears church bells ring to prayer, feels he has sinned, and goes forth to do penance. He makes a pilgrimage to the pope, who says that Tannhäuser's staff will bear leaves before he is pardoned. He plants the staff in many places, but in vain, and at last returns to the mountain and Venus. When he embraces her, the staff begins to leaf out, and soon a tree towers over the lovers while the spirit of eternal love looks down on them through its foliage. What is new is the image of the Faustian seeker and the concept that true love cannot be evil. In the ballad the hero is saved through the intercession of Mary and the vicarious damnation of the pope. Here love is its own justification. Several elements in the poem remind one of Goethe's *Faust*.

The year when Sallet composed his poem was also that in which Wagner completed the libretto of his opera, which was first performed in 1845. Wagner is important in the history of the Tannhäuser legend, not only because his opera is its most famous product, but also because he significantly altered the legend by combining it with two others. The opera begins with Tannhäuser and Venus in the Venus Mountain. The hero asks leave to go, for, although he still loves the goddess, he cannot adjust to constant pleasure. He longs for freedom, strife, and pain. Again in the upper world, he meets a former patron, Landgrave Hermann of Thuringia, who persuades him to return to the court. Tannhäuser does so, renews his acquaintanceship with Hermann's niece, Elizabeth, and the two fall in love. When the minnesingers are competing at a festival, the others praise *minne* in terms of spirituality, honor, and religion, but Tannhäuser praises physical love for its own sake, and insists that it need serve no higher value. His rivals guess that he has been in the Venus Mountain and are about to kill him as a heretic when Elizabeth intervenes. Overcome with a sense of guilt, Tannhäuser journeys to Rome to beg for absolution. He is unsuccessful and, in despair, is on his way back to the Venus Mountain when he meets his friend, Wolfram, who tries to restrain him. He entreats Tannhäuser to turn to God, and tells him that Elizabeth, who is on her deathbed, will pray for him before God's throne. Then they hear the tolling of a bell, and Tannhäuser dies. Pilgrims arrive and announce the miracle of the blooming staff.[174]

The legends which Wagner combined with the Tannhäuser material are those concerning the Thuringian saint, Elizabeth, and the singer's contest at Wartburg. The latter goes back to a thirteenth-century dramatic poem, fragments of which appear in many manuscripts of the following two centuries. One of the contestants is a Heinrich von Ofterdingen who is opposed by most of the other singers and who becomes the hero of the legend. The first modern treatment of the Wartburg contest was in E. T. A. Hoffmann's "Der Kampf der Sänger," with which the composer was familiar. He also knew the legend through a collection of medieval tales, *Der Sagenschatz und die Sagenkreise des Thüringerlandes* (1835 -1837),[175] which includes the stories of Tannhäuser and Saint Elizabeth as well. The Tannhäuser account, as it appears here, is linked to the Wartburg contest by a statement that the singer was on his way there when he was led astray by Venus. The story of Saint Elizabeth is connected to the Wartburg contest not only because she was the daughter-in-law of Landgrave Hermann, at whose court the contest is held, but also because the legend about her in the collection comes immediately after that of the contest. Moreover, E. T. A. Hoffmann's tale contains a prophesy of her birth. Although Wagner makes liberal use of the legend of the Wartburg contest, he takes only the name of his heroine and her devout nature from the Saint Elizabeth legend. The character of the heroine also owes a considerable number of traits to Mathilde in E. T. A. Hoffmann's work.

---

174 The final scene was altered in the second and third versions of the opera.
175 Wolfgang Golther, "Die Quellen der Dichtung des 'Tannhäuser'," *Bayreuther Blätter*, 12 (1889), 132-49, quotes Wagner as saying that he had read about Tannhäuser and the Wartburg contest in a German folk book and was familiar with Tieck's story, the Tannhäuser ballad, and a tale by Hoffmann. Wagner may also have known Fouqué's "Der Sängerkrieg auf der Wartburg" (1828).

Wagner's most obvious contribution to the Tannhäuser legend lies in his expansion of the subject matter. In addition, he presented it with a new type of hero. Drawing from both E. T. A. Hoffmann and Heine,[176] Wagner created a Tannhäuser who is both modern and medieval. In some respects he is a typical Romantic hero: torn by inner conflict, tortured by pangs of love, easily sated with pleasure, desirous of freedom, strife, and pain. At the same time, he is medieval enough to accept sensual pleasure as sin and to be burdened by feelings of guilt. He is also a Dionysian-Apollonian figure who is strongly attracted both to the sensual (Venus) and the spiritual (Elizabeth) and cannot reconcile the warring aspects of his personality.

The success of Wagner's opera and the controversy surrounding the composer made the legend very popular and made it the subject of scores of works: lyric poems, verse epics, short stories, novels, dramas, musicals, and operas. Frequently one can see the direct influence of Wagner on the works which followed; often, however, they utilize aspects of the legend which he left untouched. Heinrich von Levitschnigg was obviously impressed with Wagner's exploitation of the extravaganza possibilities of the Venus Mountain, for the musical, *Der Tannhäuser*, which he prepared in 1852 with the collaboration of the Viennese composer Franz von Suppé, presents spectacles which have few rivals, even in an artistic medium that traditionally stresses color and pageantry. A Count Lichtenried is in love with Tannhäuser's wife, Marie, so he has a will-o-the-wisp lead the knight into the vicinity of the Venus Mountain at midnight, where he falls under its spell. Eckard warns him in vain, and he enters. Lichtenried tells Marie what has happened and declares his love for her, but she scorns him and hurries to join her husband. The heavenly spirit of love appears to Eckard, commands him to help Marie, and gives him a staff which will protect the innocent. Eckard leads her into the mountain as the marriage of Venus and Tannhäuser is about to begin. The minions of the goddess are driven back by the power of the staff, and Venus agrees to renounce her claim to Tannhäuser if he can make the dry staff send forth roses and, in a year's time, perform other seemingly impossible tasks, some of which will lead him to Italy. Eventually he arrives in Rome as a pilgrim, having been unable to complete any of his labors. He learns of a plot to kill Lichtenried, who is also in the city, and saves the life of his enemy. Eckard appears and announces that God, who can forgive all, has pardoned Tannhäuser because he, too, has been able to forgive. With Eckard's aid the tasks are performed, the staff takes root and produces white roses, a crown from the depth of Etna and a wondrous pearl from the sea are delivered to an emissary of Venus to complete Tannhäuser's ransom, and Marie appears in front of the rose bush.

Little which is included in the ballad or the medieval legend has been left

---

176 Elster, *Tannhäuser in Geschichte, Sage und Dichtung*, p. 18, maintains that E. T. A. Hoffmann exerted a stronger influence than any other on Wagner's text. Others have particularly stressed the influence of Heine.

out. From the ballad was taken the quarrel between Venus and Tannhäuser, the intervention of Mary-Marie, the pilgrimage to Rome, and the blooming staff. From the medieval legend came Eckard, the dancing and splendor of the Venus Mountain, the twelve months of grace, and the insistence on the power of God to forgive any sinner. The influence of the medieval minnesinger is seen in the presenting of impossible demands, and that of Wagner in the staging of the immense spectacle of the marriage scene. Another author who left a definite imprint on the work is Goethe. The scene where the will-o-the-wisp leads Tannhäuser into the mountain and that of the approaching wedding remind one strongly of the "Walpurgisnacht," "Walpurgisnachtstraum," and "Classische Walpurgisnacht" scenes of *Faust.* The conditions laid down by Venus whereby Tannhäuser can gain his freedom and redeem his soul are stated in language which recalls that of the pact with Mephistopheles. Many passages echo lines in Goethe's work. However, the musical is not purely imitative. The verse is good, and the libretto reads well in spite of the emphasis on the fantastic, an idea of which can be gained by a partial list of the figures who appear: the graces, the four seasons, Morpheus, Bacchus, sirens, Hercules, Mercury, Paris, sea nymph, giants, pygmies, lamias, Tritons, naiads, dryads, oreads, fauns, Bacchantes, and amorettos. The work was performed one hundred times in three years at Vienna's Theater an der Wien.

Whereas the supernatural and miraculous is stressed in Levitschnigg's musical, it is minimized in the verse novel, *Der Tannhäuser,* which was published two years later. The author, Adolf Franckel, fits his story into an accurate and detailed account of the history of Germany from about 1240 to about 1275, including the conflict between papacy and the Hohenstaufens, the struggle of Guelphs against Ghibellines, the invasion of the Mongols, and the establishment of the Hapsburg dynasty. Against an imposing background of war, intrigue, and change, the story is told of a Franconian knight, Heinrich der Tannhäuser, who, after a youthful tutelage under Eckard, begins the wandering life of a soldier. He fights against the Mongols in Silesia, and serves with Pope Innocence IV and later under Emperor Friedrich II, with whom he receives the papal ban. After Friedrich's death, Tannhäuser returns to his ancestral home and becomes engaged to his childhood sweetheart, but before they are married he chances to enter a mountain, the Hörselberg, and finds there a beautiful woman whom he had seen briefly years before. The wars continue; Konrad, Manfred, and Konradin go to their graves, as do Innocence, Alexander, Urban, and Clemens. Tannhäuser's mother dies, his sweetheart becomes a nun, Eckard disappears, and Tannhaus Castle becomes a ruin. Meanwhile its lord lives happily in the mountain with the beautiful goddess Holda.

Here the story of Tannhäuser is little more than a device through which the author gives an intimate view of history. The ballad supplies the goddess, the mountain, and the papal curse; Wagner is responsible for a brief reference to the singers' contest, the first name (Heinrich) of the hero, and the identification of the Venus Mountain with the Hörselberg. The substitution of the traditional goddess of this mountain for Venus is merely an extension of Wagner's localization and a step toward an increased realism in keeping with the historical setting.

In the same year as the publication of Franckel's epic poem appeared the first of half a dozen parodies of Wagner's opera, the best of which was the *Tannhäuser-Parodie. Burleske Operette in vier Bildern*, by Johann Nestroy and Karl Binder.[177] This work, first performed in 1857, was a revision of a student musical that had been put on several years before in Breslau, soon after a presentation of Wagner's opera. Nestroy moved it from a Breslau-student to a Viennese atmosphere and substituted theater wit for academic jokes. In the first *Bild* we find Tannhäuser in the Venuskeller, an establishment of which Venus is both proprietress and waitress. He feels called back to earth, an argument ensues, and he leaves. He awakes in an idyllic scene to the song of a shepherd, and soon Count Purzl with his retinue comes by and persuades him to return to the court. In the second *Bild* Elizabeth reveals her love, Tannhäuser lets it slip that he has been with Venus, and Purzl bans him from the court. The third *Bild* shows a mountain region where Wolfram is waiting for the pilgrims to return from Rome. At last Tannhäuser appears and tells his friend that the penance imposed by the pope was too strict — he would rather go back to Venus. Elizabeth's body is carried past on a bier, and Tannhäuser falls on it and dies of remorse. In the last *Bild* Venus steps forth, brings them back to life, and tells them that they may live only as long as they refrain from quarreling. To supplement the witty dialogues and lyrics by Nestroy, the operetta appropriates (and often alters) songs from Goethe, Schiller, Heine, and Wagner, as well as from Mozart's *Magic Flute* and Weber's *Freischütz*. Besides parodying Wagner, there is parody of Shakespeare's *Romeo and Juliet* and Goethe's *Faust*. In addition to Wagner's main characters, Nestroy presents such figures from opera as Figaro, Othello, Wilhelm Tell, and Aida. Wagner enjoyed the performance.[178]

The parodies of Wagner's opera are eloquent witnesses to its popularity, for parody assumes a knowledge of the original. The use of a leitmotif makes a similar assumption, since it invites one to interpret a new situation in terms of another which is already familiar. The first work to employ the legend in this way was the novel, *Der Tannhäuser* (1860), by Friedrich Hackländer. The work has a nineteenth-century setting and tells of a young painter's falling under

---

177 This was the title on the program and on the booklet which was printed for the actors. The version which appears in *Johann Nestroy, Sämtliche Werke. Historisch-kritische Gesamtausgabe in zwölf Bänden*, eds. Fritz Brukner and Otto Rommel (Wien: Anton Schroll, 1924-30), IV, 201-40, is slightly different and has the title, *Tannhäuser: Zukunftsposse mit vergangener Musik und gegenwärtigen Gruppierungen in drei Aufzügen*.

178 According to Georg Richard Kruse in his edition of Nestroy's *Tannhäuser: Zukunftsposse mit vergangener Musik und gegenwärtigen Gruppierungen in drei Aufzügen* (Leipzig: Reclam, 1904), p. 5.

the spell of the beautiful Princess Lubanoff, whose eyes have "etwas dämonisch Anziehendes." She takes him away from his friends, Wulf and Francesca, and becomes his patron, mistress, and agent. To keep him dependent on her, she sells his works under a name other than his own. He finally breaks with her and — poor, sick, and without reputation — journeys on foot to Rome. At St. Peter's he has a delirious vision of a boy who leads him away and gives him a laurel stick. He finds his old friends, who nurse him back to health, and begins to paint again. The laurel is planted and starts to grow, and Tannhäuser and Francesca are soon to be married. Wulf, whose name recalls that of Wolfram in the legend of the singers' contest and in Wagner's opera, plays his namesake's role of loyal friend and also that of Eckart, the warner. He frequently refers to the ballad and several times quotes from Heine's poem in order to remind Tannhäuser of the danger of his infatuation. The princess, whose name resembles the Russian word for love, is a sympathetic, though sinister figure. The hero, like the historical minnesinger, sings and plays an instrument. The blooming staff, since it is of laurel, takes on additional significance: Tannhäuser is forgiven and will become famous. This is Hackländer's contribution to the legend, for the rest he drew from the ballad, Heine, and Wagner.

The employment of the legend as a leitmotif and the name Tannhäuser as a symbol was repeated in other works of the later nineteenth century, among them two by the scholar and poet, Eduard Grisebach. *Der neue Tanhäuser* [sic] (1869) calls attention by means of the title to a dominant trait of the nineteenth-century hero. The work is a series of poems in the first person about the erotic experiences of a young man who sees an irresistible Venus in many women. The name of the title figure thus acquires connotations similar to, but not identical with those of Don Juan. The hero of Grisebach's verse novel, *Tanhäuser* [sic] *in Rom* (1875), is also a modern character and has the same nature. He becomes acquainted with a lady who is waiting for a divorce so that she can marry her lover. She and Tanhäuser are at once strongly attracted to each other, and he asks her to marry him. But, although her passion for him knows no restraint, she decides that she cannot forsake her lover. One night the despairing Tanhäuser is in the temple of Venus, and the statue of the goddess seems to awaken and look down sympathetically on him. In a niche in the wall there is an icon of the Virgin, and he feels her influence too. Venus and Mary represent to him body and soul, physical and spiritual love, and he feels torn between them. At last he renounces the former and declares his devotion to Mary. The same emotional conflict has already been seen in the lady, for she is at times a nymphomaniac, and once also called on Mary for aid.

In making the Tannhäuser figure a symbol of sexuality, Grisebach may have been influenced by Wagner, although the latter's hero is more complex. For other elements the author drew from the ballad and even from the verse of the minnesinger, as when he tells of the breaking of the hero's guitar string and discusses the strife between the Hohenstaufens and the pope. Moreover, he paraphrases a short passage from *Tristan* and compares his hero and heroine with those of Gottfried.

In the verse novel, *Tannhäuser. Ein Minnesang* (1880), by the popular exploiter of medieval lore, Julius Wolff, Tannhäuser is also described as one whose fate it is to love and be loved, a destiny foreshadowed by a vision of Venus which his mother saw before his birth. The work is set in the thirteenth century and is practically an encyclopedia of Middle High German literati. All of the important poets and many of the secondary and even obscure writers take part in the events recounted, and a great deal of medieval verse is mentioned, quoted, or altered for the author's own use. With regard to the hero, almost everything which any previous poet or scholar has associated with him has been included: the adventures ascribed to the historical Tannhäuser, the incidents of the ballad, the identity of Heinrich von Ofterdingen and the episodes of the singers' contest, and nearly all else that the legend has produced. To this a considerable amount of new invention has been added, interwoven with actual and fictionalized history. After many colorful experiences the hero, cursed by the pope, settles down in isolation to write his greatest work, *Das Nibelungslied*. The miracle of the blooming staff causes the lifting of the papal ban, but his name is to be expunged from all records and he cannot sign his masterpiece. Heinrich von Ofterdingen, alias Tannhäuser, leaves Germany to join the retinue of Emperor Friedrich II and is never heard of again.

Max Burckhard, then director of the Vienna Burgtheater, likewise used the form of the verse novel for his treatment of the legend. In *Das Lied vom Tannhäuser* (1889), he tells how the boy Tannhäuser, because of a feud, has to flee from his half-burned castle and support himself by wandering from court to court singing minnesongs. Later, as an errant knight with the army of Emperor Friedrich II, he takes part in the invasion of Denmark and in a crusade to the Holy Land. On the way home to his ancestral castle Tannhäuser is enticed into the Höllenberg, the realm of Dame Venus, where he spends a year. However, his insatiable quest for new experiences drives him back to the world outside. Venus permits him to be gone for a time, and says that he will be entirely free of his enchantment if he spends a year in a relationship of pure and unselfish love with an innocent girl. He finds such a one in a childhood sweetheart, but learns after several months that she has promised the Virgin never to marry. He manages to seduce her without changing her mind about her promise. In despair and remorse Tannhäuser journeys to the pope in a vain attempt to gain absolution. Returning home, he learns that his sweetheart has entered a nunnery to atone for her sin. He follows her there to ask her again to marry him, and, when she refuses, he gathers a band of outlaws, forces his way into the cloister — and finds that she has just died. He says farewell to the body of his sweetheart and goes off alone into the night. When messengers come from the pope, carrying the blooming staff, he cannot be found. Shepherds and hunters sometimes tell of seeing him on May nights, standing silently by as nymphs dance.

The influence of several writers, medieval and modern, can be seen in the novel. A long conversation with a hermit recalls that between Parzival and Trevrizent, while a tale the hermit relates was obviously borrowed from the Gretchen episode of *Faust*. The scene where the outlaws force their way into the cloister reminds one of Schiller's *Die Räuber*. And the identification of the Venus Mountain as the Höllenberg (or Hörselberg), the love triangle, and the death of Tannhäuser's sweetheart point to Wagner. New to the legend is the psychological state of Burckhard's hero after he leaves the Venus Mountain, for he is not merely burdened by a sense of guilt, but rather is driven by evil spirits as Orestes by the furies.

The love triangle is the only part of the legend to appear in Georg Hoecker's sentimental novel, *Der Tannhäuser* (1898), and only the title refers to the minnesinger or the hero of the ballad. The work has a contemporary setting. It tells of a haughty, selfish woman (the Venus figure) who steals the love of a young husband and father. After the death of his child and the attempted suicide of his wife, the hero throws off the enchantment of the other woman, and the young couple is completely reconciled. The Tannhäuser figure is not distinguished by strong sexualism or by a Faustian longing for experience and knowledge. His dominant characteristic is weakness.

The interest of the nineteenth century in the Tannhäuser theme spilled over into the first decades of the following century, but in general the legend has not appealed to more recent writers. Paul Eberhardt's *Tannhäuser. Eine Tragödie* (1912) continues the Romantic tradition in a drama that links the fate of Tannhäuser and his sweetheart with the struggle of Venus and Lucifer against God. The latter two — both sympathetic characters — are banished to the lower regions; the hero and heroine die, but their souls are saved. Two works of the fifties have a more contemporary spirit. *Der Tannhäuser. Spiel in drei Akten*, which concludes Julius Schütz' *Die tragische Trilogie* (1956), gives the story in retrospect as Tannhäuser, now a partly senile old man, returns home after many years of wandering. He is under the papal ban, and the emperor he has served is dead. While some young people dance, he plays his fiddle and sings a song which borrows a dozen or so lines from *Leiche* of the historical minnesinger. Later, while his imagination is calling forth people and episodes of the past, he dies. He does not believe that his connection with Venus has separated him from God. An early scene contains a Mignon-like character and a song which reflects Goethe's "Kennst du das Land, wo die Zitronen blühn." In the short story, "Tannhäuser im Chiemgau" (1959), Felix Fischer makes fun of Tannhäuser, the Tannhäuser legend, and the scholars who have developed impressive theories as to the life of the one and the origin of the other. His hero, Heinrich, is a younger member of a peasant family that lives in the village of Tann by the Tannberg. He doesn't want to be his brother's hired man, so he decides to become a priest. However, a wanton life ends his novitiate rather soon, and he finds support for a while at the court of Friedrich II of Austria. A Venus statue on a mountain not far from his home caused the mountain to be called the Venusberg and a farm nearby to be named the Venusberghof. Heinrich seduces the two daughters of a peasant who works the farm, and for this act is condemned to die. However, the hero insists on getting a judgment from Pope Urban IV in Rome, and is allowed to do so, but receives no absolution. When the pope's staff begins to grow, he sends messengers to look for Heinrich, who, however, did not return home and cannot be found. This, Fischer suggests, is the true history of the singer and the beginning of the legend. Stanzas from Tannhäuser's Songs X and XII and from Heine's "Tannhäuser" are included in the tale.

There are other twentieth-century works which treat Tannhäuser material, but the modern legend remains essentially a nineteenth-century, Romantic phenomenon. It differs from the medieval legend in that Tannhäuser sometimes assumes the identity of the Heinrich von Ofterdingen of the singers' contest, but more especially because of a shift of interest from the Venus Mountain to the character and motivations of the hero, especially with respect to the libido. In seeking a reason for Tannhäuser's leaving the Venus Mountain, Tieck finds that he cannot endure pleasure long and has an inherent need for pain. Heine develops this trait into a Faustian longing to experience all emotions, and adds the masochistic twist that the hero, though tortured by the pangs of love, does not really want the pope to free him. This motif of *l'amour fatale* appears in many subsequent treatments of the legend. However, a counter-development which justifies the sensual love of Tannhäuser as natural and healthy, as in Sallet's poem, can also be seen. Differing from the approaches of both Heine and Sallet is that of Grisebach, whose hero is simply oversexed. So too is Wolff's Tannhäuser, and his problem is complicated by the irresistible attraction he has for women. The mental state of Burckhard's hero is not dominated by the libido in itself, but his erotic experiences in the Venus Mountain have caused a general alienation from the world outside which is close to insanity. In some works, such as those by Hackländer, Grisebach, and Eberhardt, the Venus figure is as problematic and tragic as that of Tannhäuser.

In addition to the potentialities of the maladjusted hero, the legend offered a historical background which was particularly appealing to many writers of the period which preceded and followed the re-establishment of the German Empire in 1871. Among the novels about the remote German past which flooded the book market were many that dealt with the Hohenstaufens, and either the Tannhäuser reflected in the verse of the minnesinger or the hero of the ballad could offer a suitable foil to display the political or literary history of those times. The works by Franckel and Wolff are among the best examples of this use of the Tannhäuser theme, but it appears in many others.

Just as the medieval legend influenced and was in turn influenced by the stories of the Italian sibyl, Melusina, and magically prolonged sleep, the Romantic Tannhäuser legend was affected by subjects of a like nature. One, of course, was that dealing with the singer's contest, another was *Faust*. One can see in most of the longer Tannhäuser works similarities to Goethe's poem in the character of the hero, in the language, and in individual episodes. There are prologues of devils and deities, pacts, Gretchens, *Walpurgnisnächte*, and associations with emperors. And it is probably due to the influence of *Faust* that most treatments of the legend are in verse. The borrowings from *Faust* result from a basic resemblance in the situations of Goethe's hero and that of the ballad. The souls of both are the prizes in a conflict which involves not only their own volitions, but also superhuman forces: God and Mephisto, Mary and Venus. There are many works which have been affected by the Romantic Tannhäuser legend without having become a part of it. The best known of these are Hauptmann's *Versunkene Glocke*, whose hero, Heinrich, falls under the spell of a mountain peopled by heathen spirits; Mann's *Zauberberg*, the spirits of which are psychological, rather than corporeal; and Mann's *Tod in Venedig*, where the Venus figure is a boy.

If it is surprising that a medieval ballad about a heathen goddess, a penitent, and a blooming staff should have a significant impact on modern literature, it is no less so that the ballad itself should become an authentic modern folksong. Since the beginning of the nineteenth century, twenty-seven versions have been collected by folklorists (five since 1935), many with their melodies, some from purely oral sources.[179] All have come from the South and Southeast: eight from Switzerland, seventeen from Austria, and two from Bohemia. The Swiss variants are older and stem from one or more printed versions of the sixteenth or seventeenth centuries. The Austrian-Bohemian songs apparently go back to a common source of the early nineteenth century.

The two groups differ primarily in that the former have added to and the latter subtracted from the original. Drawing from the Melusine legend and from tales of the Italian sibyl, several Swiss songs tell of inhabitants of the Venus Mountain who turn to snakes on Sundays; one reports of creatures there who are women from the waist up, but like snakes and toads below; another borrows a motif from the legend of the enchanted emperor and ends with Tannhäuser sleeping at a stone table in the mountain: when his beard grows around it three times, Judgment Day will come. Other additions include magically accelerated time — a year in the mountain is like an hour — and the statement that Tannhäuser remained there for seven years before going to Rome. The dialogue between Tannhäuser and Venus is considerably shortened in the Swiss songs, but in most cases is not omitted.

The Austrian, Bohemian, and one of the Swiss versions are only penitent songs, with no reference to Venus or the nature of the sin. Some do not give the sinner's name, and the only vestige of the Venus Mountain is in the fact that most of them have the hero die on a high mountain. The pope is never damned, and in several cases is described as being unable to help. Christ is the one who brings

---

179 Meier, pp. 145-61, and Leopold Schmidt, "Zur österreichischen Form der Tannhäuser-Ballade," *Jahrbuch des österreichischen Volksliedwerkes,* 1 (1925), 9-18, give the fullest accounts of recent acquisitions.

about the miracle of the blooming staff, and some variants have him announce the sinner's redemption. One of the latest to be collected reduces the ballad to only four stanzas: the first tells of the sinner's decision to go to Rome and confess, another of the pope's wrath, the third of the condition set for salvation, and the last of the blooming of the staff. A further development is revealed in a song first printed in 1930, which leaves out the pope and substitutes a dead tree for the staff: Jesus tells an unnamed sinner that he is to kneel for seven years under the tree and that he will be forgiven when it becomes green. The specifically medieval ballad has become no more than a brief parable illustrating God's willingness to forgive a repentant sinner. The trend of the oral tradition thus parallels the literary tendency to drop characteristic details of the legend and concentrate on the psychology of the hero. This development foreshadows the end of the legend as such, for the details are what give it identity. An examination of the more recent literary treatments of the Tannhäuser material shows, however, that while the legend has become thinner and less frequently used, writers have demonstrated an increased familiarity with the works of the minnesinger himself. If the demise of the legendary Tannhäuser is accompanied by a rediscovery of the poet, literature will gain more than it loses. For Tannhäuser's ironical humor enabled him to look at the conventions of his day in much the same way as we do and he treated them with an enjoyable irreverence. The poet was more modern than the hero of the ballad, and, when allowed to speak for himself without the interpretation of scholars, should find an appreciative and lasting audience.

TANNHÄUSER'S VERSE

Manesse Manuscript[180]

I

(f. 264^(va)) Uns kvmt ein wunneklichu zit.
des froit sich alles dc dir ist.
Du manigem hohgemvte git.
so wol dir meie dc dv bist.

5 so rehte wunnekliche komen.
dc ist mines herzen spil.
wir han dc alle wol vernomen.
wie der furste leben wil.

In osterriche vnd anderswa.
10 wil er behalden ie den pris.
Beide hie dort vnd da.
ist er an allen dingen wis.

Er hat sin ding vollebraht also.
dc man dem werden danken mvs.
15 er mag wol iemer wesen fro.
swem er da butet sinen grus.

Mit eren richet er der helt.
von iar zeiare bc vnd bas.
In weis ob irs geloben welt.
20 er lat es niht durh smehen has.

Nach siner wirde in nieman gar geloben kan.
Swc er getut wer getar sich des genemen an.

For us a wondrous time's begun,
so all the world around is gay;
it gives delight to everyone.
You should be praised for this, O May,

5   that with such splendor you appear;
it's the pleasure of my heart!
One thing indeed we all did hear:
how the prince would play his part.

Inside of Austria and out
10   he'll surely always take the prize,
for here as in the lands about
in all things he is skilled and wise.

The justice which he gives is such
as merit thanks. The man has cause
15   to be delighted very much
who's subject to his court and laws.

Each year better than the past,
with honor does our champion reign.
Though you may doubt that it can last,
20   he'll never cease through mean disdain.

The praise he merits can't be told by anyone.
Who would presume to claim the deeds which he has done?

---

181 In making the translations, the textual emendations of Siebert, *Der Dichter Tann-häuser*; S. Singer, *Tannhäuser* (Tübingen: Mohr, 1922); G. Rosenhagen, rev. of Tann-häuser, by S. Singer, *ZfdPh*, 51 (1926), 351-53; Anton Wallner, "Tannhäuser-Kri-tik," *ZfdA*, 71 (1934), 213-26, and "Tannhäuser," *ZfdA*, 72 (1935), 278-80, have been examined, but with a very few exceptions the translator preferred to follow the medieval scribe.
Several of Tannhäuser's poems have previously been translated into English. Bayard Quincy Morgan in *A Critical Bibliography of German Literature in English Transla-tion 1481-1927*, rev. ed. (1938; rpt. New York and London: Scarecrow Press, 1965), lists seven anthologies which include one to three poems by Tannhäuser. Morgan's *A Critical Bibliography of German Literature in English Translation: Supplement Embracing the Years 1928-1955* (New York and London: Scarecrow Press, 1965) lists no translations of poems by Tannhäuser.

Der habe ich noch bi minen tagen niht vil gesehen.
des hört man ime die wisen vnd die besten iehen.
25 Si slafent noch er weket si des dunket mih.
es wc ein spil gar vnz an her nv hůten sich.

Dc si den helt erzůrnen niht.
dc ist min rat es mag geschaden.
In weis ob sis gelŏbent iht.
30 si sint mit im gar vberladen.

vnd můssen alle wichen vor.
swa er vert hin mit siner schar.
er sweibet ob in hoh embor.
vil schone alsam ein adelar.

35 Sinem rate bin ich holt er lêret niht wan werdekeit.
sin widerratent niht sin ere die sint vollekliche breit.
er hat vnd mag vnd getar getůn der stolze waleis vnverzaget.
wer lebt von dem man nv so vil der wunderlichen dinge saget.
Er hat niht wandels vmb ein har.
40 swas er geredet dc lat er war.

Mit im so varnt ivden cristen kriechen valwen heiden vil.
vnger půlan rússen behein swer eht schone leben wil.
Der ist behalden swannen er vert bi im ist er ein fromer man.
Manigen armen er beratet ich hebe an mir selben an.
45 da bi schaffet er den besten vride vber ellů sinů lant.
gůten kŏf vmbe alles ding er wendet rŏb vnd brant.

Sin herze blůt alsam ein bŏn.
der zallen ziten frŏide birt.
Ir aller milte ist gar ein trŏn.
50 wider im er ist der eren wirt.
Min gelŏbe ist dc swer in zer wochen eines mag gesehen.
dc dem vngelúkes niht enkeiner slahte mag geschehen.

I've witnessed little of such things in all my days
as wise and good men say of him in praise.
25 His foes still sleep; he'll wake them up, it seems to me.
It was a game till now, but they'd do well to see

our hero's anger be not stirred,
for truly it could do them harm.
I know not if they'll take my word,
30 but they're not equal to his arm

and all of them must soon fall back
when he leads forth his warrior band.
He'll hover o'er them to attack
as does an eagle, swift and grand.

35 I like his counsel, he instructs in excellence and naught beside.
None venture to deny his fame, for it is carried far and wide.
He can and will and dares to act, this knightly hero, proud and bold.
What man is living now of whom so many wondrous things are told?
Constant and faultless through and through,
40 he makes his promises come true.

With him march Christians, Jews, Walachians, Greeks, and many an
infidel,
Hungarians, Poles, Bohemians, Russians; whoever wishes to live well
can gain the lord's support and be, whene'er with him, an honored guest.
He gives assistance to the poor; I'll name myself before the rest.
45 What's more, he's taken care that all within his lands may live in peace,
that costs of everything are fair, that robbery and burning cease.

His heart blooms always, like a tree
which every season bears delight,
and others' gifts are fantasy
50 compared to those of honor's knight.
Whoever gets to see him once a week, so I believe,
will suffer no misfortune nor have any cause to grieve.

er mag wol heissen friderich.
es wirt ab*er* niem*er* sin gelich.
(264*vb*) In kurzen zite*n* dc geschiht.
dc ma*n* wol eine krone.
schone vf sine*m* hobte siht.
so vert der furste schone.

Er ist vnser wu*n*ne.
60 glanz alsam du svnne.
so ist sin tvge*n*thafter lib
milt vn*d* erebere.
ellu wol getane*n* wib.
fragent vo*n* im mere.

65 Vo*n* de*m* gute*n*.
wol gemvte*n*.
vragent si vil dike bi de*m* rine.
Allenthalbe*n*.
vf dien albe*n*.
70 lopt ma*n* in wol vn*d* die sine.

Vf dem wasser vn*d* de*m* plane ist er so v*er*messen.
in weis niht des an de*m* dege*n* iend*er* si v*er*gessen.
Trurig h*er*ze fro.
wirt vo*n* im swa*n*ne er singet dien frowe*n* de*n* reigen.
75 So hilfe ich im so.
dc ich singe mit im zaller zit gerne de*n* meien.

Sin schimpf d*er* ist gut.
wan er git.
zaller zit.
80 mit eren d*er* reine.
Da bi hoh gemvt.
offe*n*bar-
lich getar.
sin gut dc ist gemeine.

Friedrich,[182] he well deserves the name!
No one will ever match his fame.
55 Indeed, it won't be long from now
until a crown will be
gleaming brightly on his brow;
he rules so righteously.

He's our happiness.
60 His virtues are not less
in splendor than the glowing sun.
Noble, kind, and fair:
the lovely ladies, every one
discuss him everywhere.

65 Of the adored,
good-natured lord
they often speak along the Rhine.
On every hand
in the Alpine land
70 praises of him and his combine.

Upon the sea as well as on the land his acts are daring.
I know of nothing lacking in his spirit or his bearing.
Sad hearts soon are gay
when he sings out the dances to which the ladies spring.
75 I help him in this way,
that of the Maytime with him I continually sing.

The sport is fine
which through the year
the noble peer
80 so well can show:
this gay prince of mine.
Indeed, it's plain
his wealth can maintain
such fetes — as all should know.

---

[182] Friedrich: great in peace.

90 er ist zallen ziten fro.
im zimt wol dc lachen.
dc kan er vil sv̊sse also
wol mit frȏiden machen.

Vest alsam ein adamant.
95 swa mans sol beherten.
Sin lop vert dur ellv̊ lant.
dc kan nieman scherten.

Lobe in ieman bc danne ich.
der sol des geniessen.
100 alle singer dvnket mich.
mv̊ste sin verdriessen.

Nv dar.
dv̇ schar.
wirt aber michel, komen wir zesamne in der gasse von dien strassen.

105 Nv dan.
ich kan.
noch wunder machen. des ich niht wil lassen.

Mit mir.
svlt ir.
110 komen vf den anger. da man die ivngen mit scharen siht zv̊ sigen.

Da sint.
dv̇ kint.
vor dien man mv̊s beide flȏiten vnd gigen.

Wa ist nv dv̇ gv̊te.
115 mit ir pfawen hv̊te.
der vergisse ich niemer.
solde ich leben iemer.

bi der linden.
sol man vinden.
120 vns bi schonen kinden.

90 He is always light of heart.
Joy is what he's after,
and with glee and charming art
he calls forth merry laughter.

Constant as a precious stone
95 where'er one may obtain it,
his fame in every land is known.
No enemy can stain it.

Who may better praise this knight
should gain by his endeavor,
100 but there's no singer, in his sight,
I think, who would seem clever.

Come along!
The throng
will get much larger when we come together at the corner of the street.

105 Let's go!
I'll show
I still can work some wonders when we meet.

Then you
and I, too,
110 will be upon the green when groups of youths and maidens come
from all around.

Among
the young
folks there the fiddle and the flute shall sound.

Where's my loved one at
115 with her peacock hat?
I'll forget her never,
should I live forever.

We shall be
'neath the linden tree
120 in youthful company.

da svln wir singe*n*.
vn*d* springe*n*
da sol vns gelinge*n*.

Ja. wa. lat si sich vinden.
125 sa. da. bi den schone*n* kinde*n*.

Da sol niema*n* sin vnfro.
da d*er* tanhusere.
Reiget mit d*er* liebe*n* so.
dc w*ere*   im ein sw*ere*.

130 w*ere* da niht fro kunigvnt.
mit ir reide*n* loken.
du treit eine*n* rote*n* mv*n*t.
dc sint svm*er*token.

da wirt mazze.
135 mir ze drazze.
lofet si mir vor mit de*m* balle.
Gvtel gvtel.
mache ein mvtel.
dc es mir vn*d* dir wol gevalle.

140 vf vf kint pruuet dc lebe*n*.
sit vns got de*n* lib hat gegebe*n*.
So svln wir singe*n*.
froliche springe*n*.

II

(265*ra*) Went ir in ganze*n* froide*n* sin.
so wil ich u tvn helfe schin.
vn*d* sit ir fro so frowe ich mich.
sit wir de*n* svmer han gesehe*n*.
5 Du heide stat gar wu*n*neklich.
des mvs ma*n* ir vo*n* schulde*n* iehe*n*.

There we'll sing,
dance, and spring,
not wanting anything.

Oh where   might   my sweetheart tarry?
125 She's there   right   among the youth so merry.

None should be unhappy when
Tannhäuser with such vim
dances with his dear again.
It would be hard for him

130 were Dame Kunigund not there
with her lovely curls
and her lips, so red and fair.
These are pretty girls!

Matze, she's
135 who likes to tease
when she runs before me with the ball.
Gutel, let
your mind be set
on what brings joy to you and me and all.

140 Come, young folks, taste it, life is sweet!
And since God gave us voice and feet,
we'll seize this chance
to sing and dance.

II

If you are seeking merriment,
I'll try to see that you're content,
for I'll be pleased at your delight.
Since we have seen the summer days
5 the heath has been a wondrous sight
and well does it deserve our praise.

Dur kurzewile ich kan gegan.
vf eine grŭne heide breit.
Dc wc so wuñneklich der plan.
10   dc mir swant min herzeleit.

da hort ich die vogel frŏwen.
sich der wuñneklichen zit.
dc kan von den sv̈ssen dŏwen.
dc si svngen wider strit.

15   Ich hort da vil manigen don.
von den kleinen vogellin.
Dů heide gab in senften lon.
mit manigerhande blŭmen schin.

der selben blŭmen brach ich vil.
20   al da ichs vf der heide sach.
Es duhte mich ein senftes spil.
ein aventŭre mir geschah.

Da von min herze in frŏiden was.
vnd iemer mv̈s in frŏiden sin.
25   Ich sach durh dc grŭne gras.
gan ein vil schones megetin.

Min herze dc wart frŏiden rich.
do ich die schonen erest sach.
Si duhte mich so miñnenklich.
30   dc ich mich ir fŭr eigen iach.

vnd ich ir also nahe kan.
dc ich ir bot den minen grŭs.
vnd si min rehte war genan.
do wart mir aller sorgen bŭs.

35   Ahy wie dů vil liebe erschrac.
do min dů schone wart gewar.
Da wc so wuñneklich der tag.
Si trŭg ein schapel rosevar.

Pleasure bent I wandered where
the heath extended, broad and green.
My sorrow quickly vanished there,
10   so gay and lovely was the scene.

I heard the birds rejoicing too
and loudly hail the wondrous day.
Drunk with sweet wine of morning dew,
they had to vie in song this way.

15   I heard the merry music swell
of all the little birds combined.
The radiant heath repaid them well
with blooming flowers of every kind.

Upon the heath I gathered then
20   some of the many I could see
and thought it very pleasant when
a rare event occurred to me.

My heart was filled with joy therefrom
and happiness which ne'er shall pass.
25   I saw a pretty maiden come
across a greening field of grass.

When I beheld her in the glade
with joy my heart began to stir.
I thought her such a lovely maid
30   that I'd belong to none but her.

When I was close enough that I
could speak a word of greeting there,
and she saw who was passing by,
then I was free of every care.

35   The dear was startled, I must say,
to see me there upon the heath.
So bright and lovely was the day,
she wore a leafy, rosy wreath.

Schoner creatúre ich nie gesach
40 so rehte wol gestalt.
Da si vf der heide gie.
bi ir so wurde ich niemer alt.

Ich sprach der minneklichen zv̊.
wie sit sus eine komen ir.
45 Her an disem morgen frů.
si sprach ir svlt gelŏben mir.

Dur senften luft ich in dem tŏwe
her nah rosen blůmen gie.
Ich sprach minnekliche frowe
50 din genade sv̊che ich hie.

an sie bewande ich min gemv̊te.
vnd darzů mis herzen sin.
Frowe dur din selber gv̊te.
nim min herze mit dir hin.

55 Dc enpfa mit dinem lone.
du bist aller tvgenden vol.
Frowe mines herzen krone.
so dc geschiht so tůst dv wol.

Da wir sament in den kle.
60 traten vns wc sanfte we.
Die schonen drvhte ich her ze mir.
si glei dc es vil lute erhal.
Ir roten mvnt den kvste ich ir.
si sprach ir bringent mich in schal.

65 alsus wart ich ir redegeselle.
ich nam si bi der wissen hant.
von vns wart ein gůt gevelle.
mir wart herzeliebe erkant.

I've never seen a fairer creature
40 than she when walking through the heather.
So beautiful was every feature!
I'd ne'er grow old were we together.

I spoke to her, the fairest born,
"Why have you come out here alone
45 so early on this summer morn?"
She said, "Believe me, I must own,

because of the dew and gentle breeze
I came for roses to this place."
"Lovely lady, if you please,"
50 I said, "I seek to gain your grace."

To her I turned my thoughts and mind
and all the feeling that I know:
"Lady, since you are so kind,
take my heart with you when you go.

55 Take it for that which you will give.
In every manner you excel.
Lady fair, for whom I live,
if you'll accept it, you'll do well."

As we wandered through the flowers
60 a tender, joyful pain was ours.
I pressed the beauty close to me
and heard a startled cry ring out.
I kissed her rosy lips, and she
exclaimed, "You'll get me talked about."

65 We thus became the best of friends,
and in my arms I held her tight.
We seized the pleasure fortune sends
and I discovered love's delight.

Nieman kan geprůuen niht
was steter frőide bi vns was.
Wan dem soliches heil geschiht.
der sol gelŏben deste bas.

der nie herzeleit gewan.
der ge mit frőiden disen tanz.
75 Ob im sin herze von minne enbran.
der sol von rosen einen kranz.

Tragen der git hoh gemv̊te.
ob sin herze frőide gert.
vnd gedenke an frowen gůte.
80 so wirt er vil wol gewert.

Si git frőide michels me.
danne des vil lieben meien blůt.
al die blv̊men vnd kle.
ir sv̊sser name der ist so gůt.

85 Dc habe ich vil wol befvnden.
an der lieben frowen min.
wol der minneklichen stunden.
dc ich sach ir ŏgen schin.

Vnd ich in ir minnebanden
90 also sere gestriket wart.
Mit armen vnd mit wîssen handen.
wol der minnenklichen vart.

Da ist si gerivelieret.
grůne heide
95 Mit cleinen velden wol gezieret.
an ir stât aller min gedank.

Dem tanze svln wir vrlob geben
wan er schiere ein ende hat.
vnd svln in hohem mv̊te leben.
100 megede ir hant es minen rat.

No one can tell the happiness
70 which then was ours except the one
whom fate has given like success,
for he believes what love has done.

He to whom love's grief ne'er came
is one who should dance gaily now.
75 If love has set his heart aflame,
then he shall wear upon his brow

a wreath of roses, which can fill
with pride. And if his heart seeks pleasure
and dwells on womanly goodwill,
80 he'll be rewarded in full measure.

Love gives greater joy moreover
than does the blossoming of May:
all the flowers and the clover.
It's wonderful in every way.

85 Well did I learn the truth of this
with my dear lady whom I prize.
I bless the lovely hour of bliss
when first I looked into her eyes

and in love's strong, unyielding bands
90 became so hopelessly ensnared
(my lady's arms and fair, white hands).
Blessed be the path of love we shared!

There it winds through light and shade,
green heath [lacuna]
95 adorned with blooming field and glade.
My every thought is fixed thereon.

Now to the dance we'll say goodbye,
its end approaches and is here,
but we must keep our spirits high;
100 to my advice, you maids, give ear:

valsches truren werfent hin.
mit zühten sult ir wesen fro.
Gewinnen wir der selben sin.
so svlen wir mit in tůn also.

III

Der winter ist zergangen.
dc prüfe ich vf der heide.
Al dar kan ich gegangen.
gůt wart min ŏgenweide.

5 Uon den blůmen wol getan.
wer sach ie so schonen plan.
Der brach ich zeinem kranze.
den trůg ich mit zhoie zů den frowen an dem tanze.
Welle ieman werden hohgemůt. der hebe sich vf die schanze.

10 Da stat viol vnd kle.
svmerlatten camandre.
die werden zitelosen.
Oster cloien vant ich da die lilien vnd die rosen.
Do wunschte ich das ich sant miner frowen solte kosen.

15 Si gab mir an ir den pris.
dc ich were ir dulz amis.
mit dienste disen meien.
dur si so wil ich reigen.

Ein fores stůnt da nahen.
20 al dar bevnde ich gahen.
da horte ich mich enpfahen.
die vogel also sůsse.
so wol dem selben grůsse.

110

throw false sorrowing away!
Be joyful, but be modest too.
And when our thoughts are light and gay
then we shall act the same as you.

III

The winter has gone to stay,
the heath now blooms anew,
and when I went that way
I had a wondrous view

5   of the flowers on every hand.
Who has seen such meadowland!
I picked blooms for a wreath
and gaily took it where the ladies danced upon the heath.
Come all who look for joy and see what fortune may bequeath!

10   Germanders, violets, and clover,
new shoots springing up all over,
the crocuses were there,
Easter lilies, irises, and roses everywhere,
and I resolved to have a chat then with my lady fair.

15   She'd said that I might be
her friend and dear ami,
to serve her on this May.
I'll dance for her today.

A wood was standing near.
20   I entered and could hear
a greeting, sweet and clear,
from many a little bird.
What a lovely song I heard!

Ich horte da wol zhantieren.
25 die nahtegal tŏbieren.
al da mů̊ste ich parlieren.
zerehte wie mir were.
ich was ane alle swere.

Ein rifiere ich da gesach.
30 dvrh den fores gieng ein bach.
zetal vber ein planůre.
ich sleich ir nach vnz ich si vant. die schonen creatůre.
(265ᵛᵃ) bi dem fontane sas dů̇ clare dv̇ sů̊se von fanůre.

Ir ŏgen lieht vnd wol gestalt.
35 si was an sprůchen niht zebalt.
wan mehte si wol liden.
Ir mvnt ist rot ir kele ist blank.
ir har reit val ze mâsse lank.
gevar alsam die siden.
40 Solde ich vor ir ligen tot. in mehte ir niht vermiden.

Blank alsam ein hermelin.
waren ir dů̇ ermelin.
·ir persone dv̇ wc smal.
wol geschaffen vber al.

45 ein lů̇zel grande wc si da.
wol geschaffen anderswa.
an ir ist niht vergessen.
lindů̇ diehel slehtů̇ bein. ir fů̊sse wol gemessen.
Schoner forme ich nie gesach. dů̇ min cor hat besessen.
50 an ir ist ellů̇ volle.
do ich die werden erest sach do hů̊b sich min parolle.

Ich wart fro.
vnd sprach do.
frowe min.
55 ich bin din. dv bist min.
der strit der mv̊sse iemer sin.

112

I listened to the hail
25 of the fluting nightingale
and wished to tell my tale,
just how I felt and why;
my spirits then were high.

Soon I saw the water gleam
30 where through the forest passed a stream
and flowed across a glade.
I stole along her trail until I found the lovely maid
as she was sitting by the spring so prettily arrayed.

Her eyes were beautiful and bright;
35 she never said more than was right,
and was a joy to know.
Her lips were red; her throat was bare
and white; her long, blond, curly hair
sent forth a silken glow.
40 If it should even cost my life, I would not let her go.

Her pretty arms were slim and were
just as white as ermine fur.
Her figure was both slight and small,
and well-proportioned overall.

45 One place a little larger size,
but she was slender otherwise;
neglected was no part:
her thighs were soft, her legs were straight, her feet a work of art.
I never saw a fairer form and it has seized my heart.
50 It's perfect in every way.
When I saw this beauty I spoke up without delay.

I was gay
and spoke this way:
"Lady mine,
55 I am thine,   thou art mine,
each the other must confine.

Du bist mir vor in allen.
iemer an dem herzen min. mv̊st dv mir wol gevallen.
Swa man frowen prv̊uen sol. da mv̊s ich vůr dich schallen.

60　an hůbsch vnd ȯch an gůte.
dv gist aller contrate mit zhoie ein hoh gemv̊te.

Ich sprach der minneklichen zů.
got vnd anders nieman tů.
der dich behůten mv̊sse.
65　ir parol der was sv̊sse.

Sa neic ich der schonen do.
ich wart an minem libe vro.
da von ich ir saluieren.
si bat mich ir zhantieren.
70　von der linden esten.
vnd von des meigen glesten.

da dů tauelrvnde wc.
da wir do schone waren.
dc wc lŏp dar vnder gras
75　si kvnde wol gebaren.

Da wc niht massenie me.
wan wir zwei dort in einem kle.
si leiste dc si da solde.
vnd tet dc ich da wolde.

80　Ich tet ir vil sanfte we.
Ich wůnsche dc es noch erge.
Ir zimt wol dc lachen.
do begvnden wir beide do ein gemellichens machen.
das geschah von liebe vnd ȯch von wunderlichen sachen.

85　von amv̊re seit ich ir.
dc vergalt si dulze mir.
si iach si litte es gerne.
dc ich ir tete als man den frowen tůt dort in palerne.

You're first in every thing
for me, and you will always please me so my heart will sing.
Wherever womankind is judged I'll let your praises ring.
60   Your beauty and goodness too
are such that every land has more of joy because of you."

This I told the lovely one:
"I hope that God alone and none
is guarding you, but He."
65   Her reply was sweet to me.

I bowed to her in thanks at this,
for heart and soul were filled with bliss
that she should greet me well.
She bade me sing and tell
70   about the linden bough
and May's bright colors now.

Then was our Round Table spread on the heath
where we were surrounded with splendor,
with leaves above and grass beneath.
75   Her manner was friendly and tender.

There was no court society
in the blooming clover there but we.
She did as I thought good
and what a lady should.

80   I caused her very pleasant pain.
I'd like to do it all again;
none laughs as she at court.
We two began to play a game, a most delightful sport,
because of love and curious feelings of another sort.

85   I spoke to her of love's delight
and sweetly she repaid her knight.
She said, she'd gladly bear
from me that which one does to other ladies everywhere.

dc da geschach da denke ich an.
90   si wart min trut vnd ich ir man.
wol mich der aventüre.
erst iemer selig der si siht.
sit dc man ir des besten giht.
sist also gehüre.
95   ellü granze da geschach. von vns vf der planüre.

Ist iemen dem gelinge bc.
dc lâsse ich ane has.
Si wc so hohes mútes.
dc ich vergas der sinne.
100   got lone ir alles gútes.
so twinget mich ir minne.

(265ᵛᵇ)   wc ist dc si mir tût.
alles gût.   hohen mût.
habe ich von ir iemer.
105   in vergisse ir niemer.

Wol vf adelheit.
dv solt sant mir sin gemeit.
wol vf wol vf irmengart.
dv mûst aber an die vart.
110   dû da niht enspringet dû treit ein kint.
sich frôwent algemeine die dir sint.

Dort hôre ich die flôiten wegen.
hie hôre ich den svmber regen.
Der vns helfe singen.
115   disen reigen springen.
dem mvsse wol gelingen.
zallen sinen dingen.

wa sint nv die ivngen kint.
dc si bi vns niht ensint.
120   Sor ie so selig si min künigvnt.
solt ich si küssen tusent stunt.
an ir vil rose varwen mvnt.
so were ich iemer me gesvnt.

The memory will never fade
90 of us two lovers in the glade.
Such fortune then was mine!
Whoever looks at her is blessed,
since all say she's the very best.
My darling is so sweet!
95 There on the heath without restraint we made our love complete.

Were someone's fortune better still,
I'm sure, I'd never take it ill.
Her spirits were so high
that mine were quite enraptured.
100 God bless her, as do I
whom love has fully captured.

What did she give me when she could?
All that's good.   And I should
have joy from her forever.
105 I'll forget her never.

Come on, come, Adelaide, away,
for we'll have merriment today.
And hurry, Irmgard, don't be slow!
The time has come for you to go.
110 Who doesn't dance must be with child.
By merriment are all beguiled.

There I hear the flutes awaking,
here the tambourines are shaking.
Who would help us sing
115 and in the dances spring,
to him the fates must bring
success in everything.

Where are now the maidens dear
that they should not be with us here?
120 Blessed may my Kunigund be!
A thousand kisses as a fee
on lips which bloom so rosily
and I'd forever more be free.

dü mir dc he*r*ze hat *ve*rwu*n*t.

125 vaste vnz vf de*r* mi*n*ne gru*n*t.

Der ist enzwei.

heia nv hei.

des fidelleres seite der ist enzwei.

IV

Ich lobe ein wib dü ist noch besser da*n*ne gůt.

sist schone vn*d* ist schone*r* vil vn*d* hohgemv̊t.

si hat vor alle*n* valschen dinge*n* sich behv̊t.

Ich gehorte nie wib so wol gelobe*n* als ma*n* si tůt.

5 Ysalde wart so schône nie.

noch trone dü ei*n* gúttin wc.

Medea swc dü noch ie begie.

des half ir mit wisheit fro pallas.

Juno gab richeit dur die mi*n*ne hóre ich iehe*n*.

10 swc dydo hatte dc wart geteilet vbe*r* al.

Latricia dü lie sich tȯge*n*lichen sehe*n*.

Palatrica de*n* frowe*n* vil de*r* kinde stal.

Helena wc eins kv̇niges wib.

zů de*r* kam ein discordia.

15 Dc gieng in ȯch beide*n* an de*n* lib.

des engalt ȯch amarodia.

Es schv̊f ein wib dc troia wart

zerstóret. dü hies avenant.

Lunet dü wc vo*n* hohe*r* art.

20 ir vatter de*r* hies willebrant.

Venus ei*n* apfel wart gegebe*n*.

da vo*n* so hůb sich michel not.

dar vmbe gap paris sin lebe*n*.

da lag ȯch menalavs tot.

She has wounded my heart for me
125   down to the bottom of love's sea.
It broke in two.
O! What's to do!
The fiddler's string is broken too.

IV

The woman I extoll is kinder yet than kind,
she's fair and more than fair and of a noble mind,
she's kept herself from all that falseness has designed,
her praise leaves that of other women far behind.

  5 Isolde never was so fair,
nor Trone, a goddess and a maid.
Medea, too, could not compare,
for all of wise Athena's aid.

In hope of winning love did Juno give great wealth;
10 and all that Dido had she gave, as I've heard say.
Latricia was seen in secret and by stealth;
Palatrica stole many a lady's child away.

Helen was married to a king;
to her appeared Discordia,
15 which proved for both a deadly thing,
also for Amarodia.

A woman once caused Troy to be
destroyed. They called her Avenant.
Lunette was of nobility;
20 her father's name was Willebrant.

To Venus was an apple given
which brought distress on every head.
From life was Paris rudely driven
and Menelaus too lay dead.

9

25 Sibille wc ein vil listig wib.
bi der amabilia.
Si rieten vf senatoren lip.
dc tet dů leide inuidia.

Fro planzhiflůr dv̇ was allen dingen klůk.
30 Dar vmbe walheis sit vil lange wart vertriben.
Cawan der den anker werdekliche trůg.
der klegte dc ywin in dem fores wc beliben.

Sarmena klegte grôs vngemach.
dc Camv̇ret als mv̊ssig sas.
35 ze Cvraze si do mit zorne sprach.
da lanzlet sich des vermas.

dc er mich reche an parcifale.
der hectore sin veste brach.
(266ʳᵃ) Er nam ze karidol den gral.
40 da des achilles niht en rach.

so richet es mir galogriant.
Swas opris mir zeleide tůt.
tyspe was elyon bekant.
gegen piramus stůnt ir mv̊t.
45 Dů clare amye sprach zir massenie so.
Min gvmpenie sol der stŏrie wesen vro.

Ginofer vs britanie lant.
die artus hat ze wibe erkorn.
die man in hoher zhoie ie vant.
50 der brahte vs prouenzal ein horn.

von portigal ein pezhelier. dc wc so wunderlicher art.
swer dar vs trank der wandel hete. dc er da mit begossen wart.
Porthtram dů was von lunders so geborn her.
das schůf der wigol gegen dem prouenzal ein sper.

55 her wigamv̇r da vor Camvoleis.
wol tet ers als wirs han vernomen.

120

25 The woman Sibyl was very wise;
so too was Amabilia.
Of senators would they advise;
as did the base Invidia.

That Blanchefleur in all was fair is thus revealed
30 that Walheis long was banned from home and comfortless.
Gawain, who nobly wore an anchor on his shield,
was grieved that Iwein did not leave the wilderness.

Sarmena once was greatly pained
that Gahmuret should be so cold;
35 to Curaz she with wrath complained:
"When Lancelot was overbold,

he would revenge me on Parzival,
who took to Karidol the grail
and broke down Hector's city wall
40 (Achilles was of no avail),

as Galogriant avenges me
for that which Opris now has done."
Thisbe wanted Pyramus; she
was also known to Elion.
45 This ladylove addressed her retinue:
"You'll like the entertainment planned for you."

She who became King Arthur's wife,
Brittany's fair Guinevere
who always led a merry life,
50 received from a Portuguese chevalier

a Provençal enchanted horn the wondrous powers of which were thus
that it spilled wine on those who drank therefrom and were not virtuous.
Porhtram of Lunders' race was so esteemed by all
that Wigol brought a spear against the Provençal.

55 Sir Wigamur did well at Kamvoleis,
as we have oft heard men declare.

gegen dem so hielt her wigoleis.
der was den vrowen zedienste komen.

Tristran erwarb die künigin
60 von Marroch als wir hören sagen.
Ein mörin wc du̇ heidenin.
der alden svln wir hie gedagen.

vnd loben min gůten.
Die reinen wol gemůten.
65 Swa si gat an dem tanze.[183]
mit ir rôsen kranze.
dar obe ein ander krenzel.
ein wis gevalden swenzel.
Ir har gelich dem golde.
70 als es got wu̇nschen solde.
Chrus alsam die siden.
wan mehte si wol liden.
Swa minne wer genême.
du̇ liebe da wol zeme.

75 von orient
vnz ze occident.
wart nie schoner wib geborn.
Ich han die gůten.
wol gemůten.
80 iemer mere zetroste erkorn.

Ir mvnt gewelwet.
niht geselwet.
ist ir wengel vnd kel.
ob ich iehe.
85 das ich sehe.
da ir lib ist sinewel.

des ensol ich melden. seht dc zeme niht.
wan der si mit minen ǒgen ane siht.

---

183 This line is repeated in the manuscript.

He was opposed by brave Sir Wigoleis
who came to serve the ladies there.

Tristan won a royal moor,
60 Morocco's queen, the story goes,
who was a heathen to be sure.
But let us say no more of those

and praise my lovely one,
so nice and full of fun,
65 decked out for dancing now
with rose wreath on her brow.
Above's another crown:
a white shawl, hanging down;
her hair is so like gold
70 as God might e'er behold,
as silk her tresses curl.
One must adore the girl;
wherever one is free
to love, she ought to be.

75 The Orient
or Occident
a fairer woman never bore.
I chose the dear,
this soul of cheer,
80 to be my comfort evermore.

Throat and cheek
are bright and sleek,
lips are curved into a bow.
Should it be,
85 I might see
where her form is round, I know

that ought not be mentioned; it would not be wise.
But whoever looks her over with my eyes

dem mv̊s si wol gevallen.
90 zewunsche vor in allen.

Ich lobe ir zuht ir gv̊te.
ir stete ir hohgemv̊te.
ir lib der ist so wol gestalt.
swer bi ir solde werden alt.
95 der hat der werlte lob vil gar.
si ist so minneklich gevar.
an ir ist niht vergessen.
zewunsche ist si gemessen.

vf ir hůfel vber al.
100 da sol ein borte ligen smal.
vil wol gesenket hin zetal.
da man ir reiet an den sal.
da ist lib gedrollen.
zewunsche wol die vollen.

105 volge mir.
sam tv̊n ich dir.
herzeliebů reine. du gv̊te du sv̊sse.
(266rb) tv̊st dv dc.
so wirt mir bas.
110 dc dich got vristen mv̊sse.

Minne mich.
sam tv̊n ich dich.
sol ich iemer helfe alde frȯide gewinnen.
frowe min
115 dc mv̊ste sin.
vil gar von dinen minnen.

wol gemv̊ten.
lânt die gv̊ten.
iv behagen.
120 Si sol von rehter arte der eren krone tragen.

finds that she's the best
90 compared to all the rest.

Her constancy I bless,
her mirth, her friendliness;
her form's so lovely to behold,
who in her company grows old
95 will have the world's abundant praise:
such grace has she and charming ways.
There was no oversight
with her; she's built just right.

At her hips, as I recall,
100 hangs a trimming: narrow, small,
like a sash or silken shawl.
Where one dances in her hall
she is shaped as well
as one could wish or tell.

105 Do my will
and I'll fulfill
your every wish, my darling, sweet and fair.
If you would,
I'd feel good.
110 God keep you is my prayer!

Love me too
as I love you!
If ever I shall win relief or bliss,
it will be
115 your love for me,
my dear, which brings me this.

All you so merry,
may she carry
forth your praise!
120 She has earned the crown of honor many ways.

Swa si gat zv̊ der linden.
mit wol gemv̊ten kinden.
da zimt ir wol dc reigen.
si zieret wol den meigen.
125   Ir zimt wol dc lachen.
dc kan si sv̊sse machen.

si machet trurig herze fro balt.
si ivnget den der ê wc alt.
Lopt ieman sine frowen bas.
130   dc lasse ich iemer svnder has.

Nv heia tanhvsere.
zergangen ist din swere.
Swa dů liebe bi dir were.
dů ist so frȏidebere.
135   Da wurde wol gesvngen.
getanzet vnd gesprvngen.

Nv dar.
nement war.
wa dů liebe springet.
140   vor mir.
nach mir.
swie der seite erklinget.
gestriket wol zeprise.
ze bliken also lise.

145   wa ist min fro mazze.
der springe ich zetrazze.
Nv seht an ir fůsse.
die machent es so sv̊sse.
seht an ir beinel
150   reit brvn ist ir meinel.

Wa ist min fro ivzze. dů liebe also lange.
dc elle an dem tanze.
niht springet gedrange.
Nv wol vf zerlinden. ir kint also ivngen.

When in the linden's shade
with merry youth and maid,
she likes to dance and play;
she well adorns the May.
125   Laughter fits completely
her self — she laughs so sweetly.

She makes the saddened spirit bold,
and makes him young who once was old.
Still it would not arouse my ire
130   should someone praise his lady higher.

Well, Tannhäuser, heigh-ho!
Gone is all your woe.
Whene'er the darling one is near
whose spirit is so filled with cheer,
135   there's certain to be singing,
dancing and lively springing.

Now there!
See where
the dear one leaps around,
140   before me,
behind me,
howe'er the string may sound;
decked out to take the prize,
so pleasing to the eyes.

145   Where's Mattie now? To tease her
I'll dance as to displease her.
Just see her pretty feet,
how nimble and how sweet!
Those legs beneath her gown!
150   (Her mons is curly brown.)

Where's my lady Jutta, the darling, been so long?
And why has Ella fled
the dancing and song?
Come now to the linden, you, so gay and young.

155 da wirt vnder kranze
zetanze gesvnge*n*.
heia sum*er* wu*n*ne.
sw*er* vns din erbvnne.

Hie nimt d*er* tanz ein ende.
160 sw*er* vns die frôide wende.
de*n* v*er*mide*n* rosen.
vn*d* alle zitelose*n*.
vn*d* aller vogelline*n* sang.
mich twinget dc mich e da twang.
165 Nv singe ich ab*er* hei.
heia nv hey.
Nv ist de*m* videllere sin videlboge enzwei.

V

Der kv̓nig vo*n* marroch hat d*er* b*er*ge noch genv̊g.
die guldin sint zegŏcasals des hôre ich iehe*n*.
Swie rich er si min wille mich nie dar getrůg.
Ich han ŏch de*n* vo*n* barbarie wol gesehen.

5 vo*n* dem vo*n* p*er*syan hôre ich wund*er* sage*n*.
so hat noch mer gewaltes d*er* vo*n* indyan.
Den ku̇nig vo*n* Latrize hôre ich vil d*er* heide*n* klage*n*.
sam tate*n* si de*m* soldan vo*n* d*er* sitrica*n*.

Ich ke*n*ne ŏch wol de*n* pylat da vo*n* zasamang.
10 ze babilo*n*ie iehent si wie gv̊t d*er* si.
ze alexandrie so enhabe ich dekeine*n* gedank.
der kv̓nig vo*n* baldag sol min iem*er* wesen fri.

vo*n* ku̇nig cornetin habe ich vil v*er*nomen.
vu̇r thomas gat d*er* iorda*n* dc ist mir bekant.
15 ze ir*usa*lem zem cornetal bi*n* ich kome*n*.
(266^*va*) Encolie ist mir wol kvnt i*n* kiperlant.

155 A garland on each head,
      the dance will be sung.
      Heigh-ho, summer's bliss,
      who'd begrudge us this!

      We'll dance no more today.
160 Who'd take our joy away
      may all the roses shun,
      the crocuses, each one,
      and bird-song greet no more.
      I have the pain I had before,
165 but still I'll sing heigh-ho!
      Heigh-ho, heigh-ho!
      And now the fiddler stops, for he has broke his bow.

V

      Morocco's king has hills and mountains everywhere
      at Goucasals of gold, so it was told to me.
      Though rich he be, my will has never borne me there;
      I've seen as well the king of Barbary.

  5 Of Persia's ruler I've heard many a wondrous thing,
      but he of India has power still more great.
      They say, a lot of heathen fear Latrice's king,
      just as they do the sultan of the Sitrian State.

      "How good our lord!" say those in Babylonia;
10 Pilate of Zazamank is one whom I know well.
      I'd never want to go to Alexandria,
      nor with the king of Baldak shall I ever dwell.

      About King Cornetin I've heard them say a lot;
      I know the Jordan's waters by Damascus flow.
15 The Cornevale's near Jerusalem, I've seen the spot;
      the Cyprian city of Encolia I know.

In normanya ich wc.
wie kvme ich da genas.
Für anthioch kam ich ze tůrgis svnder danc.
20 Da was der taten vil.
von den ich singen wil.
Der vattan gar mit siner milte kriechen twang.

von salnegge ein Roys.
der was von mvnt fortoys.
25 ze constantinopel was ein grande merfeyn.
Dů wite troie lang.
dů wart gar an ir dank
zer stŏret. da mv̄se sit dů růmanye sin.

ze kůnis erbent ŏch dů wib vnd niht die man.
30 dar an so stôsset pulgerie hŏre ich sagen.
Die valwen sint gar vngeriht in tanagran.
des horte ich vil die ungern vnd die Rivsen klagen.

Der beheim solde wol dem richen hellen mitte.
Cecilie sol dem keiser wesen vndertan.
35 Die sarden hant ŏch manigen wunderlichen sitte.
den voget von rome ich dike wol gesehen.

kerlingen stat mit gv̊tem vride vnd da bi engellant.
Die zarle wolden iemer also wesen fri.
Dur artus wart britanie zekaridol genant.
40 die wilzen sint geborn da her von tenebrie.

Fünf sterků regna sint.
er ist vil gar ein kint.
swer der niht weis in spangen. vnd sint doch wissentlich.
Das eine ist portigal.
45 vnd hat dů richů tal.
ander ist kaliz vnd ist vnmâssen rich.

Der dritte hat genv̊g, vnd ist von arragvn.
Der vierde vert vůr kasteln hin. gegen gramyzvn.
Den fünften von nauarre. swer den welle sehen.
50 Der var da hin so mv̊s er mir der warheit iehen.

In Normania I've been,
and nearly perished then.
Near Antioch I came to Turkey, to my distress,
20 and saw a Tartar throng
of which I'll sing ere long:
Vattan conquered Greece with naught but tenderness.

Of Salonika's king,
a Montfort knight, I'll sing;
25 Constantinople had a sea nymph, wise and grand.
Great Troy stretched far until
once, quite against its will,
it was destroyed and since became Romanian land.

The woman is the heir in Künis, not the man;
30 it borders on Bulgaria, as some maintain.
The Valwen have no law at all in Tanagran,
so both the Russians and Hungarians complain.

Bohemia's king should help the empire, this is clear,
and Sicily be subject to the emperor.
35 Sardinians have many customs which are queer;
I've often seen the Roman ruler heretofore.

France is well-protected; England is secure and whole;
Arles always wished to be as free as they.
Arthur changed the name of Brittany to Karidol;
40 From Tenebre the Wilzen people made their way.

Five mighty realms remain
within the bounds of Spain
and any but a child indeed can tell you which.
The one is Portugal
45 with fertile valleys all,
the second is Galicia and very rich,

Aragon, the third, has wealth it can't conceal;
the fourth one stretches to Granada from Castille;
that of Navarre's the fifth; who wants to see it too,
50 should journey there — he'll say that what I've told is true.

Terramer der fůrte ein her. ze orense mit gewalde.
dc wc dien schampvneisen leit. si verlurn da ivnge vnd alde.
storie manigvalde.

Oravil schŏf sich grôsse not
55 den burgen do zeleide.
da lag vil manig waleis tot
ze turnis vf der heide.
dc schŏfen si do beide.

Vienne hat legisten vl [sic].
60 der kunst astronomie.
ze doleth ich niht lernen wil.
von der nigromancie.
niht gŏt ist zŏberie.

ybernia hat der schotten vil an ir gelŏben stete.
65 ze Norwege bedarf man wol vůr kelte gŏter wete.
so hat ŏch der tennemark. der yseln vil besessen.
so mag ich des von ŏsterriche. zegŏte niht vergessen.
der wc ein helt vermessen.
bi dem wc ich gesessen.

70 Der vs peierlant mag sich ze kůnigen wol gelichen.
ich gesach nie fůrsten me so milten noch so richen
so rehte lobelichen.

(266ᵛᵇ) heia tanhusere nv la dich iemer bi im vinden.
gar an allen wandel din. so liebest dich den kinden
75 vnd mag din leit verswinden.

Nime den rosen kranz.
trage in der gŏten an den tanz.
vnd strike in wol zeprise.
la din truren sin.
80 nim war der lieben frowen din.
si tanzet also lise.

Terramer once led an army to Orense, I'm told,
which caused those of Champagne distress; they lost both young and old
in squadrons manifold.

Arofel's forces brought great dread
55   to cities then, and pain.
And many a valiant knight lay dead
at Turnis on the plain:
all this done by the twain.

Vienna has many lawyers, and so,
60   to learn astronomy
through black art, I shall never go
to Toledo, for sorcery
doesn't seem right to me.

Hibernia has many Irish in its leafy towns;
65   because of frost, in Norway they need heavy coats and gowns;
Denmark's king has occupied a host of islands too.
I'll not forget to praise the lord of Austria for you:
he was a hero bold
with whom I dwelt of old.

70   The noble of Bavaria indeed is like a king;
I never saw a prince so kind, so great in everything.
His praises one should sing.

Hey Tannhäuser, you should follow him forever more
with constancy; the girls will like you better than before:
75   your cares may all be o'er.

Take a rosy wreath
to her who dances on the heath,
a nice one, woven rightly.
Leave behind despair
80   and go and see your lady fair:
she dances O so lightly.

Viuianz ist clar.
Gvnrvn nimt sin besser war.
noch bas danne echelabvre.
85 belamvr si hat.
swanne si die zerlat.
so fröit sich min parlure.

Salatin der twanc mit siner milten hant ein wunder.
sam tet der kvnig ermenrich dc lant zebelagvnder.
90 es wart nie bas gestalt. danne ich die minnekliche vant alleine.
Mache fro mich selig wib. la tanzen mich an diner hant vil reine.

Seite ich von rûlande vil. dc tet ich aber nach wane.
nv lâssen wir die reken sin. vnd alle die von trane.
vnd die von bridamâne.

95 Ein schampenie wc da bi.
ein foret stûnt da nahen.
da was manig belamye.
die dar begvnden gahen.
do si min lieb ersahen.

100 Wol vf min gûte
zv mir an den reigen.
mir ist zemvte.
wir mvssen vnsich zweigen.
nach der vil lieben der claren der svssen.
105 dv miner swere ein teil kan gebvssen.

Wa nv Jvte vnd lose.
hie gât metze vnd rose.
wa nv richi vnd tvtel.
hie get bele vnd gvtel.

110 Schone mit dem kranze.
slichet an dem tanze.
wart nie bas gestalt ein lip.
nv la dich minnen selig wib.
werdu creatvre.
115 palure.

Viviance is fair;
Gunrun's more aware
of him than Eschenboor.
85 When she makes them leave
I'll not be one to grieve,
for she has *belle amour.*

Saladin conquered hordes of warriors with a kindly hand,
King Ermrich worked like wonders in the Belagunder land,
90 but exploits such as these were matched the time I found the dear alone.
Blessed woman, make me happy! Let me dance with you, my own.

Were I to speak of Roland much, I'd give my fancy rein,
but now we'll let the heroes be and all the ones from Trane,
and those of Bridamane.

95 Close by was a field, and one could see
a forest standing near;
and there was many a *bel ami*
who quickly hurried here
when he beheld my dear.

100 My friends, let's start
to dance; no time to lose!
I've set my heart
thereon; we'll form in twos
and go to the beautiful, loveable one
105 who can pay me for some of the pining I've done.

Where are Juta and Losa?
Here are Mezza and Rosa.
Where are Richy and Tuetel?
I see Bela and Guetel.

110 Beauty with the crown,
clad in festive gown,
no form was ever more complete!
Oh, may I love you, lady sweet?
Give a tender answer,
115 fair dancer!

Ir mvnt bran als ein rubin. gegen der svnnen glaste.
ir kel ein adamaste.
der tvgende vol ein kaste.

Wa nv floter herpfer dar zv tambvrere.
120 gegen der gvten
wol gemvten.
du ist so froidebere.
wa sint nv trumbvnere.

Nu svnge ich vil mere.
125 nv furhte ich vil sere.
dc sin die verdrîesse swen ich gerne lere.

Nv ist dem videllere sin seite zerbrochen.
dc selbe geschiht im alle die wochen.

Heia tanhvsere.
130 la dir niht wesen swere.
swa man nv singe.
froliche springe
heia nv hei.

VI

Ich mvs clagen.
dc bi kurzen tagen.
dv werlt wil an froiden gar verzagen.

du ist so kranc.
5 swc ich ir ie gesang.
ze dienste des seit si mir kleinen dank.

ein ander not.
glage ich svnder spot.
dc rehtu milte ist an den herren tot.

Her lips gleamed as a ruby in the sun's full light;
her throat's a diamond bright,
a treasure chest of right.

Where is the flutist, harpist, drummer company?
120 Come to her and play
who is kind and gay
and brings such joy to me.
Where can the buglers be?

Now I would sing much more,
125 but fear that this would bore
the one with whom I'd gladly share my art and lore.

Again the fiddler's string has broken in two;
this happens to him every week the year through.

Heigh, Tannhäuser, heigh!
130 Let grief and care go by.
Wherever there's song
just dance along
light-heartedly, heigh-ho!

VI

My plaints have begun
because everyone
soon will despair of pleasure and fun.

The world's ill-at-ease
5 and I couldn't please
it by singing the best of my melodies.

Another distress
I must mourn, I confess:
the death of true princely kindliness.

10   also zel zemerste*n* an
den keise*r* frideriche*n*.
owe dc ma*n* niht vinde*n* kan.
i*n* alle*n* tůtsche*n* riche*n*.

(267*ra*) ein kůnik de*m* zeme wol
15 nach im des riches crone.
Owe dc er niht leben sol.
de*m* si stůnt also schone.

dc was de*r* milte kůnig heinrich
bi dem wc fride stête.
20 dc nieman tůt de*m* gelich
der zů de*m* riche trete.

vn*d* im mit trůwe*n* we*r*e bi.
nv ist de*r* kůnig erstorben.
vn*d* ist dc rich gar erbes vri.
25 dc [sic] bi ist vil ve*r*dorbe*n*.

des besten landes ein michel teil
die wile vn*d* dc er lebt
kůnig kůnrat. da wc manige*r* geil
de*r* nach de*m* riche strebet.

30 nv ist aller schar gelege*n*.
wa siht ma*n* noch ergleste*n*.
als ma*n* bi kůnige*n* hat gepflege*n*.
de*n* kvnde*n* vn*d* den gesten.

vs beheim lande ein kůnig rich.
35 vn*d* ŏch i*n* osterlande
ein Lůpolt vn*d* ein friderich.
die lepte*n* âne schande.

Ein ivnge*r* fůrste von miran.
vn*d* ŏch ein welf vo*n* swabe*n*.
40 die willekliche*n* manige*m* man
vil riche*r* kleide*r* gaben.

10 As first of all the lords renowned
    must Kaiser Friedrich stand.
    Alas, that there has not been found
    in any German land

    a king to fit the crown and fill
15 his place and match his fame.
    Alas, that he's not living still
    whom it so well became.

    That was King Henry, kind and good,
    who kept the peace alone
20 better than any other could
    who might ascend the throne

    and give it faithful care.
    But now the king is dead
    and the empire doesn't have an heir:
25 destruction is widespread

    and great throughout the richest land.
    Many were happy when
    King Konrad lived, who raised his hand
    to seize the empire then.

30 The sounds of revelry have waned,
    the splendor and the zest
    with which the kings once entertained
    their friends and foreign guests.

    A Czechish monarch, rich and bold,
35 such Austrian nobles too
    as Friedrich and as Leopold,
    they lived as kings should do.

    A youthful sovereign of Meran,
    also a Swabian Guelf,
40 have freely given many a man
    rich clothing for himself.

ein ivnger helt von abenberg
vnd hug ein twinger
die worhten beide herren werg
45 si bvsten manigen swere.

Ein herman vs duringen lant
dar zv ein brabandere.
Chvnrat von lantsperg genant.
dar zv der bogener

50 des milte was mir wol erkant.
wer erbet nv ir milte
ere ich vs denne marchen lant
den gabe nie bevilte.

des tvgende wankte niht ein har.
55 si ist iemer stete. truwe
da bi nim ich eines herren war.
der hat so ganze truwe.

von brennen ein grave dietrich
der hat tvgende ein wunder.
60 vil milter got von himelriche
gewer mich des besvnder

an sime svne Chvnrat genant.
die wile in treit du erde.
so wunsche ich des dvr ellu lant.
65 dc er gut richter werde.

vnd er begrife des vatter spor
nach rechtes herren lere.
die wile im gat du ivgende vor.
so hat sin alter ere.

70 also der ivnge furste wert
der selbe vs duringen lande
albrecht vil riches lob vf gat
gebruder âne schande

Von Abenberg, a gallant youth,
and Hugh, a Tübingen knight,
in doing a noble's work in truth,
45 made many burdens light.

Herman, of Thuringia's land,
Brabant's lord and pride,
also Konrad von Landsberg, and
the Bogener beside,

50 whose kindness was well-known to me:
where are the heirs of such?
Erich's of Denmark charity
considered no gift too much.

His virtue failed not by a hair,
55 is always true and kind.
There's still a lord, as I'm aware,
of such a generous mind:

Dietrich, count of Brehna, who
has righteousness to spare.
60 God in heaven, kind and true,
hear and grant my prayer

about his son, Konrad by name:
throughout his stay on earth
in every land may I proclaim
65 him a ruler of great worth.

Let him pursue his father's ways,
act as befits a lord
when young, that he have fame and praise
when old, as his reward.

70 So too the young Thuringian,
Albrecht, widely famed,
his brother also is a man
who needs not be ashamed.

vs bolon lande ein fúrste wert
75 des wil ich niht vergessen.
vro ere sin zallen ziten gert.
dů hat in wol besessen.

Herzogen heinrich eren rich.
von pressela genant [sic].
80 den wil ich loben sicherlich.
min zvnge in wol erkennet.

het er tvsent fúrsten gůt.
seit man in tiutschen richen.
dc vergebe sin milter mv̊t.
85 vnd tet es willecliche [sic].

fride vnd reht ist vs gesant.
von ime vf sine strâsse.
der ivnge kůnig vs beheim lant.
der lebt in kůniges mâsse.

(267ʳᵇ) wer gesach bi manigen ziten ie
so werdes fúrsten krone
als er in behein lande trůg.¹⁸⁴
dem si stůnde also schone.

got helf der sele vs grosser not.
95 ich meine die herren alle
die sin an rehter milte tot.
vnd ȯch mit eren schalle.

got setzes alle in sine schar.
ich wil von fúrsten singen.
100 der vinde ich leider cleinen gar.
die nv nach lobe ringen.

---

¹⁸⁴ Since it is most unlikely that Tannhäuser would have introduced a new melody at this point, it is probable that originally lines one and three rhymed.

A worthy Polish prince is he
75 whom I shall not forget;
Dame Honor wants him constantly
and holds him captive yet.

Duke Heinrich's glory will endure
(von Breslau) and I'll tell
80 his many virtues, to be sure;
my tongue has known him well.

A thousand princes' wealth, they say
throughout the German lands,
his kindly heart would give away,
85 if it were in his hands.

He sends both peace and justice out,
along his streets they spring.
Bohemia's royal youth, no doubt,
lives as befits a king.

90 Who has seen in ages now
so fine a crown as fell
to Bohemia's king, and on whose brow
would it sit and look so well?

God save their souls from deep distress!
95 I mean the princely host
who've died to noble kindliness
and still of honor boast.

God take them in his retinue!
I'd sing the princes' praise,
100 but find, alas, so very few
who seek fame nowadays.

an dem man ie des besten iach
Heinrich der mizenere.
der sine truwe nie zerbrach.
105 der ist alles wandels lere.

er solte des riches krone tragen.
der vatter mit den kinden.
Ich kvnde nie bi minen tagen.
kein wandel an im vinden.

110 an hennenberg vil eren lit.
mit tvgenden wol beschonet.
graue herman owe der zit
dc der niht wart gekronet.

des mvs ich in von schulden klagen.
115 got gebe im dort zelône.
nach siner wirde mvze er tragen.
in himelrich die crone.

vs saxen lant herzoge albreht
der wc der fursten lere.
120 er kvnde vns fride wol machen sleht.
du werlt hat sin ere.

Von babenberg bischof egebreht.
den wil ich gerne grussen.
er was an allen tvgenden reht.
125 er kvnde wol kvmber bussen.

Vs peier lant ein furste wert
den grusse ich mit gesange.
sin herze manger eren gert.
des milte mvs mich belangen.

130 sin brvder heisset lvdewig.
der hat der tvgenden ein wunder.
Den fursten da von brvnenswig.
behute vns got besvnder.

A lord of whom the best is heard
is Heinrich of Meissen, one
who's never broken yet his word
105   and no misdeeds has done.

He ought to wear the empire's crown
and after him his heir;
a fault to bring his honor down
I've seen in him nowhere.

110   Adorned by virtue's fair display,
Count Hermann is renowned,
von Henneberg. Alas the day
that left him still uncrowned!

I must bewail his fate on earth;
115   God let him wear instead
in heaven, according to his worth,
a crown upon his head.

Duke Albrecht, lord of Saxony,
a model for them all,
120   could give us peace and harmony.
His fame has not been small.

Of Egbert, the Babenberg bishop too
I shall be glad to tell.
To every virtue he was true,
125   and he cured troubles well.

Bavaria's worthy prince I greet,
saluting him in song.
His heart seeks honor; may I meet
with bounty from him ere long.

130   His brother Ludwig has a wealth
of virtues marvelous.
May God preserve the life and health
of Brunswick's prince for us.

Von brandenbvrg der hof stet wol.
135 dem ist also zemv̊te.
dc si̇u sint wisheit also vol.
du̇ wisheit stet nach gvotte [sic].

wa sol ich herren sv̊chen.
die lobes nv gerůchen.
140 die sol vro ere wisen.
swer rehtes lob kan prisen.
mit werdes fu̇rsten zvngen.
dem wirdet lob gesvngen.
ich wil den fu̇rsten nennen.
145 ob ir in welt erkennen.
Sin grůs vnd ŏch sin lachen.
dc kan mir frŏide machen.
des mvnt ist ku̇sche vnd sv̊sse wort.
dc fůget nieman bc danne reinen wiben.
150 sit ir gv̊te hilfet mangem senden man
der in ir minne banden lit.

VII

(267ᵛᵃ) Wol vf tanzen vberal.
frŏit u̇ch stolzen leigen.
wunneklichen stat der walt.
wol gelŏbet dc sint liebu̇ mere.
5 iarlang průuet sich der schal.
gegen dem liehten meigen.
da die vogel vber al
singent wol zergangen ist ir swere.
alle vber ein planu̇re.
10 die blv̊men sint entsprvngen.
elliv creatu̇re
du̇ mv̊sse da von ivngen.
wil ein wib so wirt mir wol nach der ie min herze hat gerungen.

The Lords of Brandenburg are wise
135 and rich as they can be;
their wisdom is the sort to prize
both gold and property.

Where can the lords be found
who'd have their praise resound,
140 Dame Honor, let me learn.
Who true praise can discern
and laud with princely tongue,
for him shall praise be sung.
I'll sing the prince's fame
145 that all will know his name.
His greeting and his laughter
can bring me joy thereafter.
His words are virtuous and pleasing.
None can teach that better than can fair ladies,
150 since their kindness gives solace to many a man
who languishes in the bonds of his love for them.

VII

Come! There's dancing everywhere,
fair maids and men, be gay!
Splendidly the forest gleams,
fully leaved; this news is good to hear.
5 Stilled no longer is the air
for the radiant May
which the songbirds here and there
warble sweetly. Gone is grief and fear.
From the meadow land
10 host of blooms have sprung,
life on every hand
now again is young.
I'll be happy if so wishes she to whom my heart has always clung.

Zergangen ist der leide sne.
15 von der grunen heide.
komen sint vns die blvmen rot.
des froit sich du werlt ellu gemeine.
dar zv viol vnd kle.
liehte ogen weide.
20 mit den wunnen ist mir we.
dc kan nieman wenden wan alleine.
du mich heisset singen.
der zimt wol dc lachen.
sol mir wol gelingen.
25 dc mvs ir gvte machen.
von ir schulden mvssen noch tusent herzen vnd dannoch mere
erkrachen.

Du mir an dem herzen lit.
die sach ich so schone.
an einem tanze da si gie.
30 wol mit eren bi den schonen frowen.
ich wart fro der selben zit.
got ir iemer lone.
dc si mich so wol enpfie.
solde ich si noch einest also schowen.
35 die vil tvgentrichen.
so were mir wol ze mvte.
ir kan niht gelichen.
vil selig si dv gvte.
nach ir minnen ist mir we, noch ist du werlt gar vngemeiner hute.

VIII

Iarlang blozet sich der walt.
vnd och du heide.
valwet von dem kalden sne.
wie hant sich div zit gestalt
5 owe der leide.

148

Gone is now the hateful snow,
15 which makes the green heath bright,
for in its place red flowers come,
filling all the earth with gaiety.
Violet and clover show
eyes a lovely sight;
20 yet my joy is mixed with woe.
None can alter that but only she
who has bid me sing:
her laughter is a treat.
Only she can bring
25 what makes my joy complete.
A thousand hearts and maybe even more will break because she
looks so sweet.

The one who lies within my heart —
I saw her in a dance
as with lovely grace she glided
30 beside the pretty ladies in a row.
Joy then made my fears depart:
God reward the glance
and the greeting she confided.
If again I saw her dancing so,
35 mannerly and dear,
joy would fill my breast.
She has not her peer;
may she be ever blessed.
I long to win her but the jealous world must still obstruct the lover's
quest.

VIII

Now the forest trees are bare,
the moorland too
blanches from the chilling snow;
how the season changes there!
5 Alas, it's true!

schowe*n*t wie d*er* anger ste.
zergange*n* ist d*er* grůne kle.
wil dů reine
die ich da meine.
10 min v*er*gessen so wirt mir vil dike we.

Min frůnde helfent mir.
d*er* liebe*n* danke*n*.
d*er* ich singe vf hohe*n* pris.
gůte*n* trost han ich vo*n* ir.
15 mehte ich d*er* blanke*n*.
mache*n* brvn ir rote*n* gris.
si gert des apfels vo*n* paris.
gab dur mi*n*ne.
der gůttinne.
20 fůge ich dc so mag ich heissen ir amis.

Swas ich wil dc ist ir nein.
můs ich dc lide*n*.
e. wie lange so dc were*n*.
alsvs hellen wir en ein.
25 kônde ich gemide*n*.
si dc wolde ich fůge*n* g*er*ne.
si wil vo*n* mir de*n* liehte*n* st*er*ne*n*.
tremvntane*n*.
vn*d* de*n* mane*n*.
30 zů der svunne*n*. des en wil si niht enbern.

IX

Steter dienest d*er* ist gůt.
de*n* ma*n* schonen frowe*n* tůt.
als ich miner han getan.
(267*vb*) der můs ich de*n* salama*n*d*er* bringe*n*.
5 eines hat si mir gebotte*n*.
dc ich schike ir abe de*n* rotte*n*.

150

On the meadow naught will grow.
The clover was the first to go.
If wondrous she
forgets poor me
10 who loves her, then my heart will fill with bitter woe.

Help me, friends, that I may tell
her thanks aright
to whom I sing for lover's pay.
She'd reward me very well,
15 the fair and white,
could I make brown of her red gray.
The apple Paris gave away
to Aphrodite
for love's delight —
20 if I can get it, I may be her friend some day.

She says nay to all my ayes.
Though I've endured
till now, how long is this to be?
Thus our voices harmonize.
25 Could I be cured
of her, I'd readily agree.
She asks a gleaming star of me,
the North Star; soon
she wants the moon
30 and sun. She can't do without them all, you see.

IX

Constant service one should render
to the ladies, fair and tender,
just as I have done for mine:
salamanders she would have indeed.
5 She required one thing of me:
the Rhône, and this at once should be

hin provenz in das lant
ze nv̊renberg so mag mir wol gelingen.
vnd die tv̊nȯwe vber rin
10 fv̊ge ich das so tv̊t si swes ich mv̊te.
spriche ich ia si sprichet nein.
svs so hellen wir en ein.
dank so habe dv̇ frowe min
sist geheissen gv̊te.
15 heia hei sist ze lange gewesen vs miner hv̊te.
Ia hu̇te vnd iemer mere ia.
heilalle vnd aber ia.
ziehent herze wafena.
wie tv̊t mir du̇ liebe so.
20 dv̇ reine vnd dv̇ vil gv̊te.
dc si mich niht machet fro.
des ist mir we ze mv̊te.

Mich frȏit noch bas ein lieber wan.
den ich von der schonen han.
25 so der mv̇seberg zerge
sam der sne. so lonet mir du̇ reine.
alles des min herze gert.
des bin ich an ir gewert.
minen willen tv̊t si gar.
30 buwe ich ir ein hus von helfenbeine
swa si wil vf einem se.
so habe ich ir fru̇ntschaft vnd ir hulde.
bringe ich ir von galylee
her ân alle schulde.
35 einen berk gefv̊ge ich dc.
da her adan vffe sas.
Heia hei dc were aller dienste ein vbergulde.
Ja hu̇te vnd iemer ia.

Ein bȯn stan in yndian.
40 gros den wil si von mir han.
minen willen tv̊t si gar.
seht ob ich irs alles her gewinne.

152

from Provence brought to the land
of Nuremberg; then might my suit succeed —
the Danube is to take its place.
10 This done, she'll grant me all I have in mind.
I thank my lady for such grace;
that's why they call her kind.
I say "Yes!" and she says "No!"
We agree on all things so.
15 Hey-a-hey! She's been too long without my care, I find.
"Yes," today and always, "Yes!"
"Help me, help!" and still its "Yes!"
Hearts, cry out in sore distress!
How can the dear one act so coy,
20 this perfect love of mine?
Since she will not bring me joy,
my heart must sadly pine.

This delights me even more —
a hope from her I so adore:
25 should Mouse Mountain melt away
with its snow, the dear will grant me all.
Whatsoever I prefer
I shall freely get from her,
she'll be glad to do my will
30 if I build for her an ivory hall
where she wants it, on a sea,
then I'll have her friendship and her pay.
Should I bring from Galilee,
unharmed in any way,
35 a mountain whereon Adam sat —
if I do for her all that —
hey-a-hey! All other deeds would be surpassed, I'd say.
"Yes," today and always, "Yes!" ....

A lofty tree in India stands
40 which she wishes from my hands.
She'll do anything I ask
if — but see just what she's thinking of:

ich mvs gewinnen ir den gral.
des da pflag her parcyfal.
45 vnd den apfel den paris
gab dvr minne. venvs der guttine.
vnd den mantel der beslos
gar die frowen du ist vnwandelbere.
dannoch wil si wunder gros.
50 dc ist mir worden swere.
ir ist nach der arke we.
du beslossen hat noe.
heia hei. brehte ich die wie lieb ich danne were.
    Ia hute vnd iemer ia.

X

Min frowe du wil lonen mir.
der ich so vil gedienet han.
des svlt ir alle danken ir.
si hat so wol ze mir getan.
5 si wil dc ich ir wende den rin.
dc er fur kobelenze iht ge.
so wil si tvn den willen min.
mag ir bringen von dem se.
des grienes da dv svnne vf get.
10 ze reste so wil si mich wern.
ein sterne da bi nahe stet.
des wil si von mir niht enbern.
    Ich han den mvt.
    swc si mir tut.
15   dc sol mich alles dunken gvt.
    si hat sich wol an mir behut
(268ra)   du reine.
    svnder got alleine.
    so weis die frowen nieman die ich da meine.

20 Ich mvs dem manen sinen schin.
benemen sol ich si behaben.

I must bring her without fail
Parzival's mysterious grail
45 and the apple Paris gave
Lady Venus in exchange for love,
and the mantle which enclosed
only her whose virtue has no stain.
Other wonders she's proposed
50 which cause me bitter pain:
she must have the ark that bore
Noah in the days of yore.
Hey-a-hey! If I brought that what favors I would gain!
  "Yes," today and always, "Yes!"....

X

My lady wishes to reward
my service and my loyalty.
Let's thank her, all with one accord,
for having been so kind to me.
5 I only need to cause the Rhine
to flow no more through Coblenz land
and she will grant a wish of mine.
She'd also like some grains of sand
from out the sea where sets the sun,
10 then she'll give heed to my request.
A star gleams there, and that's the one
that she'd prefer to all the rest.
  My love is strong,
  whate'er her song
15   I will not think she does me wrong.
She feels secure howe'er I long,
  my own.
  To God alone
and no one else is this fair lady known.

20 If from the moon I steal the glow,
then may I have this noble wench.

so lonet mir dů frowe mi*n*.
mag ich die w*e*rlt alvmbe grabe*n*.
meht ich gefliege*n* als ein star.
25 so tete dů liebe des ich ger.
vn*d* hohe sweibe*n* als ein ar.
vnde ich zemale tvsent sper.
zertete als min her Gamvret.
vor Camvoleis mit richer iost.
30 so tete dů frowe mine bet.
svs mv̊s ich habe*n* hohe kost.
        Ich han. et c*etera*.

Si giht mvge ich d*er* elbe ir flus.
beneme*n* so tv̊ si mir wol.
35 dar zv̊ d*er* tv̊nowe irn dvs.
ir h*er*ze ist ganzer tvge*n*de vol.
de*n* salama*n*d*er* mv̊s ich ir.
bringe*n* vs de*m* fůre her.
so wil dů liebe lone*n* mir.
40 vn*d* tv̊t zemir des ich da ger.
mag ich de*n* rege*n* vn*d* de*n* sne.
erwende*n* des hĕre ich si iehe*n*.
dar zv̊ de*n* svm*er* vn*d* de*n* kle.
so mag mir lieb vo*n* ir geschehe*n*.
45   Ich han de*n* mv̊t. et c*etera*.

        XI

Gege*n* disen winnahte*n*.
solde*n* wir ein gemelliches trahte*n*.
wir swige*n* alzelange.
nv volge*n*t mir ich kan vns frŏide mache*n*.
5 ich singe iv wol zetanze.
vn*d* nim ir war der schone*n* mit de*m* kranze.
ir rosevarwe*n* wengel.
ersehe ich dů dar zv̊ so kŏnde ich lache*n*.

And she'll reward me well, I know,
if 'round the world I dig a trench.
If like an eagle I might fly,
25 then would she welcome my advances
(that is, if none could soar so high),
or if I broke a thousand lances
within a day, as did the sire
of Parzival to win the prize,
30 she'd gladly do what I desire,
't will cost me plenty otherwise.
    My love is strong....

If I the Elbe's waters bound,
I'd be rewarded; could I make
35 the Danube flow without a sound,
she'd love me well for custom's sake.
A salamander I must bring
to her from searing fire and flame,
then she will grant me anything
40 that any loving knight might claim.
When I can turn aside the rain
and snow, I've often heard her say,
and make the summer wax and wane,
then I shall have a lover's pay.
45   My love is strong....

XI

Now we should all decide
on some diversion for this Christmastide;
for we've been still too much.
What I propose you'll find a real delight:
5 I'll sing for you to dance
and of the flower-decked beauty get a glance.
Her rosy cheeks are such
that I could laugh with pleasure at the sight.

so sich du gute
10   schreket vor so ist mir wol zemvte.
vn*d* ir gurtel senke*n*.
machet dc ich vnd*er* wile*n*t liebe mvs gede*n*ke*n*.

Dv liebes dv gvtes.
tv hin la stan. dv wu*n*d*er* wol gemvtes.
15   wol ste*n*t dine lokel.
din mundel rot din ogel als ich wolde.
rosevar din wengel.
din kelli blank da vor stet wol din spengel.
dv rehtes svm*er* tokel.
20   reit val din har. rehte als ichs wunsche*n* solde.
gedrat dine bruste.
nv tanze eht hin min liebes min geluste.
la sitvli bleken.
ein weninc dvr de*n* wille*n* mi*n*. da gege*n* mvs ich schreke*n*.

25   Nv lachet ab*er* min flehe*n*.
ich schreke so dir blozent dine zehe*n*.
die sint wol gestellet.
vil schonu forme vn*d* h*er*zeliebu minne.
nv tanze eht hin min svssel.
30   so hol so smal so wurde*n* nie kein fussel.
swe*m* dc niht gevellet.
dc wisset d*er* hat niht gvt*er* sinne.
wis sint ir beinel.
(268*rb*)   lindu diehel reit brvn ist ir meinel.
35   ir sizzel gedrolle.
swc man an frowe*n* winsche*n* sol des hat si gar die volle.

Iv si d*er* tanz erlobet.
so dc ir mine frowe*n* niht bestobet.
seht an si niht dike.
40   ich furhte dc ir v*er*liesent uwer sinne.
ir zimt so wol dc lache*n*.
dc tvsent h*er*zen mvste*n* vo*n* ir krache*n*.
ir losliche*n* blike
twinge*n*t. mich owe dc tut ir mi*n*ne.

158

When the pretty maid
10   skips forward all my troubles are allayed.
The silken sash above
her hips waves up and down and sometimes brings me thoughts of love.

You're kind and lovely, too.
But stop a bit, joyous wonder, you!
15   How fair each curly tress,
red lips and eyes as I would have them be,
your cheek is like a rose,
with your white throat how well the neck brooch goes,
you doll in summer dress
20   with yellow ringlets, just the kind for me,
how firm and round your breasts!
Now whirl my sweet — where all my longing rests —
and show your cute behind
a moment just for me and I shall nearly lose my mind.

25   Laugh at me if you will!
Whene'er you show your pretty toes I thrill,
so well-shaped and so white.
You lovely figure, darling of my heart,
dance on and on, my sweet!
30   There never were before such dainty feet,
and whom they don't delight,
I tell you, really isn't very smart.
Her legs are white and rise
to a brown and curly mons and soft, smooth thighs.
35   Her bottom's nicely curved.
And all one wants in women she possesses, I've observed.

Dance, all, if you must,
but do not soil my lady with your dust.
Don't look at her too long
40   or you will lose your senses, every one.
Her laugh fits her so well
a thousand hearts could shatter from its spell.
Her glance is gay but strong
enough to crush me. Ah, that she has done.

45 stet hoher lat slichen.
der schonen der sol man zerehte entwichen.
wc kan ir gelichen.
des wene ich niht dc ieman tv̊ in allen richen.

Ach si ist so schône.
50 dc ich ir lob mit minem sange krône.
ir wol stenden hende.
ir vinger lang als einer kv̇niginne.
so ist si wol geschaffen.
da bi so kan si gemenliche klaffen.
55 gar ane missewende.
neme ich si v̇ur eine keiserinne.
des setze ich zepfande.
min herze dc ich niender in dem lande.
so gv̊tes niht erkande.
60 sist so minneklich gestalt. vnd lebt gar ane schande.

XII

1

Hie vor do stv̊nt min ding also. dc mir die besten iahen.
ich were den lûten sanfte bi. do hat ich holde mage.
si kerent mir den rugge zv̊. die mich do gerne sahen.
sit ich des gv̊tes niht enhan so grûssent si mich trage.
5 min dink hat sich gefûget so. dc ich mv̊s dem entwichen.
der mir. ê. von rehte entweich den lâsse ich v̇ur mich slichen.
si sint alle wirte nv. die sant mir geste waren.
vnd bin ich doch der selbe der ich wc vor zwenzig iaren.
ich bin gast vnd selten wirt dc leben ist vnstête.
10 dvnke ieman dc es senfte si. der tv̊ als ich tete.

2

So mir min ding niht ebne gat. swar ich kere in dem lande.
so denke ich sa gegen nv̇renberg. wie sanfte mir da were.

45 Stand back and let her glide,
     the fair! For her one ought to step aside.
     With her what can compare?
     In all the German lands you could not find it anywhere.

     Ah, she is so fair
50 I crown her praises with my pretty air.
     Her hands are smooth and fine,
     her fingers slender like those of a queen,
     so charming is her form,
     her way of speaking is so gay and warm,
55 I'd choose her to be mine
     in place of any empress ever seen.
     I pledge my heart, I've found
     at no place in the country all around
     her peer in excellence.
60 She's beautiful in every way and lives without offense.

XII

1

     The way things used to be with me the best of men would say
     that I was welcome everywhere; my kin were kind before.
     But now who once was glad to see me turns and looks away,
     and since I've lost my property none greet me anymore.
5 I have to step aside for him (so altered is my state)
     who rightly yielded once to me, but now I have to wait.
     Who once along with me were guests have houses now, I know,
     but my condition is the same as twenty years ago.
     For I'm a guest and never host, my life's an errant one,
10 and those who think it isn't hard should live as I have done.

2

     No matter where I wander here my path is always rough,
     which makes me think of Nuremberg—how friendly they'd receive me!

ich wolde habe*n* da genvg. da ma*n* mich wol erkande.
ê ich bi de*n* fromde*n* hete niht gelobe*n*t mir ein mere.
15 ich tet vil maniges hie bi vor dc mich nv ruwet sere.
hete ich gewist dc ich nv weis. ich hete lihte m*er*e.
in erkande do min selbes niht. des mvs ich dike engelte*n*.
des lade ich die fromde*n* in mi*n* hvs nv harte selte*n*.
wol vf her gast ir svlt enweg so sprech*en*t si mir alle.
20 in weis ob iema*n* disu fure icht wol an mir gevalle.

3

(268va) Ich denke erbuwe ich mir ein hvs. nach tv*m*b*er* lute rate.
die mir des helfen welle*n*t nv die si*n*t also gene*n*net.
vnrat vn*d* her schaffe niht die koment mir vil drate.
vn*d* einer heisset selte*n* rich d*er* mich vil wol erke*n*net.
25 d*er* zadel vn*d* d*er* zwiuel sint min stetes i*n*gesinde.
her schade vn*d* och her vmbereit ich dike bi mir vinde.
vn*d* wirt min hvs also vol braht vo*n* dirre massenîe.
so wissent dc mir vo*n* de*m* bvwe her in den bvsen snîe.

4

Rome bi d*er* tyuer lit d*er* arn gat vur pise.
30 als d*er* tronte vur pitscherer hin du tvzer gat vur rezze*n*.
grimvn lit de*m* pfate bi dur safo gat div nise.
paris bi d*er* seine lit du mvsel gat fur mezze*n*.
vur basel flusset abe der rin d*er* neker vur heilig brvnne*n*.
so ist du elbe lange dur sachsen lant gerv*n*ne*n*.
35 lutche ist och der mase bi. vur pulan gat du nise.
so flusset dur der vnger lant der wag vn*d* och du tyse.
brage bi d*er* woltach lit als wiene an d*er* tvnowe.
sw*er* des geloben welle niht d*er* var vnz ers beschowe.

5

Ein wiser man d*er* hies sin liebes kint also gebare*n*.
40 er sprach so dv zehoue sist so tv nach min*er* lere.

There where the people knew me I would rather have enough
than nothing in a foreign land, and you can well believe me.
15 I've done here quite a lot of things which I must sorely rue
and, if I'd known what I know now, I might be richer too.
But then I didn't know myself, for which I'm now distressed.
That's why I can't invite another in to be my guest.
"Go on, Sir Stranger, on your way!" they all now say to me.
20 I don't know if they get some pleasure from such courtesy.

3

I think that if I build a house, as foolish men advise,
the names of them who help are those which I can quickly tell:
Worthless and Sir Do-Nought will come with counsel, prompt and
wise,
and one who's known as Seldom-Rich, a man whom I know well.
25 Jest and Fickleness will be my servants, they won't shirk;
Sir Damage and Sir Clumsiness I'll find prepared to work.
If helpers such as these should build my house, 't would be a wreck,
with snowflakes blowing through the roof and falling down my neck.

4

The Arno flows through Pisa and the Tiber flows through Rome,
30 the Tronto by Piceno and the Töss by Rüti goes,
the Po streams past Cremona and Savoy's the Isère's home,
Paris is on the Seine, in front of Metz the Moselle flows.
Heilbronn's by the Neckar, Basel's on the Rhine, and we
know the Elbe long has wandered north through Saxony,
35 Liège sits by the Meuse, beyond the Neisse Poland stands,
the Váh and Tisza Rivers hurry through Hungarian lands,
Prague's on the Moldau, on the Danube live the Viennese.
Who doesn't think this true should go and find out what he sees.

5

To his beloved child a wise man offered this advice:
40 He said, "When you are at the court, behave as I direct.

dv solt den snôden frômede sin der frvmen solt dv varen.
vnd wis in zůhtekliche bi des hast dv lob vnd ere.
swa dv sehst ůbel tůn da von solt dv dich ziehen.
vngefůges lůder solt dv zallen ziten fliehen.
45 vnd trinke ôch in der mâsse so das ieman missevalle.
dv solt den frowen sprechen wol so lobent si dich alle.
dv solt dich růmen niht ze vil dc zimt wol von wiben.
vnd tůst dv dc so maht dv deste bas bi in beliben.

XIII

1

Wol im der nv beissen sol.
zepůlle vf dem gevilde.
der birzet dem ist da mit wol.
der siht so vil von wilde.
5 svmeliche gant zem brvnnen.
die andern ritent schowen.
der frôide ist mir zervnnen.
dc bannet man bi den frowen.
des darf man mich niht zihen ich beisse ôch niht mit winden.
10 in beize ôch niht mit valken in mag niht fůhse gelagen.
man siht ôch mich niht volgen nach hirzen vnd nach hinden.
man darf ouch nieman zihen von rosen schappel tragen.
man darf ôch min niht warten.
da stet der grůne kle.
15 noch sůchen in dien garten.
(268vb) bi wol getanen kinden. ich swebe vf dem se.

2

Ich bin ein erbeit selig man.
der niene kan beliben.
wan hůte hie morne anderswan.

Stay a stranger to the base, to worthy men be nice.
Politely join them and you'll win both honor and respect.
Wherever you see evil done you never should remain.
From loose, immoral living you at all times should abstain,
45   and drink in such a measure that no one will take offense.
Speak well of womankind and all will praise your common sense.
Don't talk about yourself too much, let ladies boast for you.
You'll get along with them much better knowing what to do."

XIII

1

He's lucky who can hunt today
in Apulia with his hawk!
Some seek within its woods for prey
and there find much to stalk;
5   these stroll down to the springs,
those go out for a ride
(I can't enjoy such things)
with ladies by their side.
One can't expect that I have pleasures of this kind:
10   to hunt with dogs or falcons, or even chase a fox,
and no one sees me follow the track of stag or hind;
don't think I should be wearing a rose wreath on my locks.
There where grows the clover
so green, don't wait for me,
15   or in the park moreover
with young and pretty maidens; I'm sailing far at sea.

2

I am a man with many a care,
a vagrant with no home,
who's here today, tomorrow there.

20 sol ich dc iemer triben.
des mvs ich dike sorgen.
swie frolich ich da singe.
den abent vnd den morgen.
war mich dc wetter bringe.
25 dc ich mich so gevriste vf wasser vnd vf lande.
dc ich den lib gefure vnz vf die selben stvnt.
ob ich den luten leide in snodem gewande.
so wirt mir du reise mit freise wol kvnt.
dar an solde ich gedenken.
30 die wile ich mich vermag.
in mag im niht entwenken.
ich mvs dem wirte geltem [sic] vil gar vf einen tag.

3

Wa leit ie man so grosse not.
als ich von bosem troste.
35 ich was zekride vil nah tot.
wan dc mich got erloste.
mich slugen sturn winde.
vil nach zeinem steine.
in einer naht geswinde.
40 min froide du wc kleine.
du ruder mir zerbrachen. nv merkent wie mir were.
die segel sich zerzarten. si flugen vf den se.
die marner alle iahen. dc si so grôsse swere.
nie halbe naht gewunnen mir tet ir schrien we.
45 dc werte sicherlichen
vnz an den sehsten tag.
in mahte in niht entwichen.
ich mvs es alles liden als der niht anders mag.

4

Die winde die so sere wênt.
50 gegen mir von barbarie.
dc si so rehte vnsvsse blênt.
die andern von turggie.

20 If I should always roam,
I'll often have to worry
(though singing as I go)
both day and night, while I hurry
where'er the winds may blow,
25 how I can take such measures, ashore and when afloat,
as keep my soul and body together one more day.
If I offend the people with a worn and shabby coat,
the journey will be dreadful for me in every way.
I'll always think of this
30 while I have life and will:
I cannot be remiss;
sometime I'll meet the landlord and have to pay his bill.

3

Who's suffered such distress as I
from hope and trust betrayed?
35 Not far from Crete I thought I'd die,
but God came to my aid.
The winds with fearful might
came near to dashing all
upon a rock that night:
40 my joy was rather small.
Soon every oar was broken; think how it was with me!
The sails all tore and shredded and flew out o'er the main.
The rowers said they'd never endured such enmity
for half a night until then; their wailing caused me pain.
45 The bark was in this shape
five dreadful days, it's true,
and there was no escape;
I simply had to bear it. What else was there to do?

4

The breezes which from Barbary
50 rush on us with a roar
are just as harsh and rude to me
as those from Turkey's shore.

die welle vn*d* ŏch die v̇nde.
gent mir grôs vngemẽvte.
55 dc si fu̇r mine sv̇nde.
d*er* reine got min hûte.
min wasser dc ist trûbe. min piscop d*er* ist h*er*te.
min fleisch ist mir v*er*salzen. mir schimelget min win.
d*er* smak d*er* von d*er* svtte*n* gat, d*er* ist niht gv̊t geu*er*te.
60 da vu̇r neme ich d*er* rosen ak. vn*d* mehte es wol gesin.
zisern vn*d* bone*n*.
gent mir niht hohe*n* mv̊t.
wil mir d*er* hohste lone*n*.
so wirt dc trinke*n* sṽsse vn*d* ŏch du̇ spise gůt.

5

65 Ahi wie selig ist ein man.
d*er* fu̇r sich mag geriten.
wie kvme mir der gelŏben kan.
dc ich mv̊s winde biten.
der schok vo*n* oriende.
70 vn*d* d*er* vo*n* tremvndane.
vn*d* d*er* vo*n* occidende.
arsu̇le vo*n* de*m* plane.
d*er* meister ab den albe*n*. der krieg vs romanie.
(269^*ra*) d*er* levan dan vn*d* oster. die mir gene*n*net sint.
75 ein wint vo*n* barbarie wêt. d*er* and*er* von tu̇rggie.
vo*n* norte*n* kvmt d*er* mezzol. seht dc ist d*er* zwelfte wint.
wer ich vf dem sande
der name*n* wisse ich niht.
dvrch got ich fůr von lande.
80 vn*d* niht dvr dise vrâge. swie we halp mir geschiht.

XIV

1

Das ich ze h*er*ren niht en wart. dc mṽsse got erbarme*n*.
des git mir des goldes niht. dc ma*n* da fũrt vo*n* walhe*n*.

These waves that surge and sink
have brought me grievous woe,
55 because of sin, I think.
God help me if it's so!
My drinking water's cloudy, my biscuit really hard,
my meat is much too salty, and musty is my wine,
the stench from down below is not a shipmate one would guard.
60 I'd rather have the smell of roses if the choice were mine.
And mouldy beans and peas
bring forth no happy mood.
Would God reward and please,
He'd make the water sweeter and give me better food.

5

65 How lucky is the one on land
who rides forth as he pleases.
It's hard for him to understand
that I must wait for breezes.
Sirocco from the east,
70 the wind from Tramontane,
and Zephyr (not the least),
Arsura from the plain,
the Alps send down the Mistral, Romania the Greek,
Levanter and the Auster, all these were named to me.
75 The wind from Barbary and that from Turkey shriek.
One tells of Norte too; the twelfth is Mezzodi.
Had I remained ashore,
these names I would not know.
I left to serve God more
80 and not to learn with sorrow all the winds that blow.

XIV

1

God pity me because I was not born to be a lord.
That's why I get none of the gold which comes from Italy.

die herren teilenz vnder sich. so kapfen wir die armen.
wir sehen iemerliche dar. so fúllet man in die malhen.
5 so kvmt vns anderthalb von dúringen vil von gůte.
dc lâsse ich vf die trúwe min dc ich des niender mv̊te.
swie tvmb ich si ich vunde da den der mich gehielte schone.
ich were e iemer ane gv̊t e ich schiede von der krone.
dem kúnige sich ich wol in weis wenne er mir lone.

2

10 Ich solde wol zehove sin. da horte man min singen.
nv irret mich dc nieman weis. in kan niht gůter dône.
der mir die gebe so svnge ich. von hovelichen dingen.
ich svnge verrer vnd bas. von allen frowen schône.
ich svnge von der heide. von lo̊be vnd von dem meien.
15 ich svnge von der svmerzit. von tanze vnd o̊ch von reigen.
ich svnge von dem kalden sne. von regen vnd von winde.
ich svnge von dem vatter vnd der mv̊ter von dem kinde.
wer lőset mir dú pfant wie wening ich der vinde.

3

Dú schonen wib der gv̊te win. dú mvrsel an dem morgen.
20 vnd zwirent in der wochen baden. dc scheidet mich von gůte.
die wile ich dc verpfenden mag so lebe ich ane sorgen.
swenne es an eîn gelten gat. so wirt mir we zemv̊te.
vnd ich dú pfant sol lősen. so kvmt dc lieb zeleide.
so sint dú wib gar missevar. swenne ich mich von in scheide.
25 der gv̊te win der svret mir. swenne ich sin niht mag verpfenden.
wenne sol min tvmber mv̊t. an truren sich vol enden.
ia weis ich der herren niht. die minen kvmber wenden.

4

Ia herre wie habe ich verlorn. den helt vs österriche.
der mich so wol behvset hat. nach grôsen sinen eren.
30 von sinen schulden wc ich wirt. nv lebe ich trurekliche.
nv bin ich aber worden gast. war sol ich armer keren.
(269ʳᵇ) der mich sin noch ergetze. wer tůt nach im dc beste.
wer haltet toren als er tet. so wol die stolzen geste.

170

The mighty all divide it up, we poor are quite ignored,
and, while they have their pouches filled, must look on woefully.
5 And from Thuringia come goods to us as well, I've heard.
I do not want and shall not take a thing, upon my word.
I'd find there wealth enough for me, though short I be of wit,
but, rather than forsake the crown, I'd live without a bit.
I'll speak well of the king — I know not when I'll gain by it.

2

10 I ought to be at court, you know, so they could hear me sing.
The trouble is that no one gives me pretty melodies.
If I had some, then I would tell of every courtly thing:
of lovely ladies I'd sing well — and better far — with ease.
I'd sing about the meadow and the foliage and of May;
15 I'd sing about the summertime, of dance and roundelay.
I'd sing of chilling snow and rain, and what the winds have done;
I'd sing about the father, mother, and their infant son.
Who will redeem my pledge? Alas, how sad that I have none.

3

Choice food of a morning, pretty women, and good wine,
20 and taking baths two times a week, all make my wealth depart.
As long as there is something left to pawn, I'll do just fine,
but, when it comes to settling, I'll be very sick at heart.
When comes the time to pay my debts my joys will be despair,
and when we have to part, the women won't look half so fair;
25 the wine will sour when no unpledged properties remain.
When will my foolish spirit cease to sorrow and complain?
I don't know any lords who wish to turn aside my pain.

4

I've lost the duke of Austria; alas that this should be,
because he housed me well, in keeping with his honor rare.
30 I held a fief from him, but now I live most wretchedly,
a poor and homeless wanderer. To whom shall I repair,
and who will take his place for me, which lord would be the best,
and treat — like he — a fool as well as a proud and noble guest?

des var ich irre nvn weis wa ich die wolgemv̊ten vinde.
35 vnd lebte er noh so wolde ich selten riten gegen dem winde.
der wirt sprichet we her gast wie frṳzet v̊ch so swinde.

5

Ze wiene hat ich einen hof. der lag so rehte schone.
lṳpolz dorf wc darzv̊ min. dc lit bi lvchse nahen.
zehinperg hat ich schône gv̊t. got im der wirde lone.
40 wenne sol ich iemer mere die gṳlte dar abe enpfahen.
es sol mir nieman wîssen. ob in klage mit trṳwen.
min frôide ist ellṳ mit im tot. da von mv̊s er mich rṳwen.
wa wilt dv dich behalten iemer mere tanhvsere.
weist aber iemen der dir helfe bṳssen dine swere.
45 o we wie dc lenget sich sin tot ist klagebere.

6

Min sômer treit zeringe gar. min pferit gat zesware.
die knehte min sint vngeritten. min malhe ist worden lere.
min hvs dc stat gar ane dach. swie ich dar zv̊ gebare.
min stube stet gar ane tṳr. dc ist mir worden swere.
50 min kelr ist in gevallen min kṽche ist mir verbrvnnen.
min stadel stat gar ane bant. des hôis ist mir zerrvnnen.
mir ist gemaln noch gebachen. gebrvwen ist mir selten.
mir ist dṳ wat zetṳnne gar. des mag ich wol engelten.
mich darf dvrh gerête nieman niden noch beschelten.

XV

Dank habe der meie.
der hat maniger leie.
vṳr gesant.
vf die liehten heide
5 dṳ wunnekliche lit.

I seek in vain and do not find a host of such good will.
35 I'd never ride against the wind if he were living still.
Who has a home cries out: "Sir Wanderer, how quick you chill!"

5

I had a villa in Vienna. What a lovely place!
And Leopoldsdorf, right near Luchsee, was also mine back then.
At Himberg I had fine estates; for these God grant him grace!
40 When shall I ever get the income from this land again?
Let none reproach me, saying that I did not hold him dear,
for all my pleasure died with him: my grief must be sincere.
How will you gain a livelihood? Tannhäuser, now give heed:
do you know any other lord who'll help you in your need?
45 Alas, the search drags on and on! His death is sad indeed.

6

My charger's step is too heavy indeed, my pack horse's load is too light.
Those who attend me go on foot, my travelling bag holds naught.
There is no roof upon my house, and I can't set this right.
My chamber is without a door, which makes me sore distraught.
50 The empty cellar's fallen in, the kitchen's burned away;
the barn still stands, but has no walls, and gone is all its hay.
None bakes nor mills the grain for me, and no one brews me beer;
my clothing's gotten much too, thin, for which I'll pay, I fear.
None needs belittle my supplies nor envy me my gear.

XV

Many thanks to May
which sent forth blossoms gay
everywhere,
colorful and bright,
5 upon the lovely field.

vil zitelose*n*.
manige*r* hande rosen
ich da va*n*t.
was d*er* o̊gen weide.
10 du̇ svme*r* wu*n*ne git.
vil d*er* vogel singet.
zeschalle wider strit.
dc in de*m* walde erkli*n*get.
ir schallen si zerehte*n* fro̊iden bringet.
15 sa zehant.
liese ich vil d*er* swe*r*e du̇ mir wc e bekant.

Ich han dien ivnge*n*.
vil da her gesvnge*n*.
des ist lang.
20 als si mich des bate*n*.
gege*n* de*m* meie*n* do.
dien liebe*n* kinde*n*.
sang ich bi de*n* linde*n*.
mine*n* sang.
25 die mir liebe tate*n*.
die scho̊f ich dike fro.
dc hat sich v*er*keret.
nv leide*r* also.
swe*r* hie fůge me*r*et.
30 wirt der doch vil selte*n* drvme gêret.
an ir dank.
sang ich in zeleide dien hohgemv̊te ist krank.

Wil si du̇ gůte.
du̇ gar wol gemv̊te.
(269*va*) trȯste*n* mich.
so vinde ich ein ende
d*er* lange*n* swe*r*e min.
wil si du̇ reine.
trȯsten mich aleine.
40 so wirde ich.
fri vor missewende.

174

Saffron all around
and many a rose I found
blooming there.
What a splendid sight
10 does summer's beauty yield!
Hosts of birds now sing
with ardor unconcealed
and make the forest ring.
Their music gives them joy in everything.
15 That was when
I put away the trouble I had borne till then.

I have often sung
verses to the young.
It's been long
20 since May came o'er the earth
and they all asked me to.
For many a youth and maid
within the linden's shade
I sang my song,
25 and brought them joy and mirth
who gave me what was due.
But, sad to say, no more
is this yet true,
for he who would restore
30 good manners is not honored as before.
To spite them all,
without request, I sang to those whose joy is small.

If she, the good and kind,
of pleasing heart and mind,
35 will comfort me
I'll find an end to pain
which long has held me fast.
If she, the fair, my own,
will comfort me alone,
40 then I'll be free
from every fault and stain.

wil si mir gvnstig sin.
so lobe ich mit schalle.
si vůr des meien schin.
45 vnd vůr die blůmen alle.
dc nieman si der mir so wol gevalle.
frowe sich.
wie schone ich mich stelle swenne ich gedenke an dich.

XVI

Es slůg ein wib ir man zetode vnd al ir kint geswinde.
slůg si zetode seht dc was dem man vnmassen zorn.
zetode slůg er si her wider vnd alles ir gesinde.
slůg er zetode doch wurden sider kint von in geborn.

5 got hies werden einen man
der nie geborn wart von frowen libe.
die vatter noch dů můter nie gewan.
die nam er im ze wibe.

dar nach ein hunt erbal.
10 dc alle lůte die do lebten horten sinen schal.

dů erde ist hoher danne der himel dc hant die wisen meister wol
bevunden.
hie vor bi manigen stunden.

ein kint dc slůg den vatter sin do es in der můter was.
do er den andern kinden sang von gote vnd in die rehten warheit las.

If she will smile at last
on me her praise will swell.
I'll say that she's surpassed
45 May's fairest heatherbell
and that none other pleases me so well.
Lady, see
how proper I can act whene'er I think of thee.

XVI

A woman struck her husband dead and all her children too
she struck down dead. Now see, with such a rage the man was torn
he struck her dead in turn, and all her maids and retinue
he struck down dead. But children afterwards to them were born.

5 God once caused a man to be
who from no woman's body came to life.
Who sire or mother never had was she
who then became his wife.

And later on a hound
10 began to bay so loudly all the world could hear the sound.

The earth is higher than the heavens; this the wisest masters (as
we've learned)
ere now have oft discerned.

A child while in its mother's womb once struck its father dead,
and while he sang of God and told the other children what the
Scripture said.

1

(42vb) Ez ist hivte eyn wunnychlicher tac.
      Nv phlege myn der aller dinge walte.
      Daz ich myt selden mv̊ze wesen.
(43ra) vnde ich gebv̊ze myne groze sculde
  5 Vvente her mich wol gehelfen mac.
      Also daz ich die sele myn behalte.
      Daz ich vv̊r svnden sy genesen.
      Vnde daz ich noch irwerbe gotes hulde.
      Nv gebe her mich so steten mv̊t.
 10 Daz ez der lib vv̊rdiene so.
      Daz myr got danken mv̊ze
      Daz myr daz ende werde gv̊t.
      Vnd ouch die sele werde vro.
      Myn scheiden werde sv̊ze.
 15 Daz mich de helle gar vv̊rber.
      Des helfe mir de reyne
(43rb) Vnde vv̊ge mich des ich da ger.
      Daz mich die hoeste vreude sy gemeyne.
      Also ich der mage mv̊z vnper. Daz ich dort vrivnde vynde.
 20 Die myner kvnfte werden vro. daz ich geheyzen mv̊ge eyn
                        seldenrichez ingesynde

2

      Ich kvnde dich herre myne klage.
      Vnde wil dir sv̊ze vater wol getruwen.
      Die lazes du dir wesen leit.
      Des bitte ich dich durch dyner mv̊ter ere
 25 Ich habe gesvndeget myne tage.
      Vnde ist myr noch vil selten ë. beruwen.

---

[185] The following text is taken from f. 42^v to f. 43^v of the Jena Manuscript in the photographic reproduction of Helmut Lomnitzer and Ulrich Müller, eds., *Tannhäuser: Die lyrischen Gedichte der Handschriften C und J: Abbildungen und Materialien zur gesamten Überlieferung der Texte und ihrer Wirkungsgeschichte und zu den Melodien* (Göppingen: Kümmerle, 1973).

1

How delightful is this lovely day!
Now care for me Who over all disposes,
that I may ever live with blessing
and may do penance for my wordly blindness.
5 For He indeed will be my stay
and through His aid my soul secure reposes.
May I be healed of all transgressing
and may I yet obtain God's loving kindness.
Grant me a will which shall not bend
10 and which deserves His love so well
that God may well reward me!
Give me, I pray, a happy end,
and let my soul in rapture dwell,
a gentle death afford me.
15 May I be saved by purity,
that hell may be no danger.
What I require, give unto me,
that I to highest joy be not a stranger.
Here must I have no family, that friends I may have yonder
20 who take such pleasure in my songs that I shall be renowned among
the knights who heavenward wander.

2

I'll tell Thee, Lord, of my distress
and fully trust Thee, Father, dear and good,
to have compassion now for me.
I pray Thee, help me for Thy mother's sake.
25 I've spent my life in sinfulness
and never been repentant, as I should.

Dyn marter vnd dyn goteheit.
Die helfen myr daz ich mich hie bekere
Der svnden der ich begangen han.
30 Daz ich der hie tzů bůze ste.
Daz sie der lib irarne
Han ich tzů dynen hulden wan.
So helfe ouch daz myn wille irge.
Vnde ich mich des gewarne
(43ᵛᵃ) Daz ich die sele sende hyn.
Tzů der ymmer werenden wunne
Gib myr so kreftelichen syn.
Daz myr der tiubel nicht vůrirren kvnne
Syn lage ist so manichvalt die her hat nach dinen kynden.
40 Orloube vns herre dyne hant daz du vns mṽzes svnden bloz
nach dynem willen vynden.

3

Got herre sit du scheffer bist.
Der barmicheit vil richer got so wache.
Vnde wecke mich ë. irge daz tzil.
Dynes orteiles herre sterke myne synne
45 Vil sůze vater ihesu krist.
helf myr daz ich mich kegen dir recht gemache.
Vnde wise mich da ich hyn wil.
Daz ich dich hie mit vollem hertzen mynne
Irget min wille sůzer got.
50 Also ich gedinges an dich gere.
So werd ich selden riche
han ich tzṽbrochen din gebot
Da vmme ich dyner hulde vnpere.
Daz soltu lutterliche
55 Vůrkiesen durch die namen dry.
Vnde durch die war irstende
So lieb so dir dyn mṽter sy.
Die vůr dem krutze sere want ir hende
Vnde durch die bete der sie dir bat help myr von mynen svnden.
60 Vnde in allen die des gernt. Daz sie dich herre durch dyn
hymelriche vunden.

Thy suffering and divinity
will surely give me aid that I may break
my bonds and leave this life of sin,
30 and make amends for all at last.
May I be penitent!
If I may yet expect to win
Thy grace, then help my will hold fast
and keep my thoughts intent
35 to send my soul where it may find
and gain eternal bliss.
And give me such a constant mind,
the devil cannot make me stray from this.
The snares are manifold he sets for all Thy children still.
40 Stretch forth Thy hand to us, O Lord, that Thou mayest find us free
from sin, according to Thy will.

3

Lord God, by Whom all things were made,
since Thou art all compassion, watch o'er me,
and waken me before the day
of judgment; Lord, make strong my inner part.
45 Sweet Father, Jesus Christ, give aid
that I may reconcile myself with Thee,
and show me what I seek, the way
that I may love Thee here with all my heart.
Should I receive that from Thy hand
50 on which my hope is built,
then I'll be richly blessed.
If I've been deaf to Thy command
and lost Thy grace through guilt,
then Thou shouldst manifest
55 Thy pardon because of the Trinity,
because Christ rose again,
because Thy mother's dear to Thee
who wrung her hands beneath the cross in pain.
Because of all her prayers help me to leave my sins behind me.
60 That they may enter paradise, help all of those whose heart's desire is
that they still may find Thee.

Got leit durch vns vil groze not.
her liez sich durch vns an eyn krutze henken.
Sin marter die was manichvalt.
Die her da leit damite her vns irloste
(43vb) Sin tot irwante mynen tot.
Owe daz ich daran nicht wil gedenken.
Daz er myn so sere vntgalt.
ob ich sin gere so kome her myr tzv̊ troste
Eyn reyne maget eyn kynt gebar.
70 Daz keyne svnde nye begienc.
Daz wonet an hymelriche
Ez nympt die besten alle dar.
Der synen namen ë. vntfienc.
Durch toufe sicherliche
75 Got weiz wol waz der lib getůt.
ob er da ane altet.
daz ist der sele tzv̊ maze gůt.
her ist der hoeste der des alles waltet.
Her ist der vater. vnde der svn. her wirt uns an dem ende.
80 Eyn lewe. eyn scaf. eyn vivr. eyn heil. also ez der lib vůrdienet hat
gar ane myssewende.

For us God suffered agony,
for us upon a cross He gave His all.
O what a painful sacrifice
He made, that He might bring us to salvation!
65 His death turned death aside for me;
alas, that I should choose not to recall
how I was saved at such a price.
Whene'er I ask, he brings me consolation.
A virgin once a Child did bear
70 Who never sinned and knew no blame.
His kingdom's in the sky.
He takes the righteous to Him there,
those baptized in His holy name
and saved before they die.
75 God knows well what the flesh will do
when it grows old unshriven;
it brings the soul in danger too.
He rules on high, to Him all power is given.
When life is o'er, He'll be to us (the Father and the Son)
80 a sheep or lion, fire or blessing; we shall be rewarded justly for
the deeds we'e done.

Nun wil ichs aber heben an
von dem Danheüser zu singen,
vnd was er wunders hat gethan
mit seiner fraw Venussinnen.

5   Danheüser was ein Ritter gut,
Wann er wolt wunder schawen,
Er wolt in fraw Venus berg
Zu andern schönen frawen.

"Herr Danheüser, ir seyt mir lieb,
10 Daran solt ir mir gedencken!
Ir habt mir einen aydt geschworen:
Ir wölt von mir nit wencken."

"Fraw Venus, das enhab ich nit,
Ich wil das widersprechen,
15 Wann redt das yemant mer dan ir,
Got helff mirs an jm rechen!"

"Herr Danheüser, wie redt ir nun?
Ir solt bey mir beleyben;
Ich wil euch mein gespilen geben
20 Zu einem stetten weybe."

"Vnd nem ich nun ein ander weyb,
Ich hab in meynem sinnen,
So müst ich in der helle glut
Auch ewigklich verbrinnen."

25 "Ir sagt mir vil von der helle glut
Vnd habt es nie entpfunden;
Gedenckt an meinen rotten mundt,
Der lachet zu allen stunden."

---

[186] The text is taken from Meier, pp. 145-46.

I shall now begin to sing
Tannhäuser's song which tells
the strange adventures which he had
where Lady Venus dwells.

5 Tannhäuser was a knight who sought
adventure everywhere,
he entered Venus Mount to see
the lovely women there.

"Tannhäuser, I am fond of you;
10 hold that in memory,
and that you've sworn to me an oath
that you'd be true to me."

"Dame Venus, that I did not do!
You know it's just a lie,
15 and if some other one said this,
God helping me, he'd die."

"Tannhäuser, why must you lament?
Remain with me for life
and I shall give my friend to you
20 to be your loyal wife."

"And if I took another wife
than her for whom I yearn,
then in the flaming fire of hell
eternally I'd burn."

25 "You speak so much of flaming hell
but never felt its power:
just think about my ruby lips
which laugh at any hour."

"Was hilffet mich ewer roter mundt?
30 Er ist mir gar vnmere;
Nun gebt mir vrlaub frewlein zart,
Durch aller frawen ere!"

"Herr Danheüser, wölt ir vrlaub han,
In wil euch keinen geben;
35 Nun beleybent, edler Danheüser,
Vnd fristet ewer leben!"

"Mein leben das ist worden kranck,
Ich mag nit lenger bleyben;
Nun gebt mir vrlaub, frewlein zart,
40 Von ewrem stoltzen leybe!"

"Herr Danheüser, nit redet also,
Ir thut euch nit wol besinnen;
So geen wir in ein kemerlein
Vnd spilen der edlen minnen!"

45 "Gebrauch ich nun ein frembdes weyb,
Ich hab in meinem sinne:
Fraw Venus, edle frawe zart,
Ir seyt ein Teüffellinne!"

"Herr Danheüser, was redt ir nün,
50 Das ir mich günnet schelten?
Nun solt ir lenger hierinne sein,
Ir müstent sein dick entgelten."

"Fraw Venus, vnd das wil ich nit,
Ich mag nit lenger bleyben.
55 Maria mutter, reyne maydt,
Nun hilff mir von den weyben!"

"Herr Danheüser, ir solt vrlaub han,
Mein lob das solt ir preysen,
Wo ir do in dem landt vmbfart.
60 Nembt vrlaub von dem Greysen!"

"I care not for your ruby lips;
30 they've brought me only woe.
Do honor now to womankind,
dear lady, let me go!"

"Tannhäuser, would you take your leave?
You shall not go away!
35 Remain with us, Oh noble knight,
and let your life be gay."

"My life grows sadder all the time;
to stay is but to grieve.
Give me permission, lady fair,
40 that I may take my leave."

"Tannhäuser, do not babble so,
what are you thinking of?
Let's go into my chamber now
and play the game of love."

45 "For me your love is only pain;
I've opened up my eyes
and seen in you, my lady fair,
a devil in disguise."

"Tannhäuser, what is this you say;
50 am I the one you scold?
If you remain in here you'll wish
you hadn't been so bold."

"Dame Venus, that I shall not do;
I'll never stay in here.
55 Maria, mother, Holy Maid,
in my distress be near!"

"Tannhäuser, you may take your leave;
though you must lend your tongue
and sing my praises through the land,
60 but only to the young."

Do schiedt er wider auß dem berg
In iamer vnd in rewen:
"Ich wil gen Rom wol in die stat
Auff eines Babstes trawen.

65 "Nun far ich frölich auff die ban,
Got müß sein ymmer walten,
Zu einem Babst, der heyst Vrban,
Ob er mich möcht behalten.

"Ach Babst, lieber herre mein,
70 Ich klag euch meine sunde,
Die ich mein tag begangen hab,
Als ich euchs wil verkünde.

"Ich bin gewesen auch ein jar
Bey Venus einer frawen,
75 So wölt ich beycht vnd buß entpfahen,
Ob ich möcht got anschawen."

Der Babst het ein steblein in der handt,
Das was sich also dürre:
"Als wenig es begrünen mag,
80 Kumpst du zu gottes hulde."

"Nun solt ich leben nur ein jar,
Ein jar auff diser erden,
So wölt ich beycht vnd buß entpfahen
Vnd gottes trost erwerben."

85 Da zog er wider auß der stat
In iamer vnd in leyden:
"Maria mutter, reyne maydt,
Muß ich nun von dir scheyden?"

Er zog do wider in den berg
90 Vnd ewiglich on ende:
"Ich wil zu Venus, meiner frawen zart,
Wo mich got wil hinsende."

He left the mountain then behind
repentant and in grief.
"I'll go to Rome and trust the pope
to give my soul relief.

65   "I'll journey forth upon my way
(may God my life control)
to ask the pope who's called Urban
if he can save my soul.

"Ah, Pope, my comforter and lord,
70   my heart is filled with rue
because of all the wrong I've done
and now confess to you.

"With Venus I have spent a year,
a sin, as I know well.
75   I seek for absolution now
that I with God may dwell."

The pope was leaning on a staff
and it was dry and dead.
"This shall have leaves ere you receive
80   the grace of God," he said.

"Had I a single year to live,
I'd spend it all to win
through any penance I could do
God's pardon for my sin."

85   He went forth from the city's gate
in grief and sick at heart.
"Maria, mother, Holy Maid,
from you I now must part."

He journeyed to the mountain then
90   to stay eternally.
"I'll go to see my lady sweet
where God would have me be."

"Seyt got wilkumen, Danheüser,
Ich hab ewer lang entporen;
95 Seyt wilkumen, mein lieber herr,
Zu einem bulen außerkoren!"

Das weret biß an den dritten tag,
Der stab hub an zu grünen,
Der Babst schicket auß in alle landt:
100 Wo der Danheüser wer hinkumen?

Do was er wider in den berg
Vnd het sein lieb erkoren,
Des must der vierte Babst Vrban
Auch ewigklich sein verloren.

"Tannhäuser, welcome once again
you've been away so long.
95   I welcome you, my dearest lord
and lover, fair and strong."

The third day when he took his staff
the pope saw leaves thereon.
He sent forth men to every land
100   where Tannhäuser might have gone.

But he was in the mountain there
with Venus as before,
and so the pope, Urban the Fourth,
was lost forevermore.

BIBLIOGRAPHY

Table of Abbreviations

ADB, Allgemeine Deutsche Biographie
AfdA, Anzeiger für deutsches Altertum
Archiv, Archiv für das Studium der neueren Sprachen und Literaturen
DVjs, Deutsche Vierteljahrsschrift für Literaturwissenschaft und Geistesgeschichte
JEGP, Journal of English and Germanic Philology
MLN, Modern Language Notes
PMLA, Publications of the Modern Language Association of America
ZfdA, Zeitschrift für deutsches Altertum und deutsche Literatur
ZfdPh, Zeitschrift für deutsche Philologie

Amersbach, Karl. "Zur Tannhäusersage." *Alemannia*, 23 (1895), 74-83.
Amman, Adolf N. *Tannhäuser im Venusberg*. Zürich: Origo, 1964.
Barto, Philip S. "Studies in the Tannhäuserlegend." *JEGP*, 9 (1910), 293-320.
Barto, Philip S. "The German Venusberg." *JEGP*, 12 (1913), 295-303.
Barto, Philip S. *Tannhäuser and the Mountain of Venus*. New York: Oxford University Press, 1916.
Bartsch, Karl, ed. *Deutsche Liederdichter des zwölften bis vierzehnten Jahrhunderts*. 4th ed. Berlin: Behr, 1901, pp. LXVIII-LXIX, 244-52.
Bartsch, Karl, ed. *Die Schweizer Minnesänger*. 1886; rpt. Darmstadt: Wissenschaftliche Buchgesellschaft, 1964.
Bechstein, Ludwig. *Der Sagenschatz und die Sagenkreise des Thüringerlandes*. Hildburghausen: Kesselring, 1835, I, 34-44.
Bernhardt, Ernst. "Vom Tannhäuser und dem Sängerkrieg auf der Wartburg." *Jahrbücher der Königlichen Akademie gemeinnütziger Wissenschaft zu Erfurt*. Erfurt: Carl Villaret, 1900, pp. 87-112.
Bezzenberger, H. E., ed. *Fridankes Bescheidenheit*. 1872; rpt. Aalen: Otto Zeller, 1962.
Böckel, Otto. "Zur Sage vom Venusberg." *Alemannia*, 13 (1885), 141-42.
Boor, Helmut de. *Die höfische Literatur: Vorbereitung, Blüte, Ausklang. 1170-1250*. 8th ed. München: Beck, 1969, pp. 370-76.
Boor, Helmut de. *Das späte Mittelalter: Zerfall und Neubeginn. 1250-1350*. 3rd ed. München: Beck, 1967, pp. 356-64.
Brauns, Wilhelm. "Zur Heimatfrage der Carmina Burana." *ZfdA*, 73 (1936), 177-95.
Brinkmann, Hennig. *Zu Wesen und Form mittelalterlicher Dichtung*. Halle: Niemeyer, 1928.
Burckhard, Max Eugen. *Das Lied vom Tannhäuser*. Leipzig: Klinkhardt, 1889.
Carmina Burana: Faksimile-Ausgabe der Benediktbeuerer Liederhandschrift. Ed. Bernhard Bischoff. München: Prestet, 1967.
Creizenach, Wilhelm. *Geschichte des neueren Dramas*. 2nd ed. Halle: Niemeyer, 1923. III, 140.
Currle, Günther. "Die Kreuzlyrik Neidharts, Tannhäusers und Freidanks und ihre Stellung in der mittelhochdeutschen Kreuzzugslyrik." Diss. Tübingen, 1957.
Denk, Otto. "Der Minnesänger Tannhäuser und seine Heimat." *Das Bayerland*, 28 (1916-17), 225-28.
Desonay, Fernand. "Der italienische Ursprung der Tannhäuser-Sage." *Universitas*, 3 (1948), 149-61.

Drees, Heinrich. "Die politische Dichtung der deutschen Minnesinger seit Walther von der Vogelweide." *Jahres-Bericht des Gräflichen Stolbergischen Gymnasiums zu Wernigerode.* Wernigerode, 1887, pp. 1-28. Review by Reinhold Becker, *Literaturblatt für germanische und romanische Philologie,* 9 (1888), 294.

Dübi, Heinrich. "Drei spätmittelalterliche Legenden in ihrer Wanderung aus Italien durch die Schweiz nach Deutschland." *Zeitschrift des Vereins für Volkskunde,* 17 (1907), 42-65, 143-60, 249-64.

Eberhardt, Paul. *Tannhäuser: Eine Tragödie.* Leipzig: Haessel, 1912.

Ehrisman, Gustav. *Geschichte der deutschen Literatur bis zum Ausgang des Mittelalters. Schlussband.* 1935; rpt. München: Beck, 1966, pp. 265-67.

Eichendorff, Joseph von. *Werke.* Leipzig: Bibliographisches Institut, 1891. II, 329-70.

Eis, Gerhard. "Die Tannhäusersage bei Gaunern und Walen." *Archiv,* 191 (1955), 221-23.

Eis, Gerhard. "Die Sage vom Venusberg bei Rudolf Rebmann." *Studia Neophilologica,* 33 (1961), 159-62.

Elster, Ernst. *Tannhäuser in Geschichte, Sage und Dichtung.* Veröffentlichungen der Abteilung für Literatur der deutschen Gesellschaft für Kunst und Wissenschaft zu Bromberg, 3. Bromberg, 1908.

Faber, Felix. *Evagatorium in Terrae Sanctae, Arabiae et Egypti Peregrinationem.* Ed. Konrad Dietrich Hassler. Bibliothek des literarischen Vereins in Stuttgart, 4. Stuttgart, 1849.

Fischer, Felix. *Tannhäuser im Chiemgau: Erzählung.* Chiemgau: Siegsdorf, 1959.

Franckel, Adolf. *Der Tannhäuser.* Weimar: Böhlau, 1854.

Geibel, Emanuel. *Gesammelte Werke.* Stuttgart: Cotta, 1883. I, 119-21.

Geiger, Emil. "Bericht über die Verhandlungen der germanistischen Section der 49. Versammlung deutscher Philologen und Schulmänner zu Basel." *ZfdPh,* 40 (1908), 93-107.

Glasenapp, C. Fr. "Aus dem 'deutschen Dichterwald'." *Bayreuther Blätter,* 3 (1880), 31-45.

Goedeke, Karl. "Meisterlieder." *Germania,* 28 (1883), 38-45.

Golther, Wolfgang. "Die Quellen der Dichtung des 'Tannhäuser'." *Bayreuther Blätter,* 12 (1889), 132-49.

Golther, Wolfgang. "Geschichte der Tannhäusersage und Dichtung." *Bayreuther Taschenbuch,* 7 (1891), 8-29.

Golther, Wolfgang. "Tannhäuser in Sage und Dichtung des Mittelalters und der neuen Zeit." *Walhalla,* 3 (1907), 15-67.

Golther, Wolfgang. *Die deutsche Dichtung im Mittelalter.* Stuttgart: Metzler, 1912, pp. 384-87.

Götze, Alfred. "Tannhäuser und Venusberg." *Neue Jahrbücher für das klassische Altertum, Geschichte und deutsche Literatur,* 53 (1924), 57-58.

Grässe, Johann Georg. *Die Sage vom Ritter Tannhäuser.* Dresden and Leipzig: Arnold, 1846.

Grässe, Johann Georg. *Der Tannhäuser und Ewige Jude.* 2nd ed. Dresden: Schönfeld, 1861.

Grisebach, Eduard. *Der neue Tanhäuser.* 3rd ed. Wien: Rosner, 1873.

Grisebach, Eduard. *Tanhäuser in Rom.* 3rd ed. Wien: Rosner, 1876.

Güntert, Hermann. *Kalypso.* Halle: Niemeyer, 1919, pp. 89-110.

Hackländer, Friedrich. *Der Tannhäuser: Eine Künstlergeschichte.* 2 vols. Stuttgart: Adolph Krabbe, 1860.

Hagen, Friedrich von der, ed. *Minnesinger: Deutsche Liederdichter des zwölften, dreizehnten und vierzehnten Jahrhunderts.* 5 vols. 1838-61; rpt. Aalen: Zeller, 1963. II, 81-97; III, 48; IV, 421-34.

Hamerling, Robert. "Über die deutsche Venus-Tannhäuser-Sage. Mit Beziehung auf die Dichtung 'Venus im Exil'." *Westermanns illustrierte deutsche Monatshefte,* 79 (1896), 53-62.

Hannemann, Kurt. "Der Tannhäuser." *Die deutsche Literatur des Mittelalters: Verfasserlexikon,* V. Ed. Karl Langosch. Berlin: Walter de Gruyter, 1955, 1078.

Haupt, Jos. "Die Sage vom Venusberg und dem Tannhäuser." *Berichte und Mittheilungen des Altertums-Vereins zu Wien*, 10 (1869), 315-23.

Heine, Heinrich. *Sämtliche Werke*. Leipzig: Hesse & Becker, n.d. II, 124-32, 226-32.

Heinrich, Gustav. "Die Tannhäuser-Sage." *Ungarische Revue*, 6 (1886), 827-29.

Heinrich, Gusztav. *Tannhäuser*. Budapest: Franklin-Társulat Nyomdája, 1915.

Hermann von Sachsenheim. *Die Mörin*. Bibliothek des literarischen Vereins in Stuttgart, 137. Stuttgart, 1878.

Hirsch, Selma. "Die älteste Gestalt der Ballade vom Tannhäuser." *Jahrbuch des Vereins für niederdeutsche Sprachforschung*, 56-57 (1930-31), 194-204.

Hoecker, Georg. *Der Tannhäuser*. Wien: Derflinger and Fischer, 1898.

Hoffmann, E. T. A. *Werke*. Berlin and Leipzig: Bong, n.d. VI, 24-63.

Holland, H. *Geschichte der altdeutschen Dichtkunst in Bayern*. Regensburg: Friedrich Pustet, 1862, pp. 505-27.

Horowitz, Hilda. "Tannhäuserdichtungen seit Richard Wagner." Diss. Wien, 1932.

Jans Enikel. *Weltchronik*. Deutsche Chroniken und andere Geschichtsbücher des Mittelalters, 3. Leipzig and Hannover: Hahn, 1900.

Jenaer Liederhandschrift, Die. Ed. Georg Holz, Franz Saran, and Eduard Bernoulli. 2 vols. 1901; rpt. Hildesheim: Georg Olm, 1966.

John, Alois. "Tannhäuser im Fichtelgebirge." *Literarisches Jahrbuch: Central-Organ für die wissenschaftlichen, literarischen und künstlerischen Interessen Nordwest-Böhmens und der deutschen Grenzlande*, 3 (1893), 70-73.

Junk, Victor. *Tannhäuser in Sage und Dichtung*. München: Beck, 1911.

Keller, Adelbert von, ed. *Fastnachtspiele aus dem fünfzehnten Jahrhundert*. Bibliothek des literarischen Vereins in Stuttgart, 46. Stuttgart, 1858.

Kluckhohn, Paul. "Ministerialität und Ritterdichtung." *ZfdA*, 52 (1910), 135-68.

Kluge, Friedrich. "Der Venusberg." *Bunte Blätter*. Freiburg: Bielefeld, 1908, pp. 28-61.

Koegel, Dora. "Die Auswertung der Tannhäuser-Sage in der deutschen Literatur des 19. und 20. Jahrhunderts." Diss. München, 1922.

Köhler, Reinhold. *Kleinere Schriften zur neueren Litteraturgeschichte, Volkskunde und Wortforschung*. Berlin: Felber 1900. III, 263-65.

Komorzynski, Egon von. "Litterarische Vorläufer des 'Tannhäuser'." *Bayreuther Blätter*, 27 (1904), 302—05.

Körner, Josef. *Nibelungenforschungen der deutschen Romantik*. Leipzig: Haessel, 1911.

Kornmann, Heinrich. *De miraculis vivorum*. N.p., 1614, p. 186.

Kornmann, Heinrich. *Mons Veneris: Fraw Veneris Berg*. Frankfurt: Fischer, 1614.

Krappe, Alexander. "Die Sage vom Tannhäuser." *Mitteilungen der schlesischen Gesellschaft für Volkskunde*, 36 (1937), 106-32.

Kraus, Carl von, ed. *Heinrich von Morungen*. München: Bremer, 1925, 117-19.

Kraus, Carl von, ed. *Deutsche Liederdichter des 13. Jahrhunderts*. 2 vols. Tübingen: Niemeyer, 1952-58.

Kück, E. "Zu Tannhäusers Rätselspruch." *AfdA*, 17 (1891), 79-80.

Kuhn, Hugo. *Minnesangs Wende*. Tübingen: Niemeyer, 1952, pp. 110-19.

Kummer, Karl F., ed. *Die poetischen Erzählungen des Herrand von Wildonie und die kleinen innerösterreichischen Minnesinger*. Wien: Hölder, 1880, pp. 67-68.

Lachmann, Karl, ed. *Die Gedichte Walthers von der Vogelweide*. 13th ed., rev. by Hugo Kuhn. Berlin: Walter de Gruyter, 1965.

Lachmann, Karl, Moriz Haupt, and Friedrich Vogt, eds. *Des Minnesangs Frühling*. 34th ed., rev. by Carl von Kraus. Stuttgart: S. Hirzel, 1967.

Lang, Margarete. *Tannhäuser*. Von deutscher Poeterey, 17. Leipzig: Weber, 1936.

Lang, Margarete and Hans Naumann. "Zu Tannhäusers Balladengestalt." *Jahrbuch für Volksliedforschung*, 5 (1936), 123-30.

Lehmann, Paul. *Die Parodie im Mittelalter*. 2nd ed. Stuttgart: Anton Hiersemann, 1963.

Leitzmann, Albert, ed. *Wolfram von Eschenbach.* Altdeutsche Textbibliothek, 13 and 14. 6th ed. Tübingen: Niemeyer, 1963, 1965.

Lennartz, Werner. *Die Lieder und Leiche Tannhäusers im Lichte der neueren Metrik.* Diss. Köln, 1931.

Levissohn, Robert. "Eine obersteirische Fassung des Volksliedes vom Tannhäuser." *ZfdA*, 35 (1891), 439-40.

Levitschnigg, Heinrich von. *Der Tannhäuser: Dramatisches Gedicht mit Gesang und Tanz in 3 Akten.* Wien: Theater-Agentur des Adalbert Prix, 1852.

Liebleitner, Karl. "Ein Tannhäuserlied." *Das deutsche Volkslied,* 22 (1920), 34-35.

Liebleitner, Karl. "Ein Tannhäuserlied aus Kärnten." *Reichspost,* 192 (14 July, 1935), 15.

Lied von dem edlen Tannhäuser, Das. Nürnberg: Kunegund Hergotin [ca. 1530]. Zwickauer Facsimiledrucke, 8. N.p., Ullmann, 1912.

Loewenthal, Fritz. *Studien zum germanischen Rätsel.* Heidelberg: Winter, 1914, pp. 64-67.

Löhmann, Otto. "Die Entstehung der Tannhäusersage." *Fabula,* 3 (1960), 224-53.

Loomis, Roger S. "Morgain la Fée in Oral Tradition." *Romania,* 80 (1959), 337-67.

Lomnitzer, Helmut and Ulrich Müller, eds. *Tannhäuser: Die lyrischen Gedichte der Handschriften C und J: Abbildungen und Materialien zur gesamten Überlieferung der Texte und ihrer Wirkungsgeschichte und zu deñ Melodien.* Litterae: Göppinger Beiträge zur Textgeschichte, 13. Göttingen: Kümmerle, 1973.

Lucas, C. T. L. *Ueber den Krieg von Wartburg.* Historische und literarische Abhandlungen der königlichen Deutschen Gesellschaft zu Königsberg, No. 4, Part 2, 1838.

Manessische Liederhandschrift, Die: Faksimile Ausgabe. Leipzig: Insel, 1929.

Martin, Franz. "Der Tannhäuser — kein Salzburger." *Mitteilungen der Gesellschaft für Salzburger Landeskunde,* 80 (1940), 85-86.

Meier, John, ed. *Deutsche Volkslieder: Balladen.* Berlin and Leipzig: Walter de Gruyter, 1935, pp. 145-61.

Meyer, Richard M. "Tannhäuser." *ADB,* 73 (1894) 385-88; rpt. Berlin: Duncker and Humblot, 1971.

Meyer, Richard M. *Deutsche Charaktere.* Berlin: Hofmann, 1897, pp. 60-68.

Meyer, Richard M. "Tannhäuser und die Tannhäusersage." *Zeitschrift des Vereins für Volkskunde,* NS 21 (1911), 1-31.

Mohr, Ferdinand. *Das unhöfische Element in der mittelhochdeutschen Lyrik von Walther an.* Diss. Tübingen, 1913, pp. 60-68.

Mohr, Wolfgang. "Tanhusers Kreuzlied." *DVjs,* 34 (1960), 338-55.

Morgan, Bayard Quincy. *A Critical Bibliography of German Literature in English Translation 1481-1927.* Rev. ed. 1938; rpt. New York and London: Scarecrow Press, 1965.

Morgan, Bayard Quincy. *A Critical Bibliography of German Literature in English Translation: Supplement Embracing the Years 1928—1955.* New York and London: Scarecrow Press, 1965.

Müller, Günther. "Strophenbindung bei Ulrich von Lichtenstein." *ZfdA,* 60 (1923), 33-69.

Nadler, Josef. *Literaturgeschichte des deutschen Volkes.* 4th ed. Berlin: Propyläen, n.d. I, 138-39.

Nestroy, Johann and Karl Binder. *Tannhäuser-Parodie: Burleske Operette in vier Bildern.* Leipzig: Joseph Weinberger, n.d.

Nestroy, Johann. *Tannhäuser: Zukunftsposse mit vergangener Musik und gegenwärtigen Gruppierungen in drei Aufzügen.* Ed. Georg Richard Kruse. Leipzig: Reclam, 1904.

Nestroy, Johann. *Sämtliche Werke: Historisch-kritische Gesamtausgabe in zwölf Bänden.* Ed. Fritz Brukner and Otto Rommel. Wien: Anton Schroll, 1924-30. IV, 201-40.

Nodnagel, A. "Die Tanhäusersage und ihre Bearbeitungen." *Archiv,* 6 (1849), 119-40.

Nover, Jakob. *Die Tannhäusersage und ihre poetische Gestaltung.* Hamburg: Königliche Hofverlagshandlung, 1897.

Nyrop, Kristoffer. *Tannhäuser i Venusbjaerget.* Copenhagen: Gyldendal, 1909.

Oehlke, Alfred. *Zu Tannhäusers Leben und Dichten*. Diss. Königsberg, 1890. Review by E. Kück, *AfdA*, 17 (1891), 207-13.

Pabst, Walter. *Venus und die missverstandene Dido: Literarische Ursprünge des Sibyllen- und des Venusberges*. Hamburger Romanische Studien, Series A, 40. Hamburg: Cram de Gruyter, 1955.

Paris, Gaston. "La légende du Tannhäuser." *Legendes du moyen age*. Paris: Hachette, 1903, pp. 111-49.

Paur, Theodor, ed. *Leben und Wirken Friedrich von Sallet's*. Breslau: August Schulz, 1844.

Pfaff, Fridrich. *Der Minnesang des 12. bis 14. Jahrhunderts*. Deutsche National-Litteratur, 8, 1. Stuttgart: Union Deutsche Verlagsgesellschaft, n.d., pp. 185-88.

Pfaff, Fridrich. "Die Tannhäusersage." *ZfdPh*, 40 (1908), 97-99.

Poag, James F. "Heinrich von Veldeke's *Minne*; Wolfram von Eschenbach's *Liebe* and *Triuwe*." *JEGP*, 61 (1962), 735.

Puls, Alfred. "Tannhäuserlied und Maria tzart." *Jahrbuch des Vereins für niederdeutsche Sprachforschung*, 16 (1890), 65-68.

Raab, Robert von. "Die Tannhausen im Mittelalter." *Mittheilungen der Gesellschaft für Salzburger Landeskunde*, 12 (1872), 1-33.

Ranke, Friedrich, ed. *Gottfried von Strassburg: Tristan und Isold*. 14th ed. Dublin and Zürich: Weidmann, 1969.

Reischl, Friedrich and Luigi Kasimir. *Das Buch von der schönen Stadt Salzburg*. Wien: Heller, 1923, pp. 134-47.

Remy, Arthur F. "The Origin of the Tannhäuserlegend." *JEGP*, 12 (1913), 32-77.

Reuschel, Karl. "Die Tannhäusersage." *Neue Jahrbücher für das klassische Altertum, Geschichte und deutsche Literatur*, 13 (1904), 653-67.

Roethe, Gustav. "Tannhäusers Rätselspruch." *ZfdA*, 30 (1886), 419-20.

Roethe, Gustav, ed. *Die Gedichte Reinmars von Zweter*. 1887; rpt. Amsterdam: Rodopi, 1967, pp. 317-18.

Rosenhagen, G. "Die Leiche des Tannhäuser und des Ulrich von Winterstetten." *ZfdPh*, 61 (1936), 269-74.

Rostock, Fritz. *Mittelhochdeutsche Dichterheldensage*. Halle: Niemeyer, 1925, pp. 12-15.

Rottauscher, Alfred and Bernhard Paumgartner. *Das Taghorn: Dichtungen und Melodien des bayrisch-österreichischen Minnesangs*. Wien: Stephenson, 1922. I, 39-47; III, 29-34.

Rudolf, Adalbert. "Tanhäuser." *Archiv*, 68 (1882), 43-52.

Sachs, Hans. *Sämtliche Fabeln und Schwänke*. Halle: Niemeyer, 1893. I, 461-66; II, 198-201; III, 349-50.

Sandweg, Walther. *Die Fremdwörter bei Tannhäuser*. Diss. Bonn, 1931.

Schlossar, Anton. *Deutsche Volkslieder aus Steiermark*. Innsbruck: Wagner, 1881, pp. 351-52.

Schmidt, Erich. "Tannhäuser in Sage und Dichtung." *Nord und Süd*, 63 (1892), 176-95.

Schmidt, Erich. *Charakteristiken*. Berlin: Weidmann, 1901, pp. 24-50.

Schmidt, Leopold. "Zur österreichischen Form der Tannhäuser-Ballade." *Jahrbuch des österreichischen Volksliedswerkes*, 1 (1952), 9-18.

Schmitt, Franz. *Stoff- und Motivgeschichte der deutschen Literatur*. Berlin: Walter de Gruyter, 1959, pp. 173-74.

Schneider, Hermann. *Heldendichtung. Geistlichendichtung. Ritterdichtung*. Heidelberg: Carl Winter, 1925, pp. 431-32.

Schneider, Hermann. "Ursprung und Alter der deutschen Volksballade." *Vom Werden des deutschen Geistes: Festgabe Gustav Ehrismann*. Ed. Paul Merker and Wolfgang Stammler. Berlin and Leipzig: Walter de Gruyter, 1925, pp. 112-24.

Schönbach, Anton E. "Die Sprüche des Bruder Wernher, II." *Sitzungsberichte der philo- sophisch-historischen Klasse der Akademie der Wissenschaften*, 150 (1905), I, 1-106.

Schütz, Julius Franz. *Die tragische Trilogie: Der Rattenfänger, Wieland der Schmied, Der Tannhäuser*. Graz and Wien: Stiasny, 1956.

Seagrave, Barbara and Wesley Thomas. *The Songs of the Minnesingers*. Urbana and London: University of Illinois, 1966, pp. 127-31.

Siebert, Johannes. *Metrik und Rhythmik in Tannhäusers Gedichten*. Diss. Berlin, 1894.

Siebert, Johannes. *Tannhäuser: Inhalt und Form seiner Gedichte*. Berlin: Vogt, 1894.

Review by Anton E. Schönbach, *Österreichisches Litteraturblatt*, 4 (1895), 693-95.

Review by J. Wahner, *ZfdPh*, 28 (1896), 382-90.

Siebert, Johannes. "Graf Hermann von Henneberg als Bewerber um die deutsche Königskrone." *ZfdPh*, 57 (1932), 215-23.

Siebert, Johannes. *Der Dichter Tannhäuser: Leben, Gedichte, Sage*. Halle: Niemeyer, 1934.

Review by Anton Wallner, *AfdA*, 53 (1934), 175-79.

Siebert, Johannes. "Zum Tannhäuser." *ZfdA*, 77 (1940), 55-60.

Siebert, Johannes. "Tannhäusers Mäuseberg." *ZfdA*, 82 (1950), 264-67.

Simpson, Claude. "Wagner and the Tannhäuser Tradition." *PMLA*, 63 (1948), 244-61.

Singer, S., ed. *Tannhäuser*. Tübingen: Mohr, 1922.

Review by G. Rosenhagen, *ZfdPh*, 51 (1926), 351-53.

Review by Edward Schröder, *AfdA*, 41 (1922), 190-91.

Singer, S. "Der Tannhäuser." *ZfdA*, 59 (1922), 290-304.

Söderhjelm, Werner. "Antoine de La Sale et la légende de Tannhäuser." *Mémoires de la Société Néo-Philologique à Helsingfors*, 2 (1897), 101-67.

Söderhjelm, Werner. "Eine tschechische Version der Reise ins Sibyllenparadies." *Neuphilologische Mitteilungen*, 10 (1908), 72-88.

Spanke, Hans. "Eine neue Leich-Melodie." *Zeitschrift für Musikwissenschaft*, 14 (1932), 385-98.

Spanke, Hans. "Eine mittelalterliche Musikhandschrift." *ZfdA*, 69 (1932), 49-70.

Taylor, Archer. "Ze künis erbent ouch diu wip und niht die man." *MLN*, 53 (1938), 509.

Thomas, J. W. "Walther von der Vogelweide and the Tannhäuser Ballad," *Neuphilologische Mitteilungen*, 74 (1973), 340-47.

Uhland, Ludwig. *Schriften zur Geschichte der Dichtung und Sage*. Stuttgart: Cotta. II, 1866, 219-50; IV, 1868, 259-86.

Ulrich von Lichtenstein. Ed. Karl Lachmann. Berlin: Sanders, 1891.

Veckenstedt, Edm[und]. "Tanhäuser, ein Dämon des Windes." *Das Magazin für die Litteratur des In- und Auslandes*, 111 (1887), 73-75.

Voss, Ernst. *Vier Jahrzehnte in Amerika*. Stuttgart: Deutsche Verlagsanstalt, 1929, pp. 364-80.

Wagner, Peter. "Mitteilungen." *Zeitschrift für Musikwissenschaft*, 9 (1926-27), 382-84.

Wagner, Richard. *Tannhäuser und der Sängerkrieg auf Wartburg*. Berlin: Adolph Fürstner, 1901.

Wallner, Anton. "Eine Hampfel Grübelnüsse." *ZfdA*, 64 (1927), 81-83.

Wallner, Anton. "Tannhäuser-Kritik." *ZfdA*, 71 (1934), 213-26.

Wallner, Anton. "Tannhäuser." *ZfdA*, 72 (1935), 278-80.

Weller, Karl. "Zur Lebensgeschichte des Tanhäusers." *Festgabe für Karl Bohnenberger*. Ed. Hans Bihl. Tübingen: Mohr, 1938, pp. 154-63.

Werner, Richard Maria. "Zu Tannhäuser." *ZfdA*, 31 (1887), 363-64.

Wiessner, Edmund. "Die Preislieder Neidharts und des Tannhäusers auf Herzog Friedrich II. von Babenberg." *ZfdA*, 73 (1936), 117-30.

Wiessner, Edmund, ed. *Die Lieder Neidharts*. Altdeutsche Textbibliothek, 44. Tübingen: Niemeyer, 1955.

Wiora, Walter. "Alpenländische Liedweisen der Frühzeit und des Mittelalters im Lichte vergleichender Forschung." *Angebinde. John Meier zum 85. Geburtstag*. Ed. Friedrich Maurer. Lahr: Moritz Schauenburg, 1949, pp. 169-98.

Wis, Marjatta. "Ursprünge der deutschen Tannhäuserlegende: zur Geschichte mittelalterlicher Pilgertraditionen, I." *Neuphilologische Mitteilungen*, 61 (1960), 8-58.

Wolff, Julius. *Tannhäuser: Ein Minnesang*. 2 vols. 5th ed. Berlin: G. Grote, 1881.

Wolff, Ludwig. "Der Tannhäuser." *Die deutsche Literatur des Mittelalters: Verfasserlexikon*. IV. Ed. Karl Langosch. Berlin: Walter de Gruyter, 1953, 355-68.

Zack, Viktor. "Tannhäuserlieder aus Steiermark." *Das deutsche Volkslied*, 32 (1930), 77-80.

Zander, F. *Die Tanhäuser-Sage und der Minnesinger Tanhäuser: Zur öffentlichen Prüfung der Schüler des König. Friedrichs-Collegiums*. Königsberg, 1858.

Zingerle, I. V. "Zur Tanhäuser-Literatur." *Germania*, 5 (1860), 361-65.

Zoder, Raimund. "Tannhäuserlied aus Niederösterreich." *Das deutsche Volkslied*, 32 (1930), 80.

Zohner, Alois. "Die Verbindung der Eckhart- und Tannhäuser-Sagen." Diss. Wien, 1909.

UNIVERSITY OF NORTH CAROLINA
STUDIES IN THE GERMANIC LANGUAGES
AND LITERATURES

Initiated by RICHARD JENTE (1949–1952), *established by* F. E. COENEN (1952–1968)

Publication Committee

SIEGFRIED MEWS, EDITOR

JOHN G. KUNSTMANN   GEORGE S. LANE   HERBERT W. REICHERT

CHRISTOPH E. SCHWEITZER   SIDNEY R. SMITH   RIA STAMBAUGH   PETRUS W. TAX

For other volumes in the "Studies" see page ii and following pages.

Send orders to: (U.S. and Canada)
The University of North Carolina Press, P.O. Box 2288
Chapel Hill, N.C. 27514

(All other countries) Feffer and Simons, Inc., 31 Union Square, New York, N.Y. 10003

UNIVERSITY OF NORTH CAROLINA
STUDIES IN THE GERMANIC LANGUAGES
AND LITERATURES

initiated by RICHARD JENTE (1949–1952), *established by* F. E. COENEN (1952–1968)

Publication Committee

SIEGFRIED MEWS, EDITOR

For other volumes in the "Studies" see preceding and following pages and p. ii

Order reprinted books from: AMS PRESS, Inc.,
56 East 13th Street, New York, N.Y. 10003

UNIVERSITY OF NORTH CAROLINA
STUDIES IN THE GERMANIC LANGUAGES AND LITERATURES

Initiated by RICHARD JENTE (1949–1952), *established by* F. E. COENEN (1952–1968)

Publication Committee

SIEGFRIED MEWS, EDITOR

For other volumes in the "Studies" see preceding pages and p. ii